The Daily Telegraph
FOURTH BOOK OF OBITUARIES

"Hugh Massingberd single-handedly transformed the slightly stuffy formula of the newspaper 'obit' into a high comic form ... his novelistic delight in human oddity, his capacity, where due, for hero-worship (particularly of sporting, military or theatrical luminaries) and his delicately anarchic sense of fun ... Among the hundreds of us newspaper hacks today there is a tiny handful of true artists at work. Of this band, Massingberd is king. Almost every page of this extraordinary book will make you moan with laughter. But put it down and someone will instantly snatch it from under your nose."

A. N. WILSON *Country Life*

The Daily Telegraph
FOURTH BOOK OF
OBITUARIES

Rogues

Edited by
HUGH MASSINGBERD

PAN BOOKS

First published 1998 by Macmillan

This edition published 1999 by Pan Books
an imprint of Macmillan Publishers Ltd
25 Eccleston Place, London SW1W 9NF
Basingstoke and Oxford
Associated companies throughout the world
www.macmillan.co.uk

ISBN 0 330 37110 X

1 3 5 7 9 8 6 4 2

A CIP catalogue record for this book is available from
the British Library.

Typeset by SetSystems Ltd, Saffron Walden, Essex
Printed and bound in Great Britain by
Mackays of Chatham plc, Chatham, Kent

For my three successors
in the Obituaries chair —
(David) Lewis Jones, Kate Summerscale
and Christopher Howse

INTRODUCTION

I HAD rather supposed that *The Daily Telegraph Third Book of Obituaries: Entertainers* would bring down the curtain on this series of biographical short stories, but then the publishers pointed out the potential of a volume on *Rogues*. Who could resist?

From Robin Hood and Rob Roy to Falstaff and Flashman, from Fagin to Arthur Daley, the Rogues of folklore and fiction have indeed proved irresistible. I remember my late friend James Lees-Milne, who wrote several biographies of worthy figures as well as of that exotic scoundrel William Beckford, telling me that he "really much preferred writing about Rogues". That wise commentator Allan Massie has observed that the world would be a duller place without them: "There is something comforting about rogues. We enjoy their larger-than-life antics as we do a pantomime, safe in the knowledge that there is no danger that we shall get involved."

Jeffrey Bernard, a prime example of the species featured in our own Rogues' Gallery, attributed the popularity of his weekly catalogue of alcoholic and sexual disaster to *Spectator* readers' *Schadenfreude.*"If you're living where the grass is greener", he explained, "it must be reassuring to glance occasionally at the rubbish dump."

When I was occupying the hot seat at the *Telegraph* Obits desk readers would sometimes take exception to our including a notorious villain (such as, say, a Mafia hitman or an East End gangster) beside – or even, horror of horrors, above – a gallant war hero or blameless bishop in the Obituaries page. The outraged inference seemed to be that we were thereby conferring some form of moral approval by granting such unworthy figures the "honour" of an obituary at all. In reality, of course, we were merely applying straightforward "news values". (As Noël Coward wrote in the lyrics of "Twentieth Century Blues": "Ev'ry sorrow, Blues value is news value Tomorrow . . .")

My only reluctance to take on the task of lining up some suitable suspects for a set of portraits of the picaresque rested on this same tricky question of morality. By bracketing these brief lives together under a blanket, and inevitably unflattering, title, would we be presuming to make some sort of judgement? For, after all, an obituarist is no more than a recording angel, chronicling with deadpan detachment – and what one Irish reviewer of an earlier volume kindly called "bemused indifference" – the idiosyncrasies of a particular life. It is not for anonymous practitioners of the necrological trade to indulge in editorialising, sermonising or delivering judicial summings-up. As in all writing worth reading, sympathy is of the essence.

That, I hope, is the saving grace of the sub-title *Rogues*. For rogues, as we all know, can often be "lovable" – indeed it is virtually tautology to use that familiar prefix. We toyed with such formulae as *Scoundrels and Scallywags*, *Rascals and Rapscallions*, *Scamps and Scapegraces*, *Cads and Bounders*, *Con-men and Crooks* (oops, no, no . . .), but only *Rogues* seemed to cover the waterfront from real wrongdoers to colourful "larger-than-life" characters for whom the appellation is almost a term of affection. One can think of many Rogues who rejoice in the description and who add to what Dr Johnson called "the public stock of harmless pleasure". (Well, make that more or less harmless . . .)

Certainly the word has evolved into something much more wide-ranging and human than the cold dictionary definition of a "dishonest or unprincipled person". While there are, undeniably, some nasty pieces of work to be found among the "Rogues" in this book, doubtless cases could be argued for the honesty and principles (at least as they saw them) of numerous others. Thus, in the obituary of Charles Skilton, publisher of *Fanny Hill* in the 1960s, it is noted here that he "was regarded by some as a lovable old rogue, by others as a principled and firm-minded man".

A fair, balanced obituary, recording good and bad, can afford pleasure to friend and foe – albeit sometimes between the lines. The material is not presented in terms of black and white; frequently, on rereading the life stories of those who fell from grace, I was struck by how many eventually found redemption. Nor should an obituarist have an "agenda": the *Rogues* featured in this book are drawn from varied walks of life and represent a broad spectrum of political views.

Before I resort to echoing the catch-phrases of those two television characters, Francis Urquhart of *House of Cards* ("You may call them Rogues but I couldn't possibly comment") and the South African beautician in *The Fast Show* ("No offence . . ."), it is time to stop all this theorising and special pleading. Let's face it: rogues make "good copy".

What follows is simply a subjective selection of a further hundred obits that I have especially enjoyed rereading for the umpteenth time, and which seem to deserve to end up between the covers of a book. They appear in unvarnished chronological sequence (which leads to some curious, not to say embarrassing, juxtapositions);

but if one were to sort them into rough categories, politicans and lawyers would probably – unsurprisingly, one might say – score pretty heavily.

On the Labour side, for example, there are the runaway MP John Stonehouse; the controversial Attorney-General Sam Silkin; "Afghan" Roberts (who, it is noted, "vigorously denied suggestions that he had been whipped by men in SS-style uniforms while he was attired in priestly garb"); the militant Pat Wall; the reformed alcoholic Raymond Blackburn; Ian ("Is he as nice as he looks?") Mikardo; and the corrupt "Mr Newcastle", T. Dan Smith. Frank Haxell and "the Ageing Tarzan" Dick (later Lord) Briginshaw represent the "politically motivated" Trades Unions. Among the Tories are the indiscreet Lord Havers; the flamboyant Sir Nicholas Fairbairn (who described his recreations as "making love, ends meet and people laugh"); Billy Rees-Davies ("affectionately known as the 'One-Armed Bandit'"); and Nicholas Freeman, who pulled down Kensington's fine Victorian town hall before it could be listed for preservation.

Marxism lives on in the obituaries of Gerry Healy (to whom Vanessa Redgrave owes "all my subsequent development as a political woman and artist") and Sid Gold, the veteran bomb-maker. Fascism found favour with Jeffrey Hamm and the Norfolk squire Andrew Fountaine (who described the Attlee administration as "a group of conscientious objectors, national traitors, semi-alien mongrels and hermaphrodite Communists"). "Docker" Hughes of the 657 Party pledged to establish an Orange Order in Portsmouth – and also campaigned against beards.

From Ireland comes Sean MacBride (the IRA terrorist who went on to win the Nobel and Lenin Peace Prizes as "a respected statesman") and Brian Lenihan. From America, a robust cast of politicos – Spiro T. Agnew ("When you've seen one slum you've seen them all"); the Watergate convicts John Mitchell and H. R. Haldeman; Wayne L. Hays (who reportedly fornicated with his staff secretary "keeping his eye on a digital clock"); Wilbur Mills (who abandoned the pleasures of reading the tax code in bed to join a striptease *artiste* known as "the Argentinian Firecracker" on stage); and General Curtis "Old Ironpants" LeMay, who advocated bombing North Vietnam "back to the Stone Age". The "Yippie" leader Abbie Hoffman specialised in acts of "guerrilla theatre", such as throwing dollar bills on to the floor of the New York Stock Exchange.

Down Under, "Big Russ" Hinze of Queensland described himself "as the roughest, toughest bloody politician you could come across". They don't come much tougher than the formidable pair of females representing China and Spain respectively, Jiang Qing and Dolores "*La Pasionaria*" Ibarruri.

Of the lawyers, few could match the forensic skills of the serial escaper Alfie Hinds. On the right side of the Law were "Campaign Charlie" McLachlan and "Big Bambino" Rizzo ("I'm gonna be so tough as mayor [of Philadelphia], I gonna make Attila the Hun look like a faggot"). The villains include "Big Vinnie" Teresa, "Fat Tony" (a sobriquet spraringly used) Salerno, "Jimmy The Weasel" Fratianno and Lord Boothby's friend, Ronnie Kray.

The round-up of spies embraces Klaus Fuchs, Tyler Kent, Alger Hiss, John Vassall and the conspiracy theorist James Rusbridger. The Foreign Office fields the paedophile Sir Peter "Humpty Dumpty" Hayman and Sir John

Galsworthy, an overzealous functionary in the FO's post-Yalta policy of (as General Martell put it) "licking the Bolshies' boots until we were black in the face".

From the world of Science come Professor William Shockley, with his bizarre views on "retrogressive evolution" (and his ubiquitous tape-recorder); the psychiatrist R. D. Laing; the behaviourist B. F. Skinner (who taught pigeons to play ping-pong); and Timothy Leary of *Hair* fame, champion of LSD. Churchmen of various denominations include the homosexual Anglican, the Reverend Peter Gamble, Lawrence Durdin-Robertson of the Fellowship of Isis and Anton LaVey, founder of the Church of Satan, who had begun his career in the circus, putting his head into the jaws of a lion – "when the beast removed a chunk of his neck, however, he decided to look for alternative employment".

As for the Arts, there is a trio of strange musicians, John Cage (celebrated for his vegetable-blending routine), the inveterate practical joker Vivian Stanshall and Tiny Tim; and also of "TV personalities", Hughie Green, Daniel Farson and Fanny Cradock. Among the authors are Laura Riding, William Burroughs, Seth Morgan and Robin Cook, the novelist, who observed that "an Eton background is a terrific help if you are into vice at all".

From the aristocratic ranks come Prince Johannes von Thurn und Taxis; the Duke of Montrose (the Rhodesian politician who considered that "the African is a bright and promising little fellow up to the age of puberty", whereupon he becomes totally obsessed with "matters of sex"); the self-styled "Lord Herbert", "Uncrowned Queen" of Tangier; Robert "the Mad Boy" Heber-Percy; and the errant herald James Frere. "Decca" Mitford represents the Rebels. Then there are the *femmes fatales*, Margaret Duchess of Argyll, Diana Lady Delamere, Pamela Harriman ("the greatest courtesan of the century"), Barbara ("Sex is a great leveller") Skelton – and Bapsy Marchioness of Winchester, who wrote to her husband: "May a viper's fangs be forever around your throat and may you stew in the pit of your own juice". The brothel-keeper Marie-la-Jolie, Marseille's most infamous madam, could only run, we are told, to "one rotting fang".

The roll-call of businessmen includes the property developers Rudolph Palumbo and John Poulson, Armand Hammer, Lord Kagan, Bernie Cornfeld, and Sir Peter Green and Charles St George of Lloyd's. Besides the publishers Cecil King, Maurice Girodias and Guy Wayte, it seemed only fair to find space for some of the "Street of Shame's" finest – Sam White, Henry Fairlie, Sir John Junor, the "Bollinger Bolshevik" Cyril Ray and "The Tunku" of the *Telegraph* himself, Peter Eastwood.

Shortly after Eastwood's exit from the *Telegraph* in 1986, the struggle began to wrest Obits from the all-powerful clutches of News and to create a new, more or less fenced-in, fiefdom. Since my own departure from the desk in 1994 I have been impressed and gratified by the increasing amount of ground gained by Obits.

Unlike the previous three volumes, which drew their material exclusively from my own era in the chair (1986–94), this one also includes obituaries published over the last three years or so. It struck me as pointless to ignore this period, especially as some of the articles had actually been prepared "for the file" during my time; for, like an iceberg, nine-tenths of the Obits Editor's job is unseen. I have dedicated this volume to my three successors in the chair, (David) Lewis Jones, Kate Summerscale and Christopher Howse, in recognition of their major roles in its content. (It is kind of Christopher to continue to allow me to rummage about in his archives.)

Much credit is due to them, and to all those who have worked on the desk at various times over the last decade, notably David Twiston Davies, Will Cohu and George Ireland (deputy editors), Claudia FitzHerbert and Aurea Carpenter (assistant editors), Diana Heffer and Teresa Moore (editorial assistants). Teresa again was an enormous help in assembling and presenting the material for publication in book form.

I would like to pay special tribute to Robert Gray, a fine writer whom the *Telegraph* has been privileged to have as the resident biographer on the Obits desk since 1990. Some of his choicest pieces are included in the book.

Grateful thanks, too, to the following contributors: Tom Baistow, Andrew Barrow, Edward Bishop, David Bowman, Robert Chalmers, Simon Courtauld, the late George Gale, the late Stan Gebler Davies, Dean Godson, Graham Hutchings, Adam McEwen, J. R. H. McEwen, James Owen, Gavin Stamp, Damian Thompson, Martin Vander Weyer, Hugo Vickers, Ian Waller, Geoffrey Wheatcroft, Roxane Witke – and others too roguish (or perhaps too wise) to be mentioned.

HUGH MASSINGBERD
London, January 1998

CECIL KING

CECIL KING, who has died aged 86, had an idiosyncratic career which bore eloquent testimony to the truth of the aphorism that "the bigger they are the harder they fall" – and indeed to Baldwin's celebrated crack about "power without responsibility".

Having dominated the newspaper and publishing world as boss of the giant International Publishing Corporation, which then embraced the *Daily Mirror* and three other national newspapers, as well as the biggest magazine group in the world, owning 230 titles and employing a workforce of 30,000, King vanished from the scene overnight in 1968 in the most dramatic *putsch* that even Fleet Street had staged – at least pre-Wapping.

King was a man of boundless ambition and possessed a formidable ego that led to his spectacular fall. Not for nothing was his middle name Harmsworth: he was a nephew of Alfred Harmsworth, 1st and last Viscount Northcliffe, father of the British popular newspaper who eventually succumbed to megalomania.

Although Northcliffe left his nephew only £500 in his £5 million will, King hero-worshipped his uncle all his life. Like Northcliffe, King developed *folie de grandeur* that was to lead him into a fatal vendetta with Harold Wilson, then Prime Minister.

King's volumes of published diaries revealed a person of absurd self-importance, quite lacking in humour. The supreme example of his self-delusion came in 1981 when he said that he had suppressed a passage from his diary in 1968 recording his version of the controversial meeting

1

with Earl Mountbatten of Burma and Sir Solly Zucker-man – supposedly to discuss the possibility of setting up a "national government" – so as not to embarrass the Queen.

An autocrat and self-confessed intellectual snob, King was none the less a complex figure whose commanding bulk – he was 6ft 4in – and chilling aloofness with underlings masked a real concern for the underdog and a deep abhorrence of racial discrimination.

For those granted an audience with this seigneurial socialist in his suite, high in the garish Mirror building in Holborn from which he ruled his vast IPC conglomerate, it could be a daunting and fascinating experience. There was the deceptively limp handshake and soft voice that could utter such curt and cutting comments; the unexpectedly elegant ambience provided by antique furniture, pictures, old books and the real fireplace, installed at enormous cost; and, above all, the ubiquitous North-cliffe memorabilia.

Cecil Harmsworth King was born in 1901, the second son of Sir Lucas King, an Anglo-Irish pillar of the Indian Civil Service, by his wife Geraldine Harmsworth. He was educated at Winchester and Christ Church, Oxford, where he took second-class honours in history.

Young Cecil began his newspaper career as an apprentice reporter on the Glasgow *Daily Record*, owned by his uncle, Viscount Rothermere. But in 1926 he moved on and up to the *Mirror*, also then owned by Rothermere. Three years later, when he was barely 28, he was appointed a director.

This transparent piece of nepotism infuriated H. G. Bartholomew, the dynamic rough diamond, known as

"Bart", who was then transforming the formerly genteel picture paper into Britain's first mass circulation tabloid. The mutual antipathy turned to open hostility when King eventually took over the *Mirror*'s sister paper, the *Sunday Pictorial*, and set up a rival empire, rubbing salt into the wound by poaching Bart's young protégé, Hugh Cudlipp, and making him editor.

Despite his privileged background, King was no less radical in his political views than Bart, and he and Cudlipp campaigned courageously against appeasement when that line was less than fashionable in Fleet Street. They stole some of Bart's thunder by hiring no less a freelance than Winston Churchill to broadcast warnings of the Hitler peril to come – only to enrage Churchill by their criticisms when he later came to power himself.

It was the racy, populist *Mirror*, however, that established itself as the Forces' favourite paper during the Second World War and which laid the groundwork not only for the Labour landslide of 1945 but also for a soaring rise in circulation to over four million in the late 1940s.

Not until 1951 did King get his long-awaited chance to "recover" what he had always regarded as his rightful inheritance. Bart, in order to cope with such heady success for someone who had started as a cartoonist, had taken heavily to the bottle. King masterminded a boardroom coup and took over "his" chair.

But the *Mirror* alone could not contain King's burgeoning ego. First, he bought "back" the Glasgow *Daily Record*. Then, after an epic battle with Roy Thomson, he took over the huge Odhams magazine group to shore up IPC's shaky periodicals division in a deal that included the ailing *Daily Herald*, Labour's "own" paper (soon to be known as "King's Cross"), as well as the profitable down-market Sunday, the *People*.

As IPC grew, so did King's sense of mission. He had come to believe, like Northcliffe before him – and as mistakenly – that he was destined not merely to achieve fame as a press baron but to wield political power.

Undoubtedly, the four IPC papers – *Mirror*, *Herald*, *Sunday Mirror* (née *Pictorial*) and *People* – campaigning enthusiastically against "13 years of Tory misrule", had played a part in Labour's win in 1964. Such a telling contribution to Wilson's victory clearly called for an appropriate reward, an important post in the new Government.

But it was to be almost a year before the new Prime Minister offered his embittered ally a peerage and a minor export appointment. To add to King's humiliation, Wilson proved unreceptive to the advice that King showered on him, both privately and through the columns of the *Mirror*.

Patronisingly, King told the Prime Minister that while he was a "supreme Parliamentary politician" he lacked a proper grasp of the big issues (an assessment with which less prejudiced observers have concurred).

Further offers of a title failed to placate an almost paranoid King. Now obsessed by this failure to recognise his outstanding services to the party, he brought the feud to a head on May 10 1968, with his imperious signed front-page article, "ENOUGH IS ENOUGH", which demanded Wilson's resignation.

He wrote: "We are now threatened with the greatest financial crisis in our history. It is not to be removed by lies about our reserves, but only by a fresh start under a fresh leader". The phrase about "reserves" was highly significant as King had been a director of the Bank of England from 1965 until his resignation the night before the article appeared.

This extraordinary outburst was the final straw for his fellow directors, who were beginning to worry that the ramshackle IPC mammoth was heading for structural and financial trouble.

They had remembered – although apparently King had forgotten – that, despite his expansive proprietorial habit of talking about "my newspapers", King's Uncle Rothermere had sold the family holding to shareholders in 1931 and that their chairman, nephew or not, was in fact just another salaried member of staff.

He was still Cecil King, however, and it was another three weeks before they could screw their collective courage to the sticking-place and charge Hugh Cudlipp with the unnerving task of telling him to go. King went, though not before he had summoned the television cameras to that elegant office with a last monarchical flourish to tell the nation that he had been stabbed in the back by disloyal pygmies but he was not finished yet. As Cudlipp moved into his chair, Fleet Street knew that he was.

He spent the rest of his life in Dublin, which had been the home of his King forefathers (who included an 18th-century bookseller and a clergyman) as well as the birthplace of Northcliffe.

He married first, in 1923, Agnes Margaret Cooke, daughter of the Professor of Hebrew at Oxford, and had three sons (two of whom predeceased him) and one daughter.

This marriage was dissolved and he married secondly,

in 1962, Dame Ruth Railton, the founder of the National Youth Orchestra, who survives him.

April 20 1987

RUDOLPH PALUMBO

RUDOLPH PALUMBO, the property developer who has died aged 86, was a shadowy and mysterious figure even by the standards of a profession which depends upon a degree of discretion and secrecy.

His name is mainly associated with the site next to the Mansion House in the City of London which Peter Palumbo, his son, set about redeveloping and with the demolition of Norfolk House in St James's Square, one of the most serious of the many losses of great Georgian buildings in London between the wars.

Rudolph Palumbo was born in London in 1901. His father owned a café in Lower Thames Street having emigrated from Amalfi in the 1880s.

Palumbo had little formal education and was largely self-taught, always being an avid reader. According to Oliver Marriott's painstaking study of *The Property Boom*, Palumbo first emerged in 1934 in the small print of a prospectus selling Regis House in King William Street, which he had earlier built with F. G. Minter, to a company promoted by Aynsley Bridgland, an active developer with whom he was often associated.

Norfolk House, designed by Matthew Brettingham as the London palace of the Dukes of Norfolk, was secretly purchased by Palumbo and P. M. Rossdale from the 16th Duke in 1937 to the fury of the Dowager

Duchess, who joined the newly-founded Georgian Group in protest.

Despite strong representations by the group and others, London County Council would not prevent the demolition of the building in 1938 by exercising powers given by the new Town and Country Planning Act. Some of the interiors of Norfolk House were rescued by the Victoria and Albert Museum. Others were eventually recreated in the private suite occupied by Palumbo in the building he erected on the site of the old Carlton Club in Pall Mall in 1958.

Palumbo also managed to achieve notoriety by building a block of flats on the site of one half of a semi-detached pair of Regency villas in St John's Wood when the other surviving half was owned by Mrs Philip Trotter, the formidable honorary secretary of the Londoners' League, who henceforth listed her address as "The Mutilated House, Maida Vale".

Like many other astute developers, Palumbo bought up bombed sites in the City during the Second World War. His great coup was to begin rebuilding the large site between Walbrook and St Swithun's Lane early in 1948 before the development charge came into force in July, and before the 1947 plan for rebuilding the City became statutory.

From a small neo-Georgian office erected on this site next to St Stephen's, Walbrook, Palumbo ran his many companies, notably the Rugarth Investment Trust. He also began in 1958 to buy up the freeholds and leaseholds of the neighbouring Victorian buildings in the triangle formed by Poultry and Queen Victoria Street to create, eventually, one vast development almost opposite the Bank of England.

It was his son Peter Palumbo, however, who approached the famous German modernist, Mies van der Rohe, to design a single tall tower on one side of what was intended to become "Mansion House Square". It was this plan, initially deferred by the City in 1969 owing to incomplete ownership of the sites required, which was eventually rejected after the momentous public inquiry held in 1984.

Rudolph Palumbo evidently did not share his son's passionate concern with commissioning modern architecture of quality. The Norfolk House and Walbrook rebuildings were designed by the pedestrian firm of Gunton & Gunton although the block in Pall Mall was redeemed by having Donald McMorran as consultant.

Palumbo himself lived at Buckhurst Park, Ascot, a house he had commissioned in 1963 from Claud Phillimore, the neo-Georgian architect. He collected furniture, porcelain, clocks and silver, particularly of the Georgian period. Ironically, it was the activities of developers like Palumbo in the 1930s, who ruthlessly exploited the absence of protection then given to real Georgian buildings, which provoked the establishment of statutory listed building legislation and so, initially at least, prevented the redevelopment of the Victorian buildings for Mansion House Square.

That Rudolph Palumbo should have died on the very day that the Court of Common Council of the City of London decisively rejected his son's second scheme to build on the site is peculiarly poignant. (But the controversial development was, ultimately, to be realised by Lord Palumbo, as he became.)

He is survived by his second wife, the former Joan

Harper, and by his son by his first marriage in 1933 to Elsie Gregory.

July 20 1987

DIANA LADY DELAMERE

DIANA LADY DELAMERE, who has died aged 74, became the central figure in what has popularly been portrayed as one of the *crimes passionel* of the century when her elderly second husband Sir "Jock" Delves Broughton, 11th Bt, was tried in Kenya for the murder of her lover the 22nd Earl of Erroll in 1941.

Broughton was acquitted at the trial, which caused a major sensation even though it took place in the middle of the Second World War, but committed suicide the following year. His widow, who subsequently married twice more, took to her grave the full story of who was responsible for the body in the Buick on the Nairobi Road.

The case inspired James Fox's book *White Mischief* (adapted as a feature film), and also the television play *The Happy Valley*.

Fox's fellow sleuth into the mystery, Cyril Connolly, who had been at Eton with the dashing "Joss" Erroll, described Lady Delamere as "one of those creamy ash blondes of the period with a passion for clothes and jewels, both worn to perfection, and for enjoying herself and bringing out enjoyment in others".

Quite apart from her familiar role as the *femme fatale* of the Erroll case, Diana Delamere was a woman of considerable fascination. She rode fearlessly to hounds, flew with Amy Johnson, fished the sea for marlin, owned a string of racehorses, shrewdly managed vast estates and eventually became the doyenne of white Kenyan Society.

Born in 1913, she was the daughter of Seymour, Caldwell, of The Red House, Hove, an Old Etonian gambler. Following a brief marriage to Vernon Motion, who played second piano in the Savoy Orpheans, she ran a cocktail club in Mayfair called The Blue Goose.

In November 1940, at Durban Register Office, South Africa, she married Sir Henry John ("Jock") Delves Broughton, a Cheshire baronet 30 years her senior with whom she had emigrated from England. Immediately afterwards they settled in the so-called "White Highlands" of Kenya, where she soon met the 22nd Earl of Erroll, Hereditary Lord High Constable of Scotland, Chief of the Hays, Military Secretary of the East Africa Command and a philanderer notorious even by the louche standards of "Happy Valley".

By Christmas Lord Erroll and Lady Broughton were embroiled in a passionate love affair. On January 18, Lady Broughton's lover and husband confronted one another. "Diana tells me she is in love with you," was the Baronet's opening gambit according to the evidence of Lord Erroll's garden boy.

"Well, she has never told me that but I am frightfully in love with her," replied the Earl.

On January 23 Broughton dined with his wife and Erroll at the Muthaiga Club, and, in the course of a bizarre evening, proposed a toast: "I wish them every happiness and may their union be blessed with an heir. To Diana and Joss."

In the early hours of the following morning two

African milk boys discovered Erroll's corpse. The following month Lady Broughton and her husband went off on a shooting safari into the Southern Masai Reserve.

On the first day of Broughton's trial for murder in May 1941, his wife made a memorable entrance into the court attired in an elegant widow's ensemble of black hat, veil and a profusion of diamonds. She left the court only once in the three-week trial, when Erroll's ear, preserved in a jar, was handed round as a exhibit.

Following Broughton's acquittal and suicide, she married for the third time, in 1943, Gilbert Colvile, an extensive cattle-rancher at Naivasha, Kenya. They were divorced in 1955 and later that year she married fourthly and finally, the 4th Lord Delamere, who died in 1979.

Lady Delamere continued to live in semi-regal state at Soysambu, Elmenteita, where her father-in-law, the 3rd Lord Delamere, had pioneered the gilded exodus to the heady freedom of the White Highlands.

September 7 1987

ROBERT HEBER-PERCY

ROBERT HEBER-PERCY, the squire of Faringdon, Berks, who has died aged 75, was an English eccentric in the grand tradition.

Devoted to books, paintings and the beautification of his estate, he built follies, rode to hounds with his reins held at the buckle on the tips of his fingers, and was the proprietor of an undertaker's business. Known as "the Mad Boy", he had a brief but hectic career in the Cavalry, acted as an extra in Hollywood, worked in a Lyons Corner

House (until spilling soup over a customer) and helped run a night club.

During the Second World War he had a Secret Service job in Arabia ("The Arabs like good manners, and I have them"), later serving as a private, albeit one who drove a large Buick.

Legion were the tales of this larger-than-life figure, particularly following his adoption as the protégé of the equally eccentric author, painter and composer, the 14th Lord Berners, familiar to readers of Nancy Mitford as "Lord Merlin". As Miss Mitford's sister, Diana Mosley, has written, Heber-Percy's "high spirits, elegant appearance and uninhibited behaviour enchanted Gerald [Berners] who no longer needed a drug to give him contentment".

In Salzburg Heber-Percy hurled a glass tankard from an upper window, narrowly missing a pedestrian below. In Florence, following a suicide attempt, he once arrived at the Hotel Excelsior, carried semi-conscious on the shoulder of Lord Berners.

The Mad Boy had a long-running feud with Cecil Beaton which culminated, in 1974, in Heber-Percy socking the celebrated photographer on the jaw at the threshold of the writer Peter Quennell's birthday party in Chelsea. Beaton, who suffered a stroke that summer, was sent reeling into Cheyne Row. He noted in his diary that Heber-Percy "had waited his chance to take the law into his own hands, break it and give me my come-uppance".

Robert Vernon Heber-Percy was born (not inappropriately) on November 5 1911, the youngest son of Algernon Heber-Percy, a kinsman of the Dukes of Northumberland, and brought up at Hodnet Hall, a vast neo-Elizabethan pile in Shropshire. His brother, Cyril, wrote of Robert: "He was full of fun, up to every prank, could hoodwink most people, and developed a gift for repartee. To this day he is capable of the most diabolical hoaxes."

Educated at Stowe, he was commissioned into the King's Dragoon Guards but his antics cut short any prospect of a military career. In 1950, following the death of Lord Berners, Heber-Percy inherited Faringdon, the fine Georgian house celebrated for such idiosyncrasies as fantailed pigeons dyed pink, orange, green, blue.

Heber-Percy maintained and enhanced Faringdon's exotic atmosphere, constructing a magnificent swimming pool reached by high steps and overlooked by giant gryphons. The floor of the changing room was inlaid with pennies. Far from an idle aesthete, he would rise at dawn to work in the fields.

Heber-Percy married first in 1942 (dissolved 1947) Jennifer, daughter of Sir George Fry, 1st Bt, and they had a daughter. In 1985 he married secondly, Lady Dorothy ("Coote") Lygon, younger daughter of the 7th Earl Beauchamp (supposed model for Lord Marchmain in *Brideshead Revisited*). They parted amicably a year later.

October 31 1987

SEAN MACBRIDE

SEAN MACBRIDE, the holder uniquely of both the Nobel and Lenin Peace Prizes, who has died aged 83, began his career as a terrorist and ended it as a respected statesman.

That this respect was not universally granted was unsurprising considering the vehemence of his politics.

He was successively chief of staff of the IRA, Minister of External Affairs in the Irish Republic, Secretary-General of the International Committee of Jurists, Chairman of Amnesty International and United Nations Commissioner for Namibia.

Sean MacBride was born in 1904 at Pietermaritzburg, South Africa, where his father Major John MacBride had fought on the Boer side against the British by way of keeping up the Irish tradition of military resistance to the Crown. The poet W. B. Yeats was, for about 30 years, passionately in love with his mother Maud Gonne, and was bitterly disappointed when she married MacBride instead of himself. It was the execution of John MacBride in the 1916 rebellion that led Yeats to coin the phrase "a terrible beauty is born". But the rebel's widow refused the poet's renewed offer of marriage.

MacBride was educated largely in Paris and spoke with a beguiling French accent which added to his considerable charm. In 1919 he returned to Dublin, and joined the IRA, suffering his first spell of imprisonment at 14 for his pains, and taking part in ambushes and guerrilla skirmishes according to legend. During the civil war, after the treaty establishing the Irish Free State, he took the part of de Valera's Republicans and was imprisoned again. After de Valera's accession to power in 1932 he remained intransigent and was briefly chief of staff of the IRA in 1936 while dabbling in journalism.

It is said that the police were looking for him in 1937 when he was sitting for his law examinations at the National University in Dublin. A year later he was honoured by de Valera for his "stalwart military service" to Irish independence and thereafter gave up active involvement in the IRA. Hanging up his pistol for good, he was speedily called to the Bar where he made a speciality of defending Republican terrorists in the courts.

In 1947 he entered politics directly, founding the *Clann na Poblachta* party, a fractious grouping of Socialists and Republicans, and winning a by-election. As a consequence de Valera, rattled by his success, unwisely called a general election.

MacBride's party won 10 seats and he was appointed Minister for External Affairs in the unlikely coalition government which followed. In the next year Eire withdrew from the Commonwealth at the insistence of his party and declared itself the Republic of Ireland.

The new republic declined to join Nato so long as Ireland remained partitioned. MacBride suggested a bilateral defence treaty to the Americans but was rebuffed. His attitude subsequently became increasingly anti-American.

The Inter-Party coalition collapsed in 1951 and MacBride's party disintegrated. He remained in the Dail long enough to bring down a second Inter-Party government in 1957, in opposition to its policy of suppressing the IRA, or acting — as he put it — "as Britain's policeman".

Thereafter MacBride took no active part in Irish politics. His proposal to run for President of the Republic met with little enthusiasm, and he confined himself to the international stage. He was secretary-general to the International Commission of Jurists from 1963 to 1970 and chairman of Amnesty International from its foundation until 1974.

In 1973, on the nomination of Swapo, he was appointed United Nations Commissioner for South West Africa and, while holding that office, declared that he had no objection to the invasion of that territory by Cuban or other "liberation forces". The following year, somewhat to his surprise, he shared the Nobel Peace Prize for his "untiring fight for human rights". Three years later he achieved his double when the Russians gave him their own Lenin Peace Prize.

MacBride's anti-Americanisms earned him plenty of friends in the Third World. He was invited by the Iranians to act as intermediary in their quarrel with the United States, and responded by calling for the Shah to be tried before an international tribunal. President Carter questioned his impartiality.

MacBride was a close friend of Amadou Mbow, secretary-general of Unesco, with whom he devised a proposed "international information order" which would have restricted severely the freedom of journalists to report from Communist and other dictatorships. This proposal was eventually shelved, along with Mbow.

In the Dublin Supreme Court MacBride consistently opposed any legislative proposal which he thought might compromise Ireland's neutrality, by now elevated by him to an article of faith. He was the author of the MacBride Principles, a set of restrictions on employment in Northern Ireland.

MacBride, who married in 1926 Catalina Bulfin and had a son and daughter, declined to the end to condemn the IRA outright, blaming their continued existence on the British.

In his person Sean MacBride was difficult to dislike. He was unfailingly courteous and equable. A man of considerable culture and charm, there can be no doubt that his amiable characteristics contributed to his failure as an Irish politician.

As for his hatred of England, it was purely abstract,

and would surely have evaporated – as he himself proclaimed – the instant the English were converted to Irish republicanism.

January 16 1988

KLAUS FUCHS

KLAUS FUCHS, who has died aged 76, was the most important of the atom spies who betrayed the secrets of the bomb to the Soviet Union. He is thought to have saved the Russians 18 months in their frantic efforts to catch up with the West.

The most unlikely-looking spy, he appeared the epitome of the absent-minded professor with his domed forehead and spectacles. Spycraft sat uneasily with him: he was, for example, somewhat bemused when ordered to make contact with the agent who "ran" him in New York for two and a half years. Fuchs was told to go to Lower East Side carrying a tennis ball in his hand to meet a man wearing gloves and carrying an extra pair, with a green book.

Bemused or not, he made contact and passed on the West's most important secrets to Harry Gold, a man whose name he never knew.

Emil Julius Klaus Fuchs, the son of a German Lutheran pastor, was born in 1911 and joined the Communist party at about the time Hitler came to power. To get him out of trouble with the Nazis, his father sent him to live with a Quaker family in Bristol, who furthered his education and set him on the road to becoming a brilliant scientist.

At the outbreak of the Second World War, however, Fuchs was detained as an enemy alien and shipped off to Canada. It is thought likely that it was there he made his first contact with Soviet intelligence.

He was allowed to return to England and found a job as a statistician working at Birmingham University on the Tube Alloys Project, the cover name for atomic research. Fuchs received security clearance for this and became a British subject – despite having been denounced as a Communist before the war by the German Consul in Bristol.

He was already in touch with Simon Kremer of the Military Attaché's Department of the Soviet Embassy in London and when the Tube Alloy Project and its scientists were handed over to the Americans, Fuchs went with it to Los Alamos. He handed over detailed reports of test results, methods of manufacture and guidance on theory, all in his own precise handwriting, to Gold who transmitted them to Moscow.

Once the bomb had been dropped on Japan, Fuchs returned to Britain to become the head of the Theoretical Physics Division of the Atomic Energy Establishment at Harwell. There, the Russians contacted him again through an agent codenamed Sonia by the British.

It was not until two years later, in 1949, that the Americans, working on the material provided by Igor Gouzenko, the cipher clerk who had defected from the Soviet Legation in Ottawa, threw suspicion on him. For the first time Fuchs became a spy suspect although there was practically no hard evidence against him.

MI5 wanted to question him, but did not want to make its interest obvious in case this deprived it of other leads. It was Fuchs himself who came to the rescue.

A curious feature of his complicated personality was that he was a stickler for the nuts and bolts of security. His father had been appointed as a teacher at the University of Leipzig in East Germany and Fuchs went to ask the Harwell Security Officer whether that would compromise his position.

MI5 seized the opportunity to send down its chief interrogator William ("Jim") Skardon. Using the sympathetic approach for which he was already famous, the patient, pipe-smoking Skardon eventually persuaded Fuchs to confess in great detail to his double life of espionage.

In the long confession, which he signed in January 1950, Fuchs added a note of contrition: "I know that all I can do now is to try to repair the damage I have done. The first thing is to make sure that Harwell will suffer as little as possible and that I have to save for my friends as much as possible of that part that was good in my relations with them."

In his confession Fuchs revealed part of his own complicated persona when he described using his Marxist philosophy to establish two separate compartments in his mind. He called it a state of "controlled schizophrenia".

Lord Chief Justice Goddard was clearly impatient with such psychological talk at Fuchs's trial and sentenced him to the then maximum penalty, 14 years. "His state of mind merely goes to show that he is one of the most dangerous men that this country could have within its shores," declared Goddard.

In fact Fuchs spent only nine years in prison. On his release he chose to go to East Germany where he was appointed director of a nuclear research institute at Dresden, working – or so he claimed – only on peaceful uses of atomic energy.

He married Greta Keilson, a German girl he had known since childhood.

January 29 1988

JOHN STONEHOUSE

JOHN STONEHOUSE, the former Labour Minister who has died aged 62, faked his death by drowning in a bizarre attempt to escape financial ruin in Britain and estabish a new identity in Australia.

To the end of his life he blamed everyone and everything but himself for a catalogue of crime and deception that destroyed his political career, earned him a prison sentence and ruined others who were innocently caught in his wake. At his trial, Mr Justice Eveleigh described him as a "sophisticated and skilful confidence trickster . . . a persuasive, deceitful and ambitious man."

The story that unfolded from the moment his clothes were found on a Miami beach in November 1974, gripped the world's press and would have stretched a novelist's credibility. Apart from fraud on a grand scale and his "drowning", there was an extraordinary saga of round-the-world travel as he sought to shed his past and rumours that he was either the victim of a Mafia-style murder or a Soviet spy.

Stonehouse was tall, handsome and charming; in his heyday he exuded that sense of power and authority which some women seem to find irresistible. He, in turn, revelled in their adulation and was a notorious philanderer.

In the House of Commons, however, he was very

much a loner, making no effort to cultivate friends, which was strange given his political ambitions.

John Thomson Stonehouse was born on July 28 1925 and educated at elementary school and Tauntons School, Southampton. Initially he worked in the probation service before doing his National Service in the RAF as a pilot and education officer.

He then read economics at the London School of Economics where he was chairman of the Labour Society.

He entered the Commons in February 1957, as Labour Co-op Member for Wednesbury and first came to prominence when he thwarted a Communist takeover of the London Co-operative Society, of which he had been appointed director in 1956. His two-year stint as the society's president in the early 1960s gave him a taste for large-scale business and its perks.

The first question mark over Stonehouse's integrity came when it emerged that, while an MP on a fact-finding visit to the Central African Federation, he had tried to set up a private business.

At the same time, his strident speeches to African audiences angered the Federal Government of Rhodesia and Nyasaland and he was declared a prohibited immigrant. This ensured him something of a hero's welcome from many Labour MPs, particularly among the Left with whom he had not hitherto been popular.

However, there was no doubting his talents and he seemed to be in the non-doctrinaire managerial mould that Harold Wilson was eager to develop in the Labour party. He rose rapidly: in Wilson's first administration from 1964 to 1966 he was Parliamentary Secretary at the Ministry of Aviation; and then in 1967, after a spell as

Parliamentary Under-Secretary of State for the Colonies, he was briefly Minister of Aviation before being appointed Minister of State at the Ministry of Technology where he pulled off a major arms deal with Libya.

In 1968 he was appointed Postmaster-General with the task of supervising the transition of the postal and telephone services from a Government department into a commercially run corporation. Astonishingly, the Cabinet agreed to Stonehouse appointing himself Chief Executive as well as the first Minister of Posts and Telecommunications.

This proved a disaster – one of his many legacies is the two-tier postal service. It was also an illustration – to be repeated in the financial scheming that proved his downfall – of how Stonehouse's considerable abilities were overstretched by his arrogant self-confidence, persuasiveness and ruthless ambition.

After Labour's 1970 defeat, Wilson, by then thoroughly disillusioned with his protégé, dropped him from the front bench. The dream of political power fading, Stonehouse set about becoming a business tycoon in the burgeoning world of fringe banking.

Capitalising on his well-known interest in the Third World, he established the British Bangladesh Trust. It aimed to attract investment capital both from Bangladeshi immigrants in Britain and from British business interests eager to exploit the new nation's commercial potential.

He managed to procure investment from many reputable companies and businessmen, including Sir Charles Forte who joined the board of London Capital Group, the culmination of Stonehouse's grand design to establish his own secondary bank. Such was the personal domination

Stonehouse achieved that his fellow directors seemed unaware that the whole set-up was what a Board of Trade inquiry later described as a "debt-ridden pack of cards . . . saturated with offences, irregularities and improprieties".

Pride would not allow him to admit failure. So, together with his secretary at the House of Commons, co-conspirator and mistress, Mrs Sheila Buckley, Stonehouse concocted an elaborate plan whereby he would "die" and then start a new life with Mrs Buckley in Australia.

He first ascertained from a hospital in his constituency (by now Walsall North) the name of a man around his own age who had recently died, a Mr Markham, and proceeded to visit the relations, ostensibly to offer his condolences as their MP but in reality to garner information about his character and habits.

Then he obtained a copy of the birth certificate and forged a passport application form with his own photograph *alias* Markham, certified with the forged signature of a fellow MP. The next few weeks were spent opening more than 40 false bank and credit card accounts in Markham's name, raising overdrafts in his own name and taking out insurance policies on his life for his wife. Armed with these, Stonehouse flew to Miami for discussions with a bank about his companies' affairs.

At the end of one meeting he said he was going for a swim and a few hours later his clothes were found on the beach. And so while Stonehouse was assumed to have drowned, "Mr Markham" was en route for Honolulu and Melbourne. After a short stay he flew to Copenhagen to meet Mrs Buckley before returning to Melbourne.

But suspicions about the "death" grew rapidly. Beach

lifeguards were adamant no one had drowned, no body was washed ashore, and in Britain the insurance companies were questioning his policies.

On Christmas Eve in 1974, Stonehouse was caught in Melbourne by pure chance. Police watching out for the vanished Earl of Lucan, wanted for the murder of his children's nanny, had become suspicious of an Englishman regularly collecting mail from the post office and arrested him – they were in fact coded letters from Mrs Buckley.

Although Stonehouse may have been exposed and had entered Australia in an unconventional way, he was still a British MP and entitled under Australian law to enter the country freely. He claimed to be the victim of blackmail and persecution in Britain and for a time it seemed he would be allowed to stay.

After a six-month battle over extradition, during which he tried another escape, he and Mrs Buckley found themselves in court at Bow Street on fraud and conspiracy charges, with Stonehouse angrily playing the role of martyr. He refused to resign from the Commons and, until convicted, could not be expelled. But he left the Labour party to join the English National party, an eccentric group which he claimed would restore honesty to British politics under his leadership.

Stonehouse was eventually allowed bail and a few days before his trial at the Old Bailey made an hour-long speech in the Commons on the evils of "humbug, hypocrisy, moral decadence and materialism" afflicting England. It was an extraordinary display of self-righteousness, heightened by fury at having to speak to only a handful of MPs. Most of the House had boycotted the fiasco.

At the trial, which lasted 70 days, he conducted his

own defence and it was a virtuoso performance, particularly as his only legal knowledge was what he learned while on remand. He fought his conviction up to the House of Lords over what he had established, albeit to no avail, was an hitherto unresolved point of law.

Stonehouse was sentenced to seven years' imprisonment and resigned his Parliamentary seat before being expelled. Mrs Buckley received a two-year suspended sentence, the judge describing her as "unfortunate" to have met him.

Stonehouse's wife, the former Barbara Joan Smith, waited until the trial was over before divorcing him. During his time in prison he had several heart attacks and received major heart surgery.

He was released on parole after three years and immediately married Mrs Buckley. Unabashed, he was back at Westminster within a few days listening to a Lords debate on the legal system, and speaking to the Cambridge Union.

A decade later he was still indulging in self-vindication. He seized on Peter Wright's *Spycatcher* allegations of MI5's attempts to destabilise the Wilson Government to call for an inquiry into how they had destroyed him.

In spite of the millions of pounds Stonehouse had swindled, none seemed to have been salted away, for he and his second wife lived modestly on her income as a public relations consultant, while he wrote fiction.

Stonehouse's earlier books had been autobiographical – *Prohibited Immigrant* (1960), *Death of an Idealist* (1975), *My Trial* (1976). Later he switched to thrillers: *Ralph* (1982), *The Baring Fault* (1986), *Oil on the Rift* (1987). He finished his last book, *Who Sold Australia?* shortly before his death.

He is survived by his second wife and by a son and two daughters of the first marriage and a son of the second marriage.

April 15 1988

FRANK HAXELL

FRANK HAXELL, who has died aged 75, was a ruthless Communist whose control of the Electrical Trades Union wreaked havoc throughout British industry for a decade before his power was broken by the High Courts in 1961 over a ballot-rigging scandal.

This celebrated case was the culmination of a long and courageous battle by anti-Communists in the union, notably Frank Chapple, and centred around Haxell's re-election as General Secretary two years earlier. Mr Justice Winn found that "fraudulent and unlawful devices" had been used to prevent the election of his non-Communist opponent, John Byrne.

He described Haxell as "most markedly dominant, shrewd, ruthless and persuasive" and found that he and other members of the Executive had "arrogated power unfettered by democratic practices".

Although probably fewer than 2,000 of the union's 230,000 members were Communists, the electricians' vital role in every industry made it a key target for Communist disruption. By 1948 the president, general secretary and other senior officials were all Communists but the takeover did not begin in earnest until Haxell was elected assistant general secretary in that year.

26

Frank Haxell

He was already on the Communist party's national executive and a key member of its industrial committee organising disruption in industry. Although only a junior official he rapidly established his authority over the rest of the union leadership.

Haxell was a brilliant, dedicated organiser with an instinctive understanding of trouble-creating tactics; he invented the "guerrilla" strike to maximise disruption at the least cost to his union, legitimised the "unofficial" strike and in 1955 managed to halt the national press for 26 days.

He was also a singularly unattractive personality, an arid and humourless zealot and rigidly orthodox Stalinist.

Francis Leslie Haxell was born in 1913 and started working as an electrician after leaving school. He held a number of minor union posts until securing his first power base after the Second World War as leader of its powerful and Communist-controlled London Area. This gave him a seat on the National Executive.

He was elected General Secretary in 1955 by an apathetic membership. Fewer than 20 per cent bothered to vote either in this or even in the bitterly fought 1959 contest.

The Russian invasion of Hungary in 1956 proved the turning point in Haxell's fortunes with several leading members of the union, including Frank Chapple and Leslie Cannon, who were later to lead the battle against him, resigning from the Communist party. His refusal to condemn the invasion aroused the first real rank and file hostility to his leadership.

The second eruption came when Cannon won an election for office but, after a so-called inquiry by Haxell

27

into alleged voting irregularities, was declared "not elected". He then had the union rulebook rewritten to further strengthen the Communist grip.

The climate of fear that Haxell's men had created was brought home to the nation by a remarkable BBC *Panorama* investigation into what was happening in the union. Haxell's opponents would only agree to be interviewed with their backs to the screen and voices distorted. What they had to say was devastating.

In the 1959 contest Haxell was declared to have a majority of a thousand votes over Byrne. Investigations showed the votes of 100 out of 700 branches had been disqualified and many other pro-Haxell votes faked. It was this that led to the court action and to Haxell's downfall.

He was then ditched by his hitherto closest allies with the same ruthlessness he had lived by. Haxell was eventually forced to resign from the Communist party, for bringing it into disrepute by condoning "illegal and undemocratic methods".

The victorious moderate leadership wreaked its revenge, stripping Haxell of the profit he had made on his union-financed home and exposing the financial corruption that had kept him and his colleagues in comfort at their members' expense.

Haxell's wife, Queenie, divorced him in 1968. They had two children.

May 30 1988

MARIE-LA-JOLIE

MARIE-LA-JOLIE, who has died at Marseille aged 82, was a celebrated brothel-keeper in that city's criminal heyday, when the *vieux port* was a world centre for white-slaving and drug-trafficking.

Marie Paoleschi was born at Marseille in 1906 and became a prostitute aged 17, at the suggestion of a petty gangster with whom she had fallen in love at a dance.

Her career took her to the Pigalle district of Paris, and to such outposts of her trade as Saigon and Buenos Aires. But Marseille was always her home, and after many vicissitudes she set up her own establishment there.

A few years ago Marie-la-Jolie published her memoirs in two volumes, which gave a hair-raising account of film stars and gangsters – notably the Guerini brothers, notorious for the "French Connection"; of a life of smuggling, corruption, prison, vendettas and champagne.

When she was warned that her revelations might endanger her safety she was unworried: "At my age, who cares?"

Marseille's most infamous madam ended her days in a small flat near the waterfront: alone, toothless save for one rotting fang, but content to have outlived nearly all her old associates.

August 18 1988

LORD SILKIN
OF DULWICH

LORD SILKIN OF DULWICH, who has died aged 70, was, as Sam Silkin, a highly controversial Attorney-General in the successive Labour administrations from 1974 to 1979.

Though Silkin was an able lawyer, many regarded his term as Attorney-General as one of the least distinguished in modern history. Mrs Thatcher, then Leader of the Opposition, accused him of encouraging lawbreaking by his role in legislation concerning the actions of Clay Cross councillors.

Nor did he shine in the Commons, where his performance was described in *The Daily Telegraph* as one of "mesmeric torpor" and as having "the staying power of the E-K directory".

From the moment of his appointment, when he shocked the legal establishment by refusing the ritualistic knighthood that goes with the job, Silkin provoked vexed reactions. Whether his record in the following five years justified the life peerage he accepted in 1985 remains a matter of dispute among both lawyers and Labour supporters.

One controversy followed another. He made an unsuccessful attempt to obtain an injunction against the publication of the Crossman Diaries. He was accused of a cover-up over the Poulson Affair. He became imbroiled in scrimshanking over the legality of secondary picketing at Grunwick and in other disputes.

In 1977 he clashed with Lord Denning and the Court of Appeal as to whether the Attorney or the Courts were the ultimate guardian of the public interest in deciding whether to prosecute. This arose from his refusal to give consent to a privately brought action to forbid Post Office workers boycotting mail to South Africa. In the event Silkin's stand on the Attorney's historical role was vindicated by the unanimous judgment of the Law Lords.

The most uncomfortable episode of his attorneyship – and one which cast a shadow on his political and legal integrity – came over Clay Cross. When out of office he had advised his party that any future legislation to indemnify the Derbyshire councillors, who had refused to implement Tory rent rises, would set a dangerous precedent and go against "all constitutional practice".

But as Attorney he gave in to party pressure to authorise the infamous "Clay Cross Bill" which, although it did not remove existing penalties on the councillors, forbade the imposition of further surcharges and removed the ban on the offending councillors holding elected office. John Nott, then a Conservative MP, suggested that Silkin should be given the "Clay Cross" for services to socialism.

Samuel Charles Silkin was born at Neath, Glamorgan, in 1918, the grandson of a Lithuanian Jewish émigré. His father, later to become Lord Silkin (a peerage subsequently disclaimed by the eldest son, Arthur), was a solicitor and a Minister in the Attlee administration.

His brother, John, who died in 1987, held office under Wilson and Callaghan. The family was thus rare – if not unique – in having a father and two sons as Privy Councillors sitting simultaneously in Parliament.

At Westminster Sam differed sharply from his brother

John in both politics and personality. He was on the right of the Labour party and a pro-European, while John was a Bevanite and anti-Marketeer; and unlike his brother Sam was little known within the party, save as a rather dull lawyer. But their differences did not affect their personal relationship, and they founded a joint consultancy in international and Common Market law.

Young Sam made his first political speech at the age of 11, when he stood as a Labour candidate in a mock election at school. He was educated at Dulwich and Trinity Hall, Cambridge, where he took a double first in Law and played cricket for the University – although he did not win a Blue. A leg-break bowler, he also played in one game for Glamorgan.

He was called to the Bar by Middle Temple in 1941 and after service in the Second World War with the Royal Artillery – in which he rose from the ranks to become a lieutenant-colonel and was mentioned in despatches – he resumed legal practice.

Silkin, practising in the same chambers as Lord Elwyn-Jones, whom he succeded as Attorney in 1974, rapidly established himself as a highly skilled lawyer with a fine mind, but he lacked the charisma that makes many lesser ones famous.

He took Silk in 1963 and the next year scored a notable success in the leading case of *Rookes* v *Barnard*, when he persuaded The House of Lords to resurrect the tort of intimidation and established the rights of individuals against trade unions – a somewhat ironic victory in the light of his subsequent political career.

In 1964 he was elected Labour MP for the Camberwell division of Dulwich, switching 10 years later to the Southwark division. He played a major role in the passing of the Leasehold Reform Act, which gave long-leasehold-ers the right to purchase the freehold.

Silkin's right-wing views made him increasingly unpopular among the Labour activists in his constituency and contributed to his decision to leave the Commons in 1983. He had been disappointed not to be offered the high judicial office normally available to former Attorneys after Mrs Thatcher came to power – just as in the 1960s he had failed in his ambition to become Secretary-General of the Council of Europe.

In recent years Silkin turned his mind more to business than the law, becoming chairman of Waterlows and deputy chairman of Robert Maxwell's BPCC, where to employees of the company he appeared ready to accept a surprisingly subordinate role – given his political and legal experience – to the Captain.

In 1985, when he was created a Life Peer as Baron Silkin of Dulwich, he became Opposition Front Bench spokesman on legal matters in the House of Lords.

In 1941 he married Elaine Stamp, who died in 1984; he married secondly Sheila Swanston; two sons and two daughters of the first marriage survive him.

August 19 1988

SAM WHITE

SAM WHITE, the veteran Paris correspondent of the *Evening Standard*, who has died aged 77, was one of the great journalistic figures of the age.

For more than 40 years his weekly reports on every aspect of French life were one of the London newspaper's chief adornments. The *Standard* and its proprietor Lord Beaverbrook exactly suited White, and *vice versa*. He would have been wasted on a true popular paper, but he was too salty and irreverent for a true quality paper.

And, famously, he never learnt French, at least not enough to converse fluently. On being asked about his French before his appointment in 1947 he answered honestly. Beaverbook's comment was: "At least we'll have someone in Paris who won't let himself be bamboozled by the French."

He picked up his stories not through official documents or interviews, but by his fingertips: in restaurants, in Jimmy's night club in the 1950s, in the bar of the Crillon (where there was a corner and a labelled telephone reserved for him) and latterly from the Travellers' Club on the Champs Elysées.

From his first years he had natural "copy" provided by both the criminal and the upper classes: the racketeers who flourished in the black market and the rich who resumed a brilliantly ostentatious round of balls, reading about which was much to the taste of Londoners living under Mr Attlee's regime of austerity.

The *gratin* remained one of White's special subjects, notably in its financial and marital complications. One great scoop, however, never appeared in the *Standard*. In the early 1950s he came to know Jimmy Goldsmith and gave the paper the news of the young playboy's impending elopement with the heiress Isabel Patino; but the story was "spiked" because of legal worries.

From time to time White was on bad terms with the British Embassy, vexing Lady Diana Cooper when her husband Duff was Ambassador by writing about her face-lifts and later obtaining the enviable story that Lady

Diana's successor, Lady Jebb, had ordered the removal of the *bidets* from the Embassy.

He made another enemy who could answer back. In Nancy Mitford's novel *Don't Tell Alfred* there appears a slippery, trouble-making journalist Amyas Mockbar ("Amyas" Mitfordian back-slang for "Sam"; Mockbar the Russian version of Moscow, an allusion to White's origins). White was surprisingly upset by this and was only deterred from legal action by Lord Beaverbrook's insistence that his correspondents should take things like that on the chin.

Although the sillier and funnier side of life was grist to White's mill he was not merely a frivolous journalist. During the Fourth Republic it was indeed hard to take French politics seriously; it was a time when, as White put it, even the well-informed sometimes had difficulty identifying the prime minister of the day.

But if White could claim to have been right about one thing in his life it was in recognising the importance, and the greatness, of de Gaulle. White correctly predicted the general's return in 1958; that it would strengthen and not destroy French democracy; and that de Gaulle would give independence to Algeria.

He subsequently took de Gaulle's side over the blackballing of Britain from Europe (a line made easier, of course by his proprietor's hostility to the Common Market). White's collection of despatches, *de Gaulle* (1984), is worth reading by anyone interested in postwar France.

Sam White was a Russian Jew by descent, born in 1911 in the Ukraine, whence his family escaped in the turbulent years after the Bolshevik Revolution. They made their way to Australia and settled in Melbourne, where Sam grew up Australianised in everything from language to love of cricket: among his reminiscences in later life was the notorious Body-line tour of 1932–33, some of whose episodes he had witnessed.

He was educated at Melbourne University, and then "politics bit me". He joined the Australian Communist party after the rise of Hitler and wrote for obscure journals of the Left.

But the inhibitions of Communism did not suit him for long. While his friends were purged for the usual errors of Trotskyism or Left-wing deviationism, White had the distinction of being expelled from the party for "bourgeois bohemianism" – that is, for his incorrigible love of wine and women.

At the end of the 1930s White gravitated to England – where he found himself when war broke out. His first thought was to return home and join the Australian Army but when he applied for a visa a contemptuous look from a clerk, implying that he was getting out of harm's way, persuaded him to stay and join the British Army instead.

He became a despatch rider until discharged after a serious accident. He drew a 40 per cent disability pension for the rest of his life.

Recovered from his injuries he joined the *Sydney Daily Telegraph* as a war correspondent and followed the Normandy campaign from D-Day plus 3, writing also for the *Evening Standard*. He had seen Paris once only, as a weekend tripper, before entering the city with the American Army and "liberating" the Coupole, the Montparnasse restaurant.

The war over, White returned to Australia and suffered "the usual Aussie treatment for anyone who was thought to have done well abroad". Assigned the humble task of reporting from the North Sydney Police Court, he pined for Europe, neglected his work, was sacked for not turning up on time, and spent his savings on a one-way ticket to London.

In 1947, three days after an apparently unsuccessful interview at the *Evening Standard*, he was offered the job of Paris correspondent, thanks (he later discovered) to the good opinion of the news editor Ronald Hyde who had read his war despatches.

White was married twice, with two sons by the first marriage, a daughter by the second. His later years were darkened by his second wife's long illness and death, and then by his own illness.

But if sometimes in low spirits, White could always manage to be good company. His visits to London – for the annual party at the *Spectator* (to which he was a regular contributor) and to take in a match at Lord's – were eagerly awaited.

For a generation of admiring younger journalists a visit to Paris was incomplete without seeing this *parisien* of nearly a half-century's standing who yet remained an unassimilated foreigner, "filled with a foreigner's curiosity about this strange city".

September 15 1988

JOHN MITCHELL

JOHN MITCHELL, who has died at Washington aged 75, was Attorney-General in President Nixon's first administration and the first holder of that office to go to jail.

In 1975 he was the most senior of the government officials imprisoned for involvement in the Watergate scandal which had led to Nixon's resignation the previous year.

As attorney-general Mitchell moved the Justice Department, which he described as "a law-enforcement agency", steadily to the right. He had no discernible enthusiasm for civil rights and was keen on preventative detention for criminal suspects, counter-intelligence measures against radicals in the universities and the extensive use of wiretapping.

Mitchell resigned as attorney-general in 1972 in order to run the Campaign to Re-elect the President (known by the acronym "CREEP") and, as a resident of the Watergate apartment block in Washington, was a neighbour of the Democratic party offices there. These were burgled during the election campaign, apparently as part of a Republican plot to spy on their opponents.

He denied having had any part in such a conspiracy but a tape-recorded conversation between Nixon and John Erlichman, his domestic counsellor, held in March 1973, has the following exchange.

Ehrlichman: "John says he's sorry he sent those burglars in there." Nixon: "That's right." At that point Mitchell chimed in with "You are very welcome, sir," and laughter was heard.

When he was sentenced to two and a half to eight years in an Alabama prison, Mitchell took it fairly lightly, saying to reporters: "It could have been a hell of a lot worse. They could have sentenced me to spend the rest of my life with Martha" (a reference to his estranged wife, "Martha The Mouth").

Such a remark was typical of the man. He had great

self-control and never lost his temper, indeed, his restraint led some colleagues to describe him as "dour", "cold", even "inhuman". Nor was Mitchell noted for his chivalrous attitude to women. He was notorious for his remark that Katherine Graham, the proprietor of the *Washington Post* which uncovered the Watergate scandal, would "get her tit caught in the wringer".

He was released on medical grounds after serving only 19 months of his sentence and then set up a consultancy business with Jack Brennan, who was Nixon's chief aide in the early post-presidential years.

John Newton Mitchell was born in Detroit, Michigan, in 1913. His family moved to Long Island, New York, during his infancy, and he was educated at Jamaica High School, Queens, and Fordham University, Bronx.

Called to the Bar in 1938, Mitchell joined the law firm of James Caldwell and made rapid progress, becoming a partner in 1942. The next year he joined the US Navy, commanding several squadrons of torpedo boats in the Pacific, including one piloted by Lieutenant John F. Kennedy, whom he knew only slightly.

After the Second World War Mitchell returned to his law firm and established himself over the following two decades as a national expert in municipal bond finance.

In 1967 the firm merged with that of Richard Nixon, and when Nixon stood for the presidency the next year he appointed Mitchell his campaign manager. Such was his success in that role that, to general liberal dismay, Nixon went on to appoint him attorney-general.

Mitchell was twice married and is survived by a daughter from each marriage.

November 11 1988

WAYNE L. HAYS

WAYNE L. HAYS, who has died at Wheeling, West Virginia, aged 77, was a skilful practitioner of cloakroom politics and for nearly 30 years a leading member of the American Congress.

In 1976, however, Hays was forced to resign his powerful offices, and eventually his seat, over one of the most celebrated sex scandals of the day. The *Washington Post* quoted Miss Elizabeth Ray, a blonde 33-year-old who had been runner-up in a North Carolina beauty contest and was employed as Hays's staff secretary, as saying that she was paid $14,000 a year out of public funds solely to fornicate with the Democratic Congressman on demand; and that he did so regularly and in a business-like fashion, keeping his eye on a digital clock.

Miss Ray said that her typing speed had never exceeded 12 words a minute: "I can't file, I can't even answer the 'phone." Hays angrily denied this, claiming that she was at least capable of filing papers away.

Miss Ray added that she had also been intimate with two Senators and "about 10" Congressmen, and that she had decided to expose Hays because he was unkind to her. For example, when she expressed sympathy for another Congressman over the publicity surrounding his involvement with a striptease *artiste* called Fanne Foxe, Hays told her: "If a broad did that to me she wouldn't be around writing books. She'd be six feet under."

In the months after Miss Ray's revelations Hays resigned as chairman of the Democratic Congressional Campaign Committee and of the House Administration

Committee. He then took an overdose of sleeping pills and, on his release from hospital, offered his resignation to Congress; this coincided with the appearance of nude photographs in *Playboy* magazine of Miss Ray and Miss Foxe.

Wayne Levere Hays was born at Bannock, Ohio, in 1911 and educated at Ohio State University. After two years as a law student at Duke University, North Carolina, he became a high school teacher at Flushing, Ohio; but resigned when the town's board of education criticised his disregard for the achievements of the Republican party.

Hays then turned his attention to politics: he became mayor of Flushing in 1939 and two years later won a seat in the state senate, where he helped pass a bill to protect schoolteachers against summary dismissal.

He had been a member of the Officers' Reserve Corps since 1933, and two days after the Japanese attack on Pearl Harbor in 1941 he volunteered for active service, being honourably discharged the next year.

In 1948 Hays was elected for the first time to Congress, where he quickly established himself as an aggressive and articulate voice. As the *Wall Street Journal* once said of him: "Threats, bluster and intimidation are integral parts of his arsenal."

He supported public housing and health and called for the repeal of the poll tax; was a doughty Cold Warrior, a keen supporter of Nato and a notable hawk during the Vietnam War.

Hays approved the Internal Security Act of 1950, which set up the Subversive Activities Control Board and required Communists to register with the Attorney-General; but he was an outspoken opponent of political witch-hunting. Annoyed by an opponent's use of statements taken out of context to indicate Communist sympathies, Hays manoeuvred him into identifying as Communist propaganda the published remarks of two popes.

During the 1950s and 1960s he voted for every major piece of civil rights legislation, though he opposed "bussing" to achieve racial integration in schools. In 1959 he startled his colleagues by urging them to hand in their pistols at the front door before entering the House of Representatives. One member indignantly retorted: "I carry a knife, not a gun."

In the early 1970s, by collecting a number of committee chairmanships, Hays became a powerful figure in the House, the rights of which he consistently championed against the growing "executive privilege" of the presidency. Incensed by the Watergate scandal, he was among the first to call for President Nixon's resignation in 1974.

Outside politics Hays was a farmer, breeding Angus cattle and Tennessee walking horses at Belmont, Ohio. He was twice married.

February 14 1989

TYLER KENT

TYLER KENT, who has died aged 77, was the American diplomat sentenced under the Official Secrets Act to seven years' imprisonment at the Old Bailey in 1940.

Shortly after the outbreak of the Second World War, Kent had been transferred from his post in Moscow to the American Embassy in London, where he worked as a cipher clerk, encoding and decoding diplomatic messages, which he passed to Germany through Italy, then a neutral country.

Kent was virulently anti-Semitic and believed that Jews were responsible for the war in Europe; he was also influenced by the strongly anti-British attitude of his ambassador, Joseph Kennedy, the Irish-American patriarch of the future presidential clan.

MI5 suspected Kent of espionage soon after his arrival in Britain; but it did not inform Kennedy, partly because he too was under surveillance, and partly in the hope that Kent would implicate others.

Early in 1940 Hans Mackensen, the German ambassador in Rome, made a number of public statements which included references to Anglo-American naval policy. This alerted Maxwell Knight at MI5 that he was in possession of highly secret messages between Churchill and Roosevelt.

As a result the military attaché at the Italian Embassy in London was placed under surveillance, which led MI5 to Anna Wolkoff, the daughter of a Russian admiral, a fanatical anti-Bolshevik and an associate of Sir Oswald Mosley and William Joyce ("Lord Haw-Haw").

Wolkoff ran the Russian Tea Rooms in Harrington Road, Kensington, which was the meeting-place of the Right Club, an anti-war organisation headed by Wolkoff and Captain Archibald Ramsay, MP. The club's activities included posting stickers denouncing the war as a Jewish plot and organising parties of pro-fascists to sit in cinema audiences and boo Winston Churchill when he appeared in newsreels.

An MI5 agent named Joan Miller discovered that

Wolkoff was in contact with Kent, and in May 1940 Special Branch officers raided his flat in Gloucester Place, surprising him in bed with his Russian-born mistress.

The policemen found more than 1,500 secret documents, stolen from the embassy and kept by Kent in a cupboard, together with a locked book containing the names of several hundred members of the Right Club. That Kent was not arrested until 10 days after Churchill became Prime Minister suggests that he was the central figure in a Security Service "sting". Wolkoff was arrested the same day and was later sentenced to 10 years.

Kent's arrest forced the Home Secretary to introduce by cabinet fiat clause 18b of the Defence of the Realm Act, under which both Ramsay and Mosley were arrested soon afterwards.

Kennedy waived Kent's diplomatic immunity; and American diplomatic traffic was blacked out across the globe while a new code was devised. Not long after Kent's arrest Italy entered the war, which led some to conclude that Germany had kept her out of it so long as she remained a conduit for Kent's intelligence.

Kent and Wolkoff were held incommunicado for nearly five months and were finally tried in secret on the eve of Roosevelt's re-election at the end of October 1940.

Tyler Gatewood Kent was born in 1911 in China, the son of William Patton Kent, the American Consul at Newchang in Manchuria, and a distant cousin of General George Patton. He was educated at St Alban's, Princeton University, the Sorbonne and George Washington University, where he became fluent in languages, including Russian.

Following his father's career, Kent joined the State Department in 1934 as a cipher clerk and was posted to the newly established American Legation in Moscow. But despite his success in examinations he failed to win promotion as a full foreign service officer.

In Moscow he turned to high living, supported by smuggling Russian Imperial valuables to America; he also blotted his copybook with a number of sexual indiscretions.

Kent's activities during the war have never been entirely explained, and it has been suggested that he was also working for the Russians: after the war the FBI discovered that Tatiana Alexandrovna Ilovaiskaya, one of Kent's mistresses in Moscow, was an agent of the NKVD.

Documents released into the American archives some years ago show that even before Kent arrived in London there was another highly placed spy known only as "the Doctor", passing information to Rudolf Hess's office in Berlin. The Doctor was never caught.

After his release from prison in 1945 Kent was deported back to America, and the next year married Clara Hyatt Hodgson, a rich divorcée whose inheritance – from the Carter's Little Liver Pills fortune – funded Kent's purchase of a small-town Florida newspaper. In 1962 he used its editorial pages to goad Joseph Kennedy into making an incautious public statement about Kent's activities as a German spy. Kent sued for libel, but when the suit collapsed he sold out and retired to Mexico.

Devaluation of the peso in the mid-1970s greatly impoverished the couple, so they returned to America and set up home in a Texas trailer-park. A goatee beard and bootstring tie gave Kent the appearance of a querulous Colonel "Kentucky Fried Chicken" Sanders.

Kent devoted his final years to denying evidence in declassified FBI files that he had ties with Moscow and to fulminating against the war ("a tremendous mistake"), the Jews ("basically responsible for the establishment of world Communism") and the Russians.

His wife survives him.

February 17 1989

ABBIE HOFFMAN

ABBIE HOFFMAN, the political agitator who has died in Pennsylvania aged 52, emerged in the 1960s as a leader of America's "yippies" – political hippies or "fun revolutionaries" – who specialised in acts of guerrilla theatre.

The yippies' greatest coup came in 1968, when they joined with more earnest Left-wingers to disrupt the Democratic National Convention in Chicago and provoked the constabulary of that city to what a government report later termed a "police riot".

Influenced by the writings of the media guru Marshall McLuhan, Hoffman, regarded television as the central factor in modern American life; and the spectacle of Chicago's police launching ferocious attacks on peaceful protesters was reckoned by some analysts to have contributed to the Democrats' loss of the presidency to Richard Nixon – hardly the result Hoffman could have hoped for.

The next year Hoffman and seven others were indicted on charges of conspiracy and crossing state lines to incite a riot. The trial lasted 20 weeks, and the defendants managed to turn it into a circus. They wore judicial robes in mockery of the judge – Julius J. Hoffman – to whom they offered LSD and whom they addressed as "Julie".

The jury eventually acquitted the defendants of conspiracy but found five of them guilty of crossing state lines to incite a riot. Hoffman was sentenced to eight months in prison, but the trial was seen by many as a victory for the defendants in the "war of symbols".

Hoffman had begun to agitate among the largely apolitical hippies in the mid-1960s: "Personally, I always held my flower in a clenched fist. A semi-structure freak among the love children. I was determined to bring the hippie movement into a broader protest."

He organised countless demonstrations and acts of vandalism against symbolic Establishment targets. In 1967, for example, Hoffman and others threw dollar bills from the visitors' gallery on to the floor of the New York Stock Exchange, provoking pandemonium as the traders rushed to pick up the money. He once led an attempt to levitate the Pentagon by mental force, and on another occasion ran a pig as a presidential candidate.

In 1968 Hoffman and his cronies coined the word "yippie" for themselves and their followers, and soon after founded the Youth International party (YIP), which boasted, disingenuously, that it had "no leaders, no members, and no organisation".

The Chicago trial made Hoffman famous, and he went on to write several best-selling books – "It's embarrassing. You try to overthrow the government, and you end up on the best-seller list" – and to continue his political activities.

In 1972 Hoffman campaigned for the presidential election of Senator George McGovern, and later that year a federal appeals court unanimously overturned the Chicago convictions, citing innumerable serious errors by Judge Hoffman.

The next year, however, Hoffman was arrested for

selling cocaine to undercover agents. After six weeks in prison he was bailed but faced with a mandatory life sentence on conviction, he vanished before the trial began.

He spent the next seven years on the run, undergoing plastic surgery to alter his appearance; changing his walk, gestures and style of speech; and adopting dozens of aliases. In 1980 he gave himself up and was jailed for three years.

On his release he returned to politics – leading environmentalist protests against plans to divert water from the Delaware river, for example – and in 1988 made his debut as a professional comedian.

The son of a pharmacist, Abbott Hoffman was born at Worcester, Massachusetts, in 1936, and educated at the local high school, from which he was expelled; Worcester Academy (a private school); Brandeis University, where he was influenced by the radical social views of Herbert Marcuse; and Berkeley, where he became involved in student politics.

In 1963 he took a job as a travelling salesman in pharmaceuticals, but during the three years he held the job he devoted most of his energies to political organising in the burgeoning civil rights movement. In 1964 and again in 1965 he journeyed to the South, where he was often arrested.

The next year Hoffman set up a shop in New York, selling crafts made by poor co-operatives in Mississippi. But the civil rights movement was being split by the rise of "Black Power" militancy, and in 1967 Hoffman abandoned his shop to devote himself to opposing the Vietnam War. He found his natural constituency among the hippies who had thronged to New York's East Village.

Hoffman was a solidly built man, voluble, highly-strung and with an expressive face; in the 1960s his long, unruly hair was both a trademark and a political statement; in recent years, operating under the pseudonym of "Barry Freed" he was somewhat bald and had his hair cut conventionally.

In 1987 he was arrested for the 42nd time, charged with trespassing on the grounds of the University of Massachusetts, where he was protesting against the CIA recruitment of university students.

Hoffman married twice: first in 1960; then, after his divorce, in 1967, to Anita Kushner, who shared in many of his exploits. He had a son and a daughter by his first marriage; and another son by the second.

April 14 1989

STEVE RUBELL

STEVE RUBELL, who has died in New York aged 45, was a colourful and resilient figure in the social life of that city and the co-founder of Studio 54, a discotheque which enjoyed great success in the late 1970s.

Rubell, a small and gregarious man, used occasionally to act as doorman of the club, deciding who was fashionable enough to be admitted and failing to recognise such celebrities as the film actor Warren Beatty and members of the Kennedy family. Among those who did achieve admission were the artist Andy Warhol and Bianca Jagger, wife of the pop singer.

When Mrs Jagger held a birthday party at the club there were typically Bacchanalian scenes: she rode a white horse through the premises while "the man in the moon" was lowered from the ceiling, a giant cocaine spoon glued to his nose.

Eighteen months after the club opened, however, Rubell and his partner Ian Schrager were sentenced to prison for failure to pay taxes: he once described his approach to accounting as "cash in, cash out and skim".

Rubell enjoyed his time in prison at Montgomery, Alabama; and by informing on several other club owners the pair reduced their sentences and were released in 1981.

Deciding that "housing is the new entertainment", they bought a half-share in a seedy hotel on Madison Avenue and staffed it with inexperienced but attractive young people; it proved a phenomenal success. By the time of Rubell's death they were running four similar hotels.

Steven Rubell was born in a middle-class district of Brooklyn in 1944 and educated at Syracuse University, where he met Schrager. He worked for a short time on Wall Street and then persuaded his partners to invest in a restaurant; three years later he had 13, and joined with Schrager to expand the business.

When they opened their first discotheque, on a golf course in Long Island, neither of them knew anything about music or cocktails, but it drew many customers. Their neighbours tried to close them down, so they moved to Manhattan and opened Studio 54.

Seven years after their release from prison their fortune was assured and their position in society re-established — even if guests at their hotels had to do without alcohol because the partners' prison record prevented them getting a liquor licence.

Rubell was a man of simple American tastes, devoted

to McDonald's hamburgers and Coca-Cola "fresh from the can". He was unmarried.

August 3 1989

PROFESSOR
WILLIAM SHOCKLEY

PROFESSOR WILLIAM SHOCKLEY, the American physicist who has died in San Francisco aged 79, played a key part in the invention of the transistor, though his personal reputation became tarnished because of his bizarre views on "retrogressive evolution".

In 1956 he shared the Nobel Prize for Physics with his two colleagues, John Bardeen and Walter Brattain. The first successful demonstration of a crude transistor was conducted at Bell Telephone Laboratories in New Jersey on December 23 1947.

The invention of a solid state device that could amplify electronic signals made the more vulnerable, power-hungry vacuum tubes obsolete and marked the dawn of the electronic age.

He went on to found Shockley Semiconductor Laboratories in 1954, which was instrumental in the birth of California's "Silicon Valley". But Shockley himself laboured under the impression that his most valuable contribution to science lay in the quite separate field of genetics.

The physicist chose to spend the last two decades of his life propounding his own radical version of the Final Solution. He hoped to "turn the ship of civilisation away

51

from the dysgenic storm" which he saw looming on the horizon.

Shockley believed society to be in the grip of "retrogressive evolution" brought about by the "disproportionate reproduction of the genetically disadvantaged". He proposed the implementation of a voluntary bonus sterilisation plan, whereby those with below average IQs would be paid to be sterilised; the lower the IQ, the higher the bonus.

Shockley was no mere theorist. In 1978 he donated his sperm to a sperm bank in southern California founded by the plastic spectacle lens tycoon Robert Graham.

Graham's intention was to arrange for the genetic make-up of geniuses to be passed on, and he approached a number of Nobel prize-winners asking for their collaboration. Shockley was alone in enthusiastically declaring himself a donor.

He believed blacks to be genetically inferior to whites, and the National Academy of Science had repeatedly to reject his requests that it should fund research into the genetic differences between whites and blacks. Shockley wrote that a great injustice was being done to black Americans themselves who were condemned to generations of genetic enslavement as a result of the establishment's pusillanimous refusal to study the "dysgenic threat".

Litigious as well as controversial, Shockley claimed more than $1 million in damages from Roger Witherspoon, a reporter in Atlanta who had written that the professor's theories resembled reworked Hitlerian experiments. A Federal jury ruled in 1984 that he had indeed been libelled but awarded him only $1.

Shockley was a singularly difficult person to deal with. He made a habit of tape-recording almost every conversation he had during the course of a day, even those which took place within the privacy of his home, and when interviewed was wont to parry questions by snapping out a reference number to his wife.

The number was then found to refer to one of hundreds of handouts; the requisite sheet having been produced, Shockley circled the appropriate paragraph in red and considered the question answered. The tape recorder would be whirring all the while.

Interviewers who asked the professor why he insisted on recording his conversations would have a piece of paper thrust under their noses with the following paragraph underlined: *"He is forthright and positive about his own view of moral and ethical consideration involved in the use of the tape recorder – the single most important application of the transistor."*

The son of an American mining engineer, William Shockley was born in London on February 13 1910 and was brought up in California. He was one of the children tested in Louis Terman's classic study of gifted children but failed to score high enough to warrant inclusion in the follow-up study. He used often to point out that Terman had passed over two later Nobel prize-winners.

Shockley was educated at Hollywood High School and the California and Massachusetts Institutes of Technology. After receiving his doctorate in physics from the latter he joined the Bell Telephone Laboratories in 1936.

At this time, interest in semiconductors was growing. The limitations of valves, their short lives, their size, their fragility and high power consumption were becoming a serious constraint.

It was known that crystals of galena – the crystal in the "crystal set" – could transform an alternating current into a direct current. In 1939 Shockley began work on making a semiconductor amplify as well as rectify.

But his work was interrupted by the Second World War. From 1942 to 1944 he directed anti-submarine warfare research at Columbia University, and in 1945 served as an expert consultant to the Secretary of War.

When he returned to the Bell Laboratories (which had moved to New Jersey) he decided it was possible to control the flow of electrons by means of an electric field imposed from outside. That did not work, but while investigating why not, two members of Shockley's solid state physics team, Bardeen and Brattain, invented the "point contact" transistor in late 1947.

It was a thin slab of germanium, with a gold contact and a tungsten contact placed very close to each other on its surface. It was cumbersome, but it amplified. About a month later Shockley invented the junction transistor, which replaced the troublesome metal contacts by two more slices of germanium. These were dosed with a different impurity from the slice in the middle, to make a sandwich.

Each outer slice formed a transistor junction with the layer in the middle. Rectification and amplification then took place inside the crystal instead of on the surface.

During the 1950s it became clear how the problem that stopped Shockley's original idea from working could be overcome. The result was the field effect transistor – the type most commonly in use today.

Subsequently Shockley's standing as a physicist remained unchallenged but few were prepared to take him seriously after he became involved in genetics. In 1973 an offer of an honorary degree by Leeds University was suddenly withdrawn because of his racial theories.

Lord Boyle of Handsworth, vice-chancellor of the university, attempted to deal with the matter in gentlemanly fashion, but was thwarted when Shockley released a recording of the conversation they had had at the Carlton Club. The recording ended with Shockley's voice: "Time is now 7.15. That was Lord Boyd at the Carlton Club." (Names were never a Shockley strong point.)

He held the Chair of Engineering Science at Stanford University from 1963 to 1975 and was Emeritus Professor thereafter.

Shockley is survived by his second wife, the former Emmy Lanning, and by two sons and a daughter from his first marriage.

August 15 1989

R. D. LAING

R. D. LAING, the psychiatrist and author who has died at St Tropez aged 61, was an exponent of new and unorthodox views on the causes of mental illness, and a guru to the disaffected youth of the 1960s.

From the beginning of his medical career he mistrusted the conventional techniques of psychoanalysis and treatment, and he was later fiercely critical of the "heartless impersonality" of psychiatry: "Can what is morally wrong be scientifically right?" he asked.

Tranquillisers, in his view, were the biochemical equivalent of a straitjacket; and electroconvulsive therapy was no more or less effective than a bang on the head — he termed it "cosh-therapy".

"Ronnie" Laing was convinced that many delusive

actions were a form of defence or protest against an unacceptable external world. He saw "normal" life and social behaviour as shrivelled, inhuman and corrupt: "We are all fallen Sons of Prophecy," he wrote in one of his more oracular flights, "who have learned to die in the Spirit and be reborn in the Flesh."

It was this poetic and iconoclastic approach – together with his enthusiastic endorsement of such psychotropic drugs as marijuana and LSD – that earned Laing a wide following in the "counterculture" of the hippies: his first book, *The Divided Self: An Existential Study in Sanity and Madness* (1960), sold 400,000 paperback copies in Britain alone.

Laing helped to change ideas but encountered heated professional opposition – and at times disbelief. His conviction that insanity is a result of family pressure led him to such assertions as that "the initial act of brutality against the average child is the mother's first kiss"; and his sympathy for deviancy led him to champion the criminal as well as the insane.

He could be *outré*, too, in his own behaviour. It was his habit, for example, to howl at the moon. In 1984 he was in a bar in California when other drinkers took exception to his howling. Matters came to a head when he decided to exorcise a neighbouring drinker, who hit him over the head with a shovel, shouting: "I'll knock the Devil out of you!"

Laing's reaction to the incident was typical: "I don't blame the man who did it to me. I'm sure deep down he's really a gentle loving creature. I only hope I can still play the piano."

The son of working-class Presbyterians, Ronald David Laing was born on October 7 1927 in Glasgow. His childhood was unhappy – he was frequently beaten and his stern mother kept him apart from other children – and this helped shape his adult thought.

After attending a local grammar school – where he read widely, particularly in the classics – he studied medicine at Glasgow University and psychiatry at the West of Scotland Neurological Unit.

Laing then worked for two years in Army psychiatric units, before returning to Glasgow to practise at the Royal Medical Hospital and to teach in Glasgow University's department of psychological medicine. In 1956 he joined the Tavistock Clinic in London, where he himself underwent analysis.

After four years there he spent a further seven as a research fellow in psychiatry at the Tavistock Institute of Human Relations, becoming principal investigator at its schizophrenic and family research unit. He was also director of the Langham Clinic for Psychotherapy, a Jungian centre, from 1962 to 1965, when he helped establish a therapeutic clinic at Kingsley Hall, London, where patients and doctors lived together and where he experimented with the therapeutic use of mescaline and LSD.

Having made his name with his first and most influential book Laing went on to write a dozen more; in later years these became more speculative and metaphysical, and as he made wide changes in his earlier thinking he fell out of favour with his readers. He followed *The Divided Self* with *The Self and Others* (1961), which dealt with the interaction between individuals. *Sanity, Madness and the Family* (with A. A. Esterson, 1964) presented case histories based on his approach to families.

The same year Laing published *Reason and Violence* (with David Cooper), to which Jean-Paul Sartre contributed an introduction: "Like you," wrote the Frenchman, "I regard mental illness as 'the way out' that the free organism, in its total unity, invents in order to be able to live through an intolerable situation."

The Politics of Experience and The Bird of Paradise (1967) explored the illness of society, presenting the insane, the criminal and the revolutionary as mystical explorers in a vicious and mechanised world. It sold half a million copies in America.

In 1970 he published *Knots*, which described forms of blockage in interpersonal relations and was later adapted as a play by Edward Petherbridge: it was performed as a series of sketches, the best of which resembled animated Jules Feiffer cartoons. The next year came *The Politics of the Family*, after which Laing travelled for a time in the East and studied Buddhism and Hinduism.

The Facts of Life (1976) was to some extent autobiographical, describing the hardships of his early life; it also discussed the possibility of prenatal memories and influences on the psyche, and gave brief examples of psychiatric cases, sometimes sharply humorous.

Do You Love Me? (1977) explored the problems of erotic relationships in a manner that reminded some critics of Woody Allen, and was followed the next year by *Conversations with Children*, which was both earnest and arch. The same year he was charged with possession of 94 ampoules of LSD: the case was withdrawn by DPP, as Laing had obtained the drug in 1970, when possession by practitioners was legal.

The Voice of Experience (1982) was another essay on the significance of intra-uterine events. And in 1985 he published his autobiography, *Wisdom, Madness and Folly: the Making of a Psychiatrist*.

Laing was also a poet, and in 1979 published a volume of sonnets. His later verses tended to doggerel, though – "Little Billy, Plays with his Willy" and so on.

In the 1980s Laing's standing with the public declined, and his books were less widely read: but his classical reading enabled him to regard both praise and disparagement with equanimity. In his later years he worked as a psychoanalyst in private practice in Hampstead.

From 1964 to 1982 he was chairman of the Philadelphia Association, a London-based charity with the aim of "developing appropriate human responses to those distracted by misery, which in our present state of knowledge is not mitigated, or is sometimes aggravated, by most forms of psychiatric intervention".

August 25 1989

NICHOLAS FREEMAN

NICHOLAS FREEMAN, who has died aged 50, was the Conservative leader of the Royal Borough of Kensington and Chelsea Council from 1977 until 1989.

He stood as the Conservative candidate for Hartlepool in both the 1974 general elections and when Sir Brandon Rhys Williams, Conservative MP for Kensington, died suddenly in 1988, Freeman had high hopes of succeeding him. He failed to be nominated, which was no doubt partly explained by his virulent opposition to the poll tax, and by dubious rumours of his involvement in a plot to unseat the late incumbent.

Freeman, however, had long been a controversial

figure: in 1982 he had provoked a storm by using his powers as council leader to order the destruction of the borough's fine Victorian town hall on Kensington High Street. The Royal Fine Art Commission condemned the action as "official vandalism . . . decided upon covertly, implemented without warning and timed deliberately to thwart known opposition".

He remained unrepentant, arguing that by selling off the site for development the council would be able to build a more efficient and economically run town hall in its place. Freeman was particularly criticised for failing to find an alternative use for the building, and it was suggested that he had ordered in the demolition men overnight without consulting colleagues so as to thwart the preservation order which was about to be placed on it.

He survived the storm, doubtless helped by the fact that he dominated the council to a degree unusual among municipal leaders, but there was little comfort for the ratepayers: the cost of the new town hall far exceeded his original estimates.

Nicholas Hall Freeman was born on July 25 1939, and educated at Stoneygate School, Leicester, and King's School, Canterbury. He was admitted a solicitor in 1962 and called to the Bar by Middle Temple in 1968. He practised at the Criminal Bar and was appointed a Recorder in 1985.

A fine speaker with a powerful personality and strong political ambitions, Freeman was elected to Chelsea council in 1968 where his attractive and sociable personality won him many admirers among local Conservatives.

He became chairman of the borough planning committee shortly after being elected to the council and made a particular effort to clear up what he called "the sore thumb in the royal borough", the seedy area around Earls Court.

There were complaints, however, that Freeman took little real interest in north Kensington, where poverty and racial tension contrast uneasily with areas of immense wealth.

He vigorously implemented the Government's curbs on local authority spending and was able to claim that his council had the smallest staff per head of population of any British borough. It was also the first London borough to hand over some of the responsibility for rubbish collection to private enterprise.

Freeman was a member of the influential Conservative Central Office Policy Group for London which paved the way for the abolition of the Labour-controlled Greater London Council.

His rejection in 1988 as Conservative candidate for Kensington was a bitter disappointment which, he felt, ended his hopes of ever reaching Westminster. Freeman was elected mayor of Kensington and Chelsea in 1988, resigned as leader of the council the next year and announced his intention of retiring from the council altogether in 1990.

Colleagues were surprised at his decision, for the borough seemed to be Freeman's whole life. He spent almost every evening at the town hall either doing council business or entertaining generously in his room.

He was appointed OBE in 1985. He was unmarried.

November 13 1989

DOLORES IBARRURI

DOLORES IBARRURI, better known as *La Pasionaria*, who has died aged 93, was one of the moving spirits behind the Republican forces in the Spanish Civil War and the most famous Spanish woman of her generation.

Although a committed Communist from an early age, *La Pasionaria* ("the Passion Flower") inspired people as much by her undoubted courage, the power of her oratory and her presence – she was very tall and always dressed in black – as by her belief in the Russian Revolution.

In the first months of the war no face or voice on the Republican side was better known than hers. The posters in Madrid portrayed Lenin, Stalin and *La Pasionaria*, rather than the president or any other politician; it was she who led the recruiting campaign for the Republican army in rousing, often fanatical, speeches on the wireless and at mass rallies. A battalion was named after her.

The name of *La Pasionaria* is most often associated with her rallying cry at the beginning of the war, "*No pasaran!*" ("They shall not pass") – echoing Pétain at Verdun.

No less memorable were her exhortations to Republican troops to "die on your feet rather than live on your knees", and her speech of farewell to the International Brigades in Barcelona when they were withdrawn in November 1938: "You are history. You are legend. You are the heroic example of democracy's solidarity and universality. We shall not forget you, and when the olive tree of peace puts forth its leaves again, mingled with the laurels of the Spanish Republic's victory – come back!"

It was remarkable that any woman, in Spain and in time of war, should be as influential and famous – or notorious – as the Communist deputy for Asturias. Inevitably *La Pasionaria*'s reputation led to stories told on the Nationalist side of her cruelty, in particular towards prisoners and nuns.

She was described, quite wrongly, as a former nun who had married an unfrocked monk and cut a priest's jugular vein with her teeth.

In fact, in contrast to the ferocity of many of her speeches, there were several instances of *La Pasionaria*'s compassion during the war. Oddly, for the fount of revolutionary womanhood, she did not support the call for women to take up arms, urging them instead to leave the front and assist the war effort by working in factories or hospitals.

La Pasionaria also played a leading role in educating the peasant militiamen. It was said that when a soldier had been taught to read and write he would write two letters – one to his wife and the other to *La Pasionaria*, to tell her that he was not only fighting the Fascists, but learning too.

Throughout the war *La Pasionaria* held rigidly to the Communist party line, often disagreeing with Largo Caballero's and Negrin's conduct of the war and consistently opposing the Anarchists and the POUM.

In her autobiography, *El Unico Camino* (published in Britain as *They Shall Not Pass*), she writes of the Russian "volunteers" and of the "unconditional aid" given by Stalin. She maintained the position prescribed by Moscow, and at the same time devised a spurious defence of property rights to keep the middle classes in the Republican camp.

In 1939, at the end of the Spanish Civil War, *La Pasionaria* left the "rats of capitulation" for exile in Russia; she was secretary-general of the Spanish Communist party from 1942 to 1960, and then president.

When she returned to Spain after Franco's death – having slavishly followed Moscow for 60 years, with only one public protest at the time of the invasion of Czechoslovakia in 1968 – *La Pasionaria* found herself out of touch with the new generation of young "Eurocommunists". For their part they found her an embarrassment and restrained her from speaking too often in public.

Dolores Ibarruri was born on December 9 1895, the eighth of 11 children, to a mining family in the Basque country. Her upbringing was harsh, and at 15 she went to work for a seamstress, then as a domestic servant, resentful that women could not work in the mines.

Dolores's marriage, at 20, to a miner, and the birth of a daughter, did nothing to alleviate her poverty; she began to lose her previously strong religious convictions and to read Marx and Engels. Her husband was often in prison, and three of her five children were to die in infancy.

Shortly after the Russian Revolution, writing in a journal called *The Class Struggle*, Dolores signed her article *Pasionaria*, and the name stuck. She joined the Basque Communist party in 1920, and was elected to the Central Committee of the Spanish Communist party (PCE) 10 years later.

The declaration of a republic in 1931 brought little of the "democratic progress" envisaged by the Communists, and *La Pasionaria* was jailed several times in Madrid and Bilbao. She paid her first visit to Russia in 1933 for the 13th Communist International and described Moscow as "the most marvellous city in the world".

She was back in prison again in January 1936, shortly before the election of a Popular Front Government and her own election as one of 17 Communist deputies. *La Pasionaria* promptly secured the release of all the inmates of the Oviedo prison.

In Parliament *La Pasionaria* was scathing in her attacks on the "forces of reaction"; and was blamed, unfairly, for having instigated the assassination of Calvo Sotelo a few days before the uprising in July.

During the Civil War *La Pasionaria* and the Communist ministers were often critical of the Government – sometimes justifiably – for being irresolute and failing to take advantage of their military successes.

She had a special affinity with the International Brigades and foreign visitors to the Republican zone, who seemed to symbolise for her a worldwide fraternity of revolutionary idealists fighting Fascist oppression. For them it was she, staying on in Madrid after the Government moved to Valencia in November 1936, who more than anyone else gave inspiration to their cause.

After 1939 *La Pasionaria* spent 38 years living in Moscow, and travelling to most parts of the world in the Communist cause. With false passports she spent some time in France after 1945; and also made visits to Iran, Egypt, China, Cuba and Eastern Europe over the years.

La Pasionaria attended Stalin's funeral in 1953; and in the 1960s she was awarded the International Lenin Peace Prize and the Order of Lenin. There was no question of her retiring from political activity; at the age of 75 the force of her personality was still evident when she addressed 50,000 people at a rally outside Paris.

The PCE was legalised 18 months after Franco's death, in April 1977. *La Pasionaria* returned to Spain in May and served again, for a short period, as deputy for Asturias, having been first elected more than 40 years before.

In spite of her differences with the PCE, *La Pasionaria* would go almost daily, with her lifelong friend and secretary Irene Falcon, to the party's headquarters in Madrid.

The second volume of her memoirs, *Me Faltaba España* (*I Missed Spain*), was published in 1985. She made her last major public appearance at a rally that year to celebrate her 90th birthday, when she recieved the Order of the October Revolution.

La Pasionaria was acclaimed during her lifetime not only by Communist political leaders but also by artists and writers in Spain. Picasso dedicated more than one work to her, and used to visit her in exile; she is also widely believed to have inspired the character Pilar in Ernest Hemingway's *For Whom the Bell Tolls* – Ingrid Bergman played the part in the film.

The British members of the International Bragades honoured *La Pasionaria* in 1979 by depicting her image on a memorial in Glasgow.

La Pasionaria was married in 1916 to Julian Ruiz. Of her five children she is survived only by a daughter, Amaya. Her son, Ruben, was killed in the defence of Stalingrad in 1942.

November 14 1989

GERRY HEALY

GERRY HEALY, who has died aged 76, was a veteran political agitator and the founder of several revolutionary political parties.

Though generally known as a Trotskyite, he eschewed that label himself, and theorists might have called him a Nihilist. An Irish ex-Communist – he was expelled from the Communist party in 1938 – he was certainly one of the most extraordinary figures on the British political landscape.

A brilliant speaker, short, squat and entirely unpreposessing in appearance – though with a particularly magnetic appeal to young people – Healy had vast energy and an encyclopaedic knowledge of Left-wing politics, which he often deployed in factional warfare against his comrades. In 1975, for example, the newspaper of his Workers' Revolutionary party (WRP) published a series of articles accusing the Socialist Workers' party, the biggest Trotskyite organisation in America, of links with Stalin's secret police, the GPU, at the time of Trotsky's murder in Mexico.

Furore ensued in the ranks of the Fourth International: "At the moment when we are becoming accepted as a genuine force in the working-class movement," said a Belgian Trotskyite, "this fool talks of agents from the GPU and the CIA."

Healy also conducted a ceaseless war against unseen security men and was constantly searching for bugs in his party offices, which were situated above a butcher's shop in Clapham, south London.

The first party he led was the Workers' International League, from which he was expelled in 1943 for "personal opportunism and political degeneration". Then came the Revolutionary Communist party and the Socialist Labour League; he was also closely involved in the so-called Blue Union, which built up considerable support in the docks of Liverpool and Hull in the 1950s.

In 1973 the League became the WRP, which attracted such figures as the actors Corin and Vanessa Redgrave, whose own eulogy stated: "I owe to him all my subsequent development as a political woman and artist."

The party enjoyed narrow but fervent support during the 1970s and had an effective propaganda machine in its daily newspaper, *News Line*. But in 1985 Healy was expelled by its central committee for "reactionary practices" and having "abused his power for personal gratification".

As one of his supporters said at the time, "It was like Lenin being dropped by the Bolsheviks." More upsets were to follow. Soon afterwards a counter-coup was effected by 13 members of the central committee, including the Redgraves, and Healy was reinstated.

Two days later, however, *News Line* published a front page story accusing Healy of "sexual assault" and "systematic debauchery" involving 26 women members of the WRP. Undaunted, the Redgraves and Healy established a rival faction; and in 1987 founded a new organisation called simply the Marxist party.

Gerry Healy was born on December 3 1913 and joined the Communist party in 1928. He first came to national prominence in 1959, when he set up the Socialist Labour League – the Militant Tendency of its day – in conjunction with the editorial board of the agitprop weekly *Newsletter*, which he had launched three years before.

The immediate task of the League was to campaign "against Gaitskell and Gaitskellism, which we regard as a thoroughgoing betrayal of Labour principles and the interests of the working class".

Healy seemed to be deliberately courting expulsion, and in March of that year the organisation was duly proscribed by the Labour party. Like all his groupings the League was ferociously sectarian; its members would only attend the demonstrations organised by other groups in order to hand out leaflets explaining why they refused to take part.

It nevertheless became the most important Trotskyite group in Britain, well established in the docks, and with militant followers in the motor industry and Fleet Street.

In 1969 Healy launched a new organ of the League, the *Workers' Press*, the first issue of which came out on the eve of that year's Labour party conference. The timing was deliberate; he had sworn revenge when Harold Wilson had in 1964 purged the Young Socialists of the young Trotskyites infiltrated into it by the League.

Politics and the company of the young seem to have been the chief diversions of his life, and he was shy of personal publicity, especially photographs. In 1958, for example, he was leaving a conference on unemployment when a photographer took his picture from a slowly moving motor-car. Healy chased after the vehicle, with a turn of speed surprising in one of his bulk, and gave up only when the driver had reached third gear.

December 11 1989

CHARLES SKILTON

CHARLES SKILTON, who has died aged 68, was the versatile and eccentric proprietor of one of the last independent one-man publishing houses.

He made a fortune from an expurgated version of *Fanny Hill* which he published in the 1960s; frequently risked prosecution on account of his subversively sexological list; and was angrily dismissive of would-be censors.

Skilton brought his first copy of *Fanny Hill* from a dubious bookdealer in the Charing Cross Road. He took it to bed with a blue pencil and produced an expurgated version of the erotic classic which he brought out in 1963 in a hardback edition at 45 shillings.

He was alarmed to receive a telephone call the week before publication advising him that Mayflower Books were about to publish a paperback at 3s 6d. But the Mayflower text was the unexpurgated version and was immediately seized by Scotland Yard.

In 1964 Skilton published his own paperback edition at 7s 6d which sold more than half a million copies – at one point he had no fewer than three printers operating simultaneously. With the profits from the first month's sales he bought himself a handsome residence in Sussex, Oldlands Hall, which Skilton and his circle used to refer to as "Fanny Hall".

The son of a self-employed master builder in Dulwich, Charles Skilton was born on March 6 1921 and educated at Alleyn's School. At the age of 14 he procured some type and a small handpress, with which he printed a school magazine.

In 1937 he worked briefly for Stanley Gibbons, the stamp dealers, before moving to the publishing firm of George Allen & Unwin, where he became an assistant to the legendary Sir Stanley Unwin, who made a deep impression on the young Charles.

The strong seam of pacifism in the firm undoubtedly influenced Skilton's decision to become a conscientious objector during the Second World War. In 1942 he was imprisoned at Wormwood Scrubs, and he used to recall the legend on the door of his cell below the peep hole: "It is forbidden to lean out of the window".

After his release Skilton took up an administrative position in the lunatic asylum at Bexley Heath; he ventured into book publishing shortly afterwards with a capital of £50.

His first outstanding success came when he took up the author Frank Richards, creator of Billy Bunter. As is the lot of small independent publishers, he sold the rights to the Bunter books to Cassell in a period of financial stringency.

There were many publishing setbacks – in 1954 the office typewriter was pawned to buy Christmas lunch for the family – but there were also some spectacular triumphs.

Skilton always supported local booksellers brought to court and used to tell of the time he travelled to Edinburgh to stand beside a local bookseller charged with selling the Kama Sutra: "To the best of my knowledge the Kama Sutra is *still* banned in Edinburgh!"

His list was extraordinarily diverse and included a

number of scholarly tomes of genealogy, including the three sumptuous volumes of A. C. Addington's monumental work *The Royal House of Stuart*, which traced all the descendants of King James VI and I. Many of the books were characterised by fine design and typography.

Skilton was a man of great contradictions; he had a self-confessed "miscellaneous" mind which led to a huge range of personal interests: the Divorce Law Reform Union; the Independent Publishers Guild; the Society for the Protection of Ancient Buildings; and the Royal Society of Painters in Watercolour.

He was an avid collector – of everything from books and postcards to publishing businesses and country houses. "Fanny Hall" was followed by a mock medieval castle at Banwell in Somerset but his last great project was the restoration of the 86-roomed derelict Whittinge-hame House near Edinburgh, formerly the family home of A. J. Balfour, the Prime Minister.

Skilton was regarded by some as a lovable old rogue, by others as a principled and firm-minded man. He once wrote that those "publishers who have contributed to sexual enlightenment and even gratification have given more happiness to more people than all the morality councils and all the obscenity-prosecuting authorities put together".

He is survived by a daughter.

January 28 1990

HENRY FAIRLIE

HENRY FAIRLIE, the political journalist, who has died in Washington aged 66, blazed into British journalism in the 1950s and 1960s, went to America in 1966 and was never seen again on this side of the Atlantic.

His was a story of triumph and disaster. At the height of his success, when he was still in his thirties, few commentators were better known and none was more admired by his colleagues. But after little more than 10 years of celebrity in London, Fairlie's career went sharply awry.

His personal life had always been chaotic, and it was a combination of money, women and a libel action which led to his flight to America. On an edition of *Any Questions?* he had presumed upon his friendship with Lady Antonia Fraser, a fellow panellist, to offend her with a defamatory remark.

Lady Antonia sued him and the BBC for libel. He declined to respond to any letters from the BBC and his lawyer; and they, left without any defence, settled with Lady Antonia but refused to pick up Fairlie's bill. This was hanging over him when he left for America, along with telephone bills, accumulated rent and so forth.

As the years went by his refusal to return to Britain became increasingly mysterious. Lady Antonia had made it clear that she would not pursue him in the courts; his debts became things of the past; and newspapers – particularly the *Sunday Times* – made him the most generous offers.

It was not as if he was living in great comfort in

Washington. He had done so to begin with, enjoying a *ménage à trois* in Georgetown. But this was too good to last, and for most of the next 25 years he had difficulty making ends meet.

Henry Fairlie was born in Scotland on January 13 1924, one of six children of a farmer who gave up his land to come south and become news editor of the *Evening Standard*. Fairlie relished telling how one night his father – worse for drink after a dinner for Lord Beaverbrook – was put into a taxi in Fleet Street and the cabbie instructed to drive him home. "When he got there, he was dead!" Fairlie would roar. "That's how I'd like to go!"

He inherited from his father his intensely black hair, his red face, his fierce eyes, his large mouth – which spluttered whenever he got excited (this was frequently) – and that deep melancholia which sometimes strikes the Scots.

Henry was educated at Highgate School and Corpus Christi College, Oxford, where he read Modern History. He missed war service because of a suspect heart, and followed his father into newspapers – working for the *Manchester Evening News* and the *Glasgow Herald* before joining *The Times* as an obituarist, leader writer and one of the Printing House Square bohemian set.

In 1955 he moved to the *Spectator*. He spent a comparatively short time as its political columnist, first under the *nom de guerre* of "Trimmer", then under his own name; but it was there that he established himself as a gifted writer with an instinctive feeling for politics.

Doubtless the most famous piece he wrote for the *Spectator* was that in which he popularised the idea of "the Establishment", which he anatomised as the "whole matrix of official and social relations within which power is exercised". A. J. P. Taylor had used the expression before in much the same sense, but it will always be associated with Fairlie.

As a politcal columnist he followed in a tradition begun by his predecessor Hugh Massingham, of the inquisitive, intuitive essay. He took a serious, even grave view of political life, as an honourable calling whose practitioners were engaged in work of high importance.

When he left the *Spectator* Fairlie became a freelance – indeed, he threatened legal proceedings when he was described as an *"Express* man." He wrote for the *Daily Mail*, *Observer*, *Encounter*, Malcolm Muggeridge's *Punch*, Lady Rhondda's *Time and Tide* and later in the *Daily Express* and *Sunday Telegraph*, for which he covered the 1964 General Election.

His sojourns at newspapers were increasingly brief, however; in a much repeated phrase of Brian Inglis's, it could truly be said that Fairlie left many a newspaper a poorer place.

He was also a sought-after broadcaster. It was immediately after one appearance on *Any Questions?* that he had the misfortune to be arrested for contempt of court in relation to monies owed, which prompted his marvellously long-suffering wife, Lisette, to say: "At least tonight I shall know where he is." His finances were permanently in crisis, and although his friends rallied round his position was by now hopeless.

So Fairlie fled to Washington, leaving his wife and three children behind. He presented his flight as a necessary journalistic manoeuvre, to quit the effete Britain, which had never had it so good, and move centre-stage.

In his early Washington period the *Sunday Express* paid him £100 a week for a column from Washington, but this did not endure. Latterly he was sometimes reduced to sleeping in the offices of the *New Republic*, his principal employer; he also wrote occasionally for such newspapers as the *Baltimore Sun* and the *New York Times*, but he never had a regular income.

His articles about British politics were penetrating but inevitably somewhat out of date, and full of poignant nostalgia.

Fairlie wrote several books and was commissioned to write many more. Those he published included *The Life of Politics* (his masterpiece), *The Kennedy Promise*, *The Spoiled Child of the Western World* and *The Parties*. At the time of his death he was working on a book about America, from the angle of a long journey he had made through the country in the company of a young woman friend, as well as a first novel.

George Gale writes: Henry Fairlie was the most vivid of men and leaves the most vivid of memories. Apart from Randolph Churchill, no journalist writing about British politics in the 1950s and 1960s had a better understanding of the ways and means of the Tory party. He was never quite so at home with Labour politics. It is characteristic of him that he recognised the political genius of Aneurin Bevan, but knew his Burke and Bagehot far better than his Marx.

Henry was, nevertheless, fascinated by class and its historical role, though this did not pull him towards the Left: it was mixing with the liberal democratic establishment of Washington which saw to that. He had some of

Harold Macmillan's ambiguity towards privilege and deprivation, combined with a touch of that sentimental nostalgia for patrician rule which Macmillan affected.

He accompanied the British Prime Minister on his African tour at the beginning of 1960, and was one of the journalists who seized on the "wind of change" passage (which Macmillan himself had not intended as a keynote part of his crucial speech) and thereby made it of decisive significance. Fairlie enjoyed Macmillan much as someone might enjoy a cigar or a glass of port.

When he worked at *The Times* Henry would walk up Fleet Street from Printing House Square, deserting his colleagues to join Gerard Fay, Iain Hamilton and others. A year or two later they graduated to El Vino, where they would be joined by – or join – Perry Worsthorne, Colin Welch, Philip Hope-Wallace and many more.

In retrospect it was the golden age of Fleet Street and El Vino; and in that company Henry Fairlie shone at least as brightly as any other and usually shouted more loudly. They may not have been good people but they were very good days, and Henry Fairlie was a very, very good journalist.

February 27 1990

VINCENT 'BIG VINNIE' TERESA

VINCENT "BIG VINNIE" TERESA, the former *capo* in the New England Mafia who has died at Seattle aged 61, spent the last two decades of his life in hiding under the alias of Charles Cantino, having become an FBI informant in return for a reduced prison sentence.

When he was convicted for handling stolen securities in 1969 "Big Vinnie" agreed to be a federal witness against his former associates. In exchange for his testimony – which resulted in the indictment or conviction of more than 50 mobsters, including Meyer Lansky, one of their principal financiers – Teresa's prison sentence was reduced from 20 to five years.

On his release he embarked on a new career under the name Charles Cantino and wrote a best-selling book about his experiences – *My Life in the Mafia*. He became the Mafia's most wanted man – £200,000 was offered to anyone who could find and kill him, and repeated attempts were made on his life.

And yet "Big Vinnie", a vast bulk of a man who weighed 23 stone, had been one of the Mafia's most formidable criminals; he once admitted to having kept a man-eating pirhana in a fishbowl to convince his Boston gambling customers that he ran a tough outfit.

His violation of the code of *omertà* – according to which "men of respect" would never reveal their secrets, and to which he had adhered since childhood – was apparently the result of his having been betrayed within the organisation. Teresa claimed that mobsters had stolen some £1,500,000 from him and threatened his children.

But his new identity did not afford him peace for long. In 1977, within two days of his arrival in Australia to give evidence to a citizens' committee supposedly set up to campaign against the legalisation of casinos, he found himself under a deportation order.

Mr Wran, the Labour premier of New South Wales at

the time, denounced the citizens' committee as a sham and revealed that Teresa had received a visa under the name of "Santana". Teresa condemned the Australian authorities for "blowing his cover", claiming that 500 assassins would be after his blood.

Two years later he was named by the Australian authorites as head of a ring which was illegally exporting such birds as the galah from Australia to America, where they were sold for as much as £1,500 apiece.

Vincent Teresa was born in 1928, the grandson of a Mafia don who had emigrated from Sicily to America in 1895. Young Vincent was a compulsive thief from his earliest years and spent much of his childhood in the company of his uncle, Dominic "Sandy Mac" Teresa, who was a bodyguard and enforcer to Joseph Lombardo, another Mafia don.

"Big Vinnie" soon worked his way up to the top of the crime empire of Raymond Patriarca (Lombardo's successor), and by 1965 he had branched out of his New England territory to run gambling "junkets" to casinos all over the world – to Las Vegas, London, Antigua and Haiti (where he presented President "Papa Doc" Duvalier with a Cadillac) – on which the games were fixed by such "mechanics" as "Yonkers" Joe Salistino, a card-sharper of genius. Teresa boasted that he had cheated "suckers" out of millions of dollars.

After he turned FBI informant in the early 1970s Teresa lived in hiding under heavy guard: in 1977 he said that he and his family had moved eight times in half as many years because he feared that he would "one day wake up and find my head in one room and my legs in the other".

In 1978 he published his second book about his experiences in the Mafia, *The Wiseguys*.

March 11 1990

ALLAN ROBERTS

ALLAN ROBERTS, the Labour MP for Bootle and Opposition Front Bench spokesman on environmental protection and development, who has died aged 46, was a Left-winger with a particular interest in housing policy.

But, for all his environmental interests, Roberts was probably most widely known for his controversial visit – in the company of two other Left-wing Labour MPs – to Afghanistan in 1981.

The trip, which provoked a storm of protest in Britain, was exploited by the Communist regime. They encouraged the idea that it was an official visit by "a British parliamentary delegation".

"Afghan" Roberts, as he inevitably became known, was quoted as praising "the brave people of Afghanistan defending the fruits of revolution". Although he urged eventual withdrawal by the Soviet forces he insisted that the regime was the lesser of the evils faced by the country. The insurgents responded by putting up posters in Kabul accusing him of being duped by a Soviet conspiracy.

Roberts caused another sensation when, on a visit to Germany, he had to receive hospital treatment after suffering injuries at the Buddy club, a well-known haunt of homosexuals in West Berlin. But he vigorously denied suggestions that he had been whipped by men in SS-style uniforms while he was attired in priestly garb.

Allan Roberts

A baker's son, Allan Roberts was born at Droylsden, Lancs, on October 28 1943 and edcuated at the local secondary modern school. He qualified as a teacher at Didsbury College of Education, but then decided to take up social work and did an extra-mural course in social studies at Manchester University.

In 1972 Roberts joined the social services department of Lancashire County Council and from 1976 to 1979 was principal officer in child care with Salford Social Services.

He had joined the Labour party at the age of 16 and soon established a reputation as a Left-winger and CND supporter. Roberts unsuccessfully fought the Manchester parliamentary seat of Hazel Grove in the two General Elections of 1974.

Then, somewhat surprisingly, he was adopted to succeed the Right-wing Roman Catholic Labour MP for Bootle, Simon Mahon, and won the safe seat in the 1979 General Election. He won a majority of 24,477 at the 1987 General Election.

He was a member of the House of Commons Select Committee on the Environment and a former chairman of the Parliamentary Labour party's environmental group. Roberts's special knowledge was derived from his work on Manchester City Council in the 1970s when he was chairman of its housing committee.

Although he was an opponent of council house sales, he was not doctrinaire on the issue. Once it became law he advocated the right to rent as well as to buy and also that private tenants should have the same rights as council tenants to purchase their homes.

As an MP he campaigned to give council tenants more democratic control over their estates; he advocated that local authorities make better use of their housing and that they be allowed to set up estate agencies and building societies.

At Westminster Roberts followed a conventional hard-Left line. He co-nominated Anthony Wedgwood Benn for the deputy leadership of the Labour party and was an active member of the Campaign Group of Labour MPs as well as being sympathetic to Militant.

But unlike some of his fellow Left-wingers, Roberts, with his reddish fair hair and extreme informality of dress (he was the first MP to appear in the Chamber wearing jeans), had an amiable quality and was well liked at Westminster.

An ardent campaigner for the rights of minority groups – such as coloured people, homosexuals and women immigrants – he was once described as "more sincere than serious".

Roberts was unmarried.

March 23 1990

SID GOLD

SID GOLD, who has died at Wimbledon aged 102, adopted a prosaic English name which concealed a past lived in the world of Conrad's *The Secret Agent*, an atmosphere of plots, intrigue, bombs and revolution.

In his Russian youth he had helped manufacture bombs for use against the Tsarist authorities in the abortive 1905 revolution. As an eager 17-year-old revolutionary he had met at his great uncle's house Gregorii Apfelbaum, better known as Zinoviev, the imputed author of the famous letter. (Apfelbaum later married the great-uncle's daughter.)

Goldin (as he then was) trained as a watchmaker and in the classic revolutionary tradition was set to work making timing devices for bombs. His subversive activities became known to the police when they arrested a drunken fellow employee at the watchmaking works and found him in possession of a compromising printing plate.

The Tsarist authorities, with that unpredictable mercifulness which contrasts so starkly with Stalin's wholly predictable mercilessness, questioned Goldin but allowed him to go free because he was so young.

Soon afterwards Goldin followed his Apfelbaum kinsfolk to Warsaw. There he pursued his trade as a watchmaker until 1911, when the Apfelbaums, together with Lenin and others, decided to emigrate. Goldin travelled across Germany and picked up a fishing boat that took him to Grimsby.

Son of an estate manager, Solomon Borisovich Goldin was born near Mogilev on May 17 1887 and began his apprenticeship at the age of 10, after the family moved to Tula, a town famous for samovars and munitions.

His workplace was a hotbed of revolutionary fervour, and at the age of 17 he joined the Bolsheviks and plunged into *Das Kapital*. His comrades put him in charge of printing manifestos and other Marxist literature, and also made him responsible for the cleaning and safe storage of firearms pilfered by workers from the local arms factories.

After leaving the revolutionary circles of Warsaw, Sid Gold settled in Twickenham. Though he never took British citizenship, during the First World War he put his bomb-making talents at the service of his new country by making timing devices for grenades and shells used by the British Army.

Soon after the war, Gold, who had arrived in this country without a penny, set up his own watchmaking business, and in the mid-1930s, his design of a special mechanical clock earned him an award from the Royal Observatory.

Although he retained his revolutionary principles he also accumulated a certain amount of decadent capitalist pelf, and showed no eagerness to return to Russia either before, during or after the Bolshevik revolution. Perhaps this was just as well, for in 1936 Zinoviev and his wife perished in one of Stalin's purges.

Gold married first an English pianist, who died before the outbreak of the Second World War. They had a son who served in the RAF in Burma and now lives in California. Gold's second wife was Welsh, and of pronounced pro-Soviet views.

They visited Russia together in 1961, and in Moscow encountered Gold's sister Mania, who had fought as a partisan during the Second World War and later worked in the state security system.

April 1 1990

CHARLES MCLACHLAN

CHARLES MCLACHLAN, Inspector of Constabulary for south-east England who has died aged 58, was the Liverpudlian troubleshooter whose much-publicised pursuit of drunken drivers, prostitutes and illegal pickets earned him the sobriquet of "Campaign Charlie".

His robust views – expressed during a long run as Chief Constable of Nottinghamshire until his appointment as an Inspector of Constabulary in 1987 – included a call for the birching of vandals.

McLachlan made no bones about patrolling Nottingham and the M1 with armed squad cars. In a BBC Radio 4 broadcast he said that he was not prepared to have unarmed officers confronted by armed criminals.

His determination to protect his men endeared him to the force, though he was less well regarded in the red light district of Nottingham where he launched a purge of prostitutes and pimps. The *Telegraph* columnist Auberon Waugh animated against McLachlan's "detestable practice" of dressing policewomen as prostitutes to further his campaign. Waugh also assailed McLachlan for proposing, after the Hungerford massacre, that members of the public be forbidden to own or wear bullet-proof vests.

One of "Campaign Charlie's" particular enthusiasms was for wide-ranging use of the breathalyser. This practice brought him into conflict with the Police Federation in Nottingham which felt that such a campaign could only damage public relations.

But it was McLachlan's crucial role in the miners' strike which made him a national figure. As Chief Constable for Nottinghamshire and chairman of the Association of Chief Police Officers responsible for distributing reinforcements from outside forces, he was at the centre of the most controversial police operation in recent times.

McLachlan decided to halt convoys of suspected pickets from Yorkshire at the county border and turn them round on the grounds that their presence would be likely to disturb the peace. This turn-round was carried out on a scale beyond all British policing experience.

Those who tried to breach road blocks risked arrest for obstructing police. Although this action was approved by the High Court, McLachlan became a *bête noire* of civil libertarians; his strike headquarters at Nottingham became known as "Fort McLachlan".

Quite unabashed, he dedicated himself to protecting the working miners of Nottinghamshire. His steadfastness of purpose brought howls of protest from the Left and he endured angry verbal attacks – being accused variously as vain, emotional and volatile.

Latterly his duties in the south-east included responsibility for some aspects of the Metropolitan Police and in December 1989 he produced a report on crime in the London Underground.

The son of a ship's carpenter, Charles McLachlan was born at Liverpool on December 12 1931 and educated at the Liverpool Institute High School before starting work in an insurance office. He did his National Service in the Royal Military Police and received a commission.

This gave him a taste for policing; his physique, height and confident manner assured recognition. After a brief spell back on his insurance office stool he decided to make his career in the police.

As he was fond of recalling, this decision horrified his parents who told him that he was "a disgrace to the family". Notwithstanding his Army commission he had to work his way up the police ranks.

In 1962, while a sergeant, he took a law degree at

London University, and in 1968 after being appointed a Chief Inspector in Warwickshire he took an MA in criminology at Keele University. Two years later he returned to Liverpool and Bootle as Chief Superintendent.

In 1973 he moved to Lincolnshire as Deputy Chief Constable and three years later was appointed Chief Constable of Nottinghamshire. McLachlan would look anywhere for new ideas, not least in America where he enjoyed visiting the FBI, with whom he had a warm rapport.

McLachlan was president of the Association of Chiefs of Police from 1984 to 1985. He was awarded the Queen's Police Medal in 1977 and appointed CBE in 1985.

Away from his policework and broadcasting commitments, the softly-spoken McLachlan led a quiet domestic life which embraced regular worship as a Methodist, enthusiasm for Gilbert and Sullivan, caravanning among French vineyards and skiing in Austria.

He married, in 1958, Dorothy Gardner; they had three sons.

April 5 1990

Dr Jack Manahan

DR JACK MANAHAN, who has died in Virginia aged 70, played out the last part in the drama of the Grand Duchess Anastasia of Russia, espousing the cause of "Anna Anderson", giving her a home and finally granting her the identity she craved.

For whether or not Anna Anderson was the Grand Duchess Anastasia, from 1968 until her death in 1984 she addressed herself as Mrs Jack Manahan. Manahan himself once asked Gleb Botkin, a friend of his wife's: "Well, what would Tsar Nicholas think if he could see his new son-in-law?" Botkin replied: "I think he would be grateful."

For many years the couple were preoccupied with attempting to establish Mrs Manahan's identity, but they were gradually worn down by unfavourable verdicts.

The story had baffled historians ever since the Berlin police rescued a mystery girl who had tried to commit suicide in the Landwehr Canal in 1920. Huge sums had been expended on bitterly contested court cases and the saga became the subject of a play as well as a film starring Ingrid Bergman.

Although the official investigation concluded that Emperor Nicholas II, Empress Alexandra and their children were all shot on the night of July 16/17 1918 in the cellar of the house in which they had been confined at Ekaterinburg, there is some evidence to show that the Empress and her daughters were removed to Perm and were alive a few months later.

There was also evidence to support Mrs Manahan's claim to be the youngest daughter of Russia's last Emperor, but the tale of Anastasia was never fully explained.

The son of a dean of the University of Virginia, John Manahan was born in 1919 and became a professor of history and political science.

In 1968 he invited Anna Anderson to stay with him at his farm in Scottsville, Virginia. Her visa was in danger of expiry, and that December he married her, explaining that his motive was to "get history written straight, to see that she has a happy and safe life".

Numerous journalists came to see the would-be Anastasia over the years, and they were habitually greeted by the swarthy, crew-cut Manahan, who would call out "Anastasia" in his Southern drawl.

Peter Kurth, the author who put up the strongest case for her identity being that of the missing Grand Duchess, recalled that she invariably kept the press waiting, though Manahan was on hand with excuses to explain the delay.

Throughout the 1970s Manahan sent out newsletters from the University Circle in Charlottesville, informing the world of his peregrinations with his wife "Anastasia, last Grand Duchess of Russia still surviving".

Kurth described him as "a non-stop talker, unflaggingly gracious and hospitable, ebullient, opinionated, with a Southern gentleman's inscrutable courtesy and a story to tell about any subject".

As the years went by, so the way of life of the Manahans deteriorated. Mrs Manahan encouraged weeds to grow up around their house, a wire fence was erected, and the front windows were blocked with cardboard.

Strange traps consisting of branches and sacks of coal were set up in the garden. Within the house, books were piled from floor to ceiling, and the front room became a veritable Anastasia Museum.

As his wife became increasingly shy of going out, Manahan would sit in his station-wagon attended by various hounds, his hand pressed hard on the horn until she emerged. The house became a health hazard and the Manahans were taken to court for "failing to maintain clean and sanitary premises, allowing refuse to collect on their premises, and allowing weeds and brush to grow in excess of 18 ins up".

Manahan made a brief effort to improve their living

conditions, but eventually their home was so overrun with junk that the couple moved into a smaller house across the drive. Mrs Manahan's health deteriorated alarmingly and she took to a wheelchair.

Her husband – who was 20 years her junior – continued to care for her and in 1981 her official 80th birthday was celebrated with a reception on the lawn.

In 1983 there was a production of *Anastasia* at the Barboursville Playhouse, and Manahan was dully photographed beside the car with his wife sitting in the vehicle. But soon afterwards the court declared that Manahan was no longer capable of looking after his wife.

She was taken to Blue Ridge Hospital, from where, a fortnight later, her husband was seen to "grab the wheelchair, lift her into his car and drive away". Four days later she was traced and Manahan was arrested on a felony warrant, though her lawyer agreed that he had been acting out of love.

Anna Anderson died in hospital on February 12 1984. Manahan remained at large, full of fantastic stories, the victim of outbursts of paranoia, but amiable to the last.

April 15 1990

MAURICE GIRODIAS

MAURICE GIRODIAS, the French publisher who has died in Paris aged 71, specialised in literature once considered too obscene for public consumption, and became notorious as "the man who made the world safe for pornography".

Girodias lived to see works such as *Lolita* by Vladimir

Nabokov, *Sexus* and *Quiet Days in Clichy* by Henry Miller, *Naked Lunch* by William Burroughs (*qv*), *The Ginger Man* by J. P. Donleavy, and a host of daring books by authors including Lawrence Durrell, Georges Batallie and Jean Genet become respectable, often lucrative, modern classics – but from which their original sponsor derived little profit.

The publisher also emitted a score of frankly pornographic books written at his commission. Struggling British writers arriving in Paris in the 1950s and 1960s knew that they could make a bit of money "writing dirty books for Girodias". He would order these to be written according to his own specific formula – based on his thorough knowledge of the "British market for whipping, nannies and so on".

Maurice Girodias was born in Paris in 1919. Girodias was the name of his French mother; his father, Jack Kahane, founded the Obelisk Press in the 1930s and was the first to publish Henry Miller's *Tropic of Cancer*, for which Maurice designed the cover at the age of 14.

Horrified by the rise of Nazism, his father committed suicide in 1939 by drinking a full bottle of Cognac, and Girodias – who had inherited his father's taste for "forbidden" books, and wine, women and song – took over the failing family business.

In 1953 he founded Olympia Press, which made its name initially with the English language, green-covered Travellers Companion series of dirty books, or "sex fictions" as he liked to call them.

Girodias attributed much of his success to the "Bogmoletz Cure" a treatment consisting of the injection of monkey glands. This was prescribed by an unconventional psychiatrist during one of the many low points in the publisher's life: his marriage and a subsequent love affair had collapsed. He was bankrupt and not for the first time.

"The cure was miraculous," he said. "For six months I was so full of energy that I could not sleep, and my sex life became overpowering. I was 33 at the time, the same age as Christ on the Cross. It left me a huge surplus of energy. That is what started Olympia Press."

The turn-around in his fortunes came when Miller gave him the novel *Plexus* to publish. He went on to publish Beckett's *Watt*, the first English editions of *The Story of O*, *Lolita* and *The Ginger Man*, and *Candy* by Terry Southern and Mason Hoffenberg.

But he soon fell foul of the de Gaulle administration. In 1964 he estimated that nearly 70 of the 200 books published by Olympia had been declared "unsuitable" – this meant that they could not be displayed or advertised.

After numerous confrontations with French censors, Girodias was ordered not to publish for 80 years and six months, though the ban was subsequently reduced to a mere three years. A string of appeals followed, and at one stage he languished for two days in a Parisian jail.

Girodias had by now also incurred commercial problems. When *Lolita* became an international best-seller in 1955, Nabokov switched to a better known, "respectable" house. Soon afterwards Donleavy fell out with Girodias over his conduct with the publication of his novel *The Ginger Man*.

Other writers, too, fell out with him for various reasons. His practice, for example, of publishing more serious works in the same format as the best-selling dirty book series did nothing to enhance their literary reputation. Many felt that Girodias used their books to disguise the lewder side of his business.

The Olympia Press began to founder. In the early 1960s the publisher used what was left of his money to open a theatre in the basement of a Paris night club. But the establishment was closed by the *gendarmerie* in 1964 after a performance of a show inspired by the Marquis de Sade's *Philosophy in the Bedroom*.

Asked why he had proceeded to stage the show despite its obscene material, Girodias replied: "I just have a calling to be a trouble-maker."

He subsequently settled in America. But, although later in the so-called "Nineteen-Sexies" he was able to re-issue his list of pornographic novels, Girodias's sojourn in the United States ended in disaster.

In 1974 he was expelled from the country for seeking to publish a work of fiction, which depicted the Secretary of State, Dr Henry Kissinger.

To compound his woes, Olympia Press had gone into liquidation in 1970. When the company was put up for auction, Donleavy bought it. Apparently if Donleavy's name was ever mentioned to Girodias in public after the sale, he would jump up from his chair, tear tormentedly at his hair, and run for the door.

In his last years Girodias, by then in lowish water, lived in a small studio flat in Paris. A bitter man, he nurtured a particular rancour towards the Americans, and to the intellectual writers who, he complained, "treated me like a dog", in spite of the fact that, in his view, many of them owed their professional start to him.

Shortly before his death, Girodias published the first two volumes of an exhaustive autobiography *Une Journée sur la Terre* entitled, respectively, *Arrival* and *The Gardens of Eros.*

He died of a heart attack while giving a radio interview to promote his memoirs.

July 5 1990

PAT WALL

PAT WALL, Labour MP for Bradford North, who has died aged 57, was an avowed Trotskyite and supporter of the Militant Tendency.

He finally reached Westminster at the last General Election, in 1987, after years of bitter opposition from Labour party moderates to his candidature. In 1982 he had achieved national notoriety with a speech warning of a "bloody civil war in Britain" and declaring that "a Marxist Labour government" would abolish the monarchy and the House of Lords, sack the generals, admirals, air marshals, senior civil servants – and "in particular, the judges" – in order to hold on to power.

Wall combined a reverence akin to religious faith for Trotsky's memory and thinking – "a man of marvellous humanity and faith in the future of mankind" – with being an able and prosperous businessman. He was a hardware buyer for mail-order companies and in 1970 was reputed to be earning the then substantial income of £20,000.

Wall had considerable charm and a first-class analytical mind. Unlike many others on the extreme Left he was not a ranter, and his speeches in the Commons – whatever view may be taken of their content – were notable for lucidity and carefully marshalled arguments.

A typewriter salesman's son, Charles Patrick Wall was born in Liverpool on May 6 1933 and educated at the Liverpool Institute. He joined the Labour party when he was 17 and rapidly became constituency secretary for Garston, a borough councillor, a delegate for the Shopworkers' Union and then a Liverpool city councillor.

In 1964 he became a founder member of Militant, taking one of its 25 original £1 shares. After unsuccessfully seeking selection as Labour's candidate at Barons Court and then Blyth Valley, he was adopted for Bradford North in 1982, ousting the sitting MP, Ben Ford.

Ford appealed to Labour's National Executive Committee on the grounds that Wall was a Militant supporter – membership of which was banned for Labour party members – and that his constituency party had been infiltrated by other Militant supporters.

The National Executive ordered a re-selection, which Wall again won; he had sold his share in Militant, which removed any technical grounds for the NEC to deny his endorsement.

The 1983 election contest in Bradford North became a *cause célèbre* in the national campaign, with Wall's candidature becoming grist to the Conservative propaganda mill as evidence of Labour's extremism. It was all the more bitterly fought as Ben Ford stood against Wall as "Labour Independent" under the slogan "Stop the Trot". His 4,000 votes led to Wall's defeat and victory for the Conservative candidate, Geoffrey Lawler.

Wall's candidature for the 1987 election was again initially rejected by the National Executive and only reluctantly confirmed after he pledged loyalty to party policy and reaffirmed that he had broken his connection with Militant.

Wall's arrival at Westminster was clouded by his knowledge that he was suffering from an illness that would eventually prove fatal. This did not, however, deter him from throwing his energies into work at the Commons.

He found *perestroika* hard to swallow and in November 1989 wrote to Gorbachev warning him that: "A return to capitalism will not benefit the workers in any part of the Soviet Union . . . only a socialist planned economy on full workers' democracy can offer any solution."

The controversy over Salman Rushdie's *Satanic Verses* posed a dilemma for Wall in a constituency with a large Muslim population and where the book was publicly burnt. But in response to Muslim demands that he should support their call for the banning of Rushdie's book his stand was uncompromising: "As a socialist who condemns the banning of books in South Africa, Ireland, Russia and other countries I cannot support the banning of books in Britain and I am particularly opposed to the burning of books."

Wall was a passionate jazz enthusiast – heading a Commons motion regretting the death of Ken Colyer – and what he described as "a lifelong Everton FC fanatic".

He married, in 1960, Pauline Knight; they had two sons and a daughter.

August 8 1990

B. F. SKINNER

B. F. SKINNER, the psychologist who has died at Cambridge, Massachusetts aged 86, was the doyen of the American behaviourist school – the intellectural descendants of Ivan Pavlov.

Fred Skinner's views were based on his theory that free will and the unconscious mind do not exist, and that people make choices solely through environmental triggers. People do not shape the world, he said – the world shapes them. From the experiments he conducted on animals at Harvard University, where he spent most of his academic career, Skinner concluded that desirable behaviour could be achieved through operant conditioning – a system of rewards, punishments and positive reinforcement.

In pursuit of this theory he invented a device which became known as the Skinner Box – a sound-proofed enclosure with buttons or levers which are pressed by animals to receive food after they have performed specific tasks. The box provides a precise way to observe, record and measure behaviour, and is widely used by psychologists and drug researchers.

In the 1940s Skinner also introduced the air crib to the world – a roomy, insulated, temperature-controlled box with a window, in which a baby could sleep and play comfortably without blankets or clothes. One of his daughters spent her first two and a half years in his "baby box", and he hoped that it would revolutionise child-rearing, but it never quite caught on.

Skinner also published a utopian novel, *Walden Two*

(1948), in which he urged society to dispense with the notions of individual freedom and dignity in favour of the survival of the species.

Through his teaching and writings he had a considerable influence on the undergraduate generations of the 1960 and 1970s, though many of his colleagues were sceptical about his vision of a society in which everyone would be obliged to be well-behaved and happy.

"I can only feel that he was choosing these goals for others, not himself," the psychologist Carl Rogers once said. "I would hate to see Skinner become well behaved . . . and the most awful fate I can imagine for him would be to have him constantly happy. It is the fact that he is very unhappy about many things which makes me prize him."

Burrhus Frederic Skinner was born at Susquehanna, Pennsylvania, on March 20 1904. He studied English at Hamilton College, New York, and briefly tried to write fiction – until, as he put it, "I discovered the unhappy fact that I had nothing to say, and went on to graduate study in psychology, hoping to remedy that shortcoming."

Having taken his doctorate at Harvard in 1931, he taught at Minnesota and Indiana Universities before returning to join the faculty in 1947. It was at Harvard that he developed his celebrated box, which he used to teach rats, and later pigeons, to perform tricks.

Birds learned to play the piano, to dance and play ping-pong, and during the Second World War Skinner devised a way for a pigeon to guide a missile to its goal by pecking at an image of the target on a screen. Asked what he would have done differently if he had the chance, Skinner replied: "Just one thing. I performed one experiment that has never ceased to reverberate. I've been laughed at by enemies and kidded by friends. If I could do it all over again, I'd never teach those pigeons to play ping-pong."

His other books included *The Behaviour of Organisms*, *Verbal Behaviour*, *Science and Human Behaviour* and – his most controversial – *Beyond Freedom and Dignity*, which was a defence of his novel.

Skinner denied that his vision of humanity's future was a totalitarian one. "The main point", he said days before his death, "is not that I don't want to see people free . . . but think that beyond feelings of that sort we must take into account the future of the world. I want people to change their behaviour – or to create a world in which their behaviour changes – so we're not going to destroy the world as a liveable environment too soon."

He is survived by his wife, Yvonne, and two daughters.

August 21 1990

GENERAL CURTIS 'OLD IRONPANTS' LEMAY

GENERAL CURTIS "OLD IRONPANTS" LEMAY, who has died aged 83, was celebrated for his line that North Vietnam should be "bombed back to the Stone Age", though he had earned his sobriquet on account of his exploits during the Second World War.

"Old Ironapants" – or more flatteringly, the "Iron Eagle" – was fabled for the determination with which he defied flak and enemy fighters and "unacceptable" losses as he attacked or directed operations against heavily defended daylight targets in Germany and occupied Europe.

LeMay later commanded the Strategic Air Command, was US Air Force chief of staff and stood for vice-president on George Wallace's ticket in the presidential campaign of 1968.

A burly, bluff, strong-willed, heavily jowled man – he needed the cabin space of a Fortress or Superfortress to accommodate his ample figure – LeMay lived up to his nicknames into the mid-1960s. It was then that he made his notorious remarks about North Vietnam.

"We must be willing," he said, "to continue our work of bombing until we have destroyed every work of man there if this is what it takes to win the war."

The cigar-chewing general was considered by many to be the father of strategic bombing – he was also known as America's "architect of systematic destruction". LeMay was one of the men in charge of dropping atomic weapons on Hiroshima and Nagasaki in 1945, although he thought them unnecessary: "We dropped the bombs because President Truman told me to do it."

But during the presidential campaign in 1968 he was ambiguous about the possible use of nuclear weapons in Vietnam – declaring them to be almost certainly unnecessary rather than unthinkable. He said that the American public had developed an absurd phobia about nuclear weapons and that if he himself had the choice between being killed by a rusty Russian knife or a nuclear weapon, he would lean towards the latter.

LeMay was scathingly dismissive of the idea that a nuclear war would mean the end of the world, and insisted that 20 years after the Bikini tests the fish were back in the lagoon, the coconuts were growing again and the rats were bigger, fatter and healthier than ever before.

Curtis LeMay was born in 1907. Inspired by Lindbergh's epic flight from New York to Paris in 1927, he applied for flying training and immersed himself in meteorology and navigation.

After a stint in Hawaii he was posted to Air Force GHQ at Langley Field as operations and intelligence officer of the 49th Bombardment Squadron, an appointment which almost coincided with the introduction of the B-17, the Flying Fortress.

LeMay was one of that bomber's first navigator-pilots, and took part in the 1937 flag-showing visit to South America. Two years later he received command of his first Fortress. Subsequently his long-range navigational skills were in demand as American military aviation set out to shrink the globe. He pioneered ferry routes to Africa and Britain, for which he was awarded a DFC.

Shortly after the United States entered the war, LeMay was given command of the 305th Bombardment Group which he led to Britain, where it was one of the first American bomber units to see action.

Undeterred by the perils of daylight raiding and the attendant losses, LeMay – cigar clamped in his jaw – was renowned for holding his Fortress on course though assailed by flak and fighters. In one attack on St Nazaire he held course to the target for a nerve-racking seven minutes.

But others under his command wavered and it was typical that on the next day, convinced that too many pilots were missing targets because they were zigzagging, LeMay should have forbidden evasive action on the final bombing run.

The word "suicidal" went round the messes, but LeMay's results began to win admiration and were soon represented on his broad chest by the ribbons of the Air Medal and Silver Star. He assembled separate combat formations of 18 aircraft, so designed that enemy fighters would encounter firepower from any angle.

Among his more notable exploits was an attack in 1943 on the Messerschmitt aircraft works at Regensburg in Germany, a flight which ended with landings in North Africa. He was awarded the Distinguished Service Cross.

The next spring he was promoted to major-general – at 37 he was one of the youngest officers to hold this rank in the US Army – and became commander of the 8th Air Force's 3rd Bombardment Division during the invasion of Normandy in 1944. Afterwards LeMay was switched to the Far East where he led 20th Bomber Command's B-29 Superfortress raids on targets in Manchuria. On moving to 21st Bomber Command, he savoured a low-level fire-raising night raid on the Japanese capital: stripping the Superforts of defensive guns to increase their bombloads, he sent 300 aircraft in below anti-aircraft range.

He stayed with the Command when it became the 20th Air Force until he was claimed by General Spaatz, Strategic Air Force's commander, as Chief of Staff. This involved him in planning the atomic bombing of Japan.

Characteristically LeMay returned home in style after VJ Day, breaking the Japan to Chicago record with a non-stop B-29 flight. The welcome included the offer of an Ohio seat in the Senate; but, at that time, he preferred to remain an airman.

Staff appointments followed and when in 1947 the Air Force became independent of the Army he returned to Europe as US Air Commander. In the summer of 1948 he directed the Berlin airlift, sometimes flying in supplies himself and being awarded the Medal for Humane Action.

Later that year he went to Strategic Air Command. His nine years there hardened an already metallic approach to world politics, especially Communism.

LeMay always had a personal bomber ready so that he could, in the event of a Soviet nuclear attack, lead the retaliation himself. His men regarded the General with a combination of respect and abject terror.

On one memorable occasion all hell was let loose when he found a man at one of the SAC bases guarding a hangar, as LeMay put it, with a ham sandwich.

In 1961 LeMay was appointed to the top job as Chief of Staff of the US Air Force. Inevitably, his aggressive nature guaranteed fireworks, and his forthright advocacy of a build-up of nuclear and other advanced weaponry led him into a running battle with Robert McNamara, the Defense Secretary, and what he regarded as his desk-bound department.

LeMay's insistence that that manned bombers should be as important as missiles in the deterrent force eventually led to his "retirement" in 1965. He went down like one of his giant bombers with all guns firing to the last, demanding in a final blast that America should take control of outer space.

LeMay's despair at what he saw as America's drift away from the principles that had made her great led him to his ill-starred involvement with Wallace. Despite their brave proclamations of mutual admiration the General and the Governor were not well matched.

LeMay had, in fact, pioneered a policy of racial integration in the US Air Force – deeply unpalatable to Wallace, one of whose main tickets was the advocacy of racial segregation. Wallace, on the other hand, had no wish to become embroiled in the debate about nuclear weapons in Vietnam. The Governor had promised that he would, if necessary, turn the war over to the generals, but that did not make LeMay his man.

Dour at the best of times, LeMay appeared more lugubrious than ever during the campaign. The electorate seemed to agree with the conclusion of John F. Kennedy, who had once said: "If you have to go, you want LeMay in the lead bomber. But you never want LeMay deciding whether or not you have to go."

Latterly LeMay lived in a military retirement community in Southern Califorina. He was a director of the National Geographic Society.

He married, in 1934, Helen Maitland; they had a daughter.

October 3 1990

SETH MORGAN

SETH MORGAN, who has died in a motor-bicycling accident in New Orleans aged 41, was variously a drug dealer and addict, strip-joint barker, pimp, armed robber and acclaimed novelist.

In 1977 his non-literary activities landed him in Vacaville State Penitentiary, California, where he gave up drugs and made the acquaintance of the murderer Charles Manson. But on his release three years later Morgan resumed his self-destructive habits.

In emulation of Malcolm Lowry he decided to drink himself to death in New Orleans, but while there he instead wrote the novel that made his name, *Homeboy* – a roistering and largely autobiographical account of "flipside Frisco", full of sex, drugs and violence.

The anti-hero of the novel, Joe Speaker, mirrored Morgan's own career as a barker and addict, who found himself in prison; and the evocation of San Francisco's hellish netherworld – which contained dope fiends whose eyes spun "like slot machine lemons" and characters with names like "Baby Jewels" and "Big Lurleen the Sex Machine" – was evidently empowered by his first-hand experience.

At the time of his death Morgan had embarked on a second novel, a crime story set in downtown New Orleans, which was apparently an attempt to address his deranged attitude to the opposite sex.

Seth Morgan was born in New York in 1949. His mother drank herself to death when he was six, and he was brought up by his father, Frederick Morgan, a poet and editor of a New York literary magazine, the *Hudson Review*.

Morgan junior later recalled having been surrounded by "literary jawboning" in the family's Park Avenue apartment, which was frequented by such personages as e. e. cummings and Robert Lowell.

After being expelled from two boarding schools "for monied misfits" in Switzerland for a variety of extortion activities and sexual misdmeanours, he attended a more liberal establishment in Mexico, where he drank mescal, smoked mota and passed the exams to the University of California at Berkeley.

Within weeks, however, Morgan was flying noxious substances to and from New York and Los Angeles and had cast aside his books. In 1970 he tried to sell a portion of a shipment of cocaine which had turned pink to the singer Janis Joplin, who, attracted by the dealer's combination of sleaze and affluence, announced her intention of marrying him.

It was downhill from then on. In 1968 Morgan's brother John had jumped off the San Francisco Oakland Bay bridge: and within three months of moving in with Joplin, she was dead.

He went on to marry a waitress whose face he had paralysed by driving his Harley-Davidson into a wall, and when this relationship, too, broke down, he took refuge in a heroin addiction.

Morgan then married a call girl, for whom he was pimping, and embarked on the armed robberies which landed him in jail. After being released on parole, he took up with another prostitute, and vacillated between alcoholism and detoxification programmes, before settling in New Orleans to indulge his newly discovered "habit" of writing.

October 22 1990

DR ARMAND HAMMER

DR ARMAND HAMMER, who has died in Los Angeles aged 92, was variously a pharmacist, a manufacturer of pencils, a merchant banker, a doctor, an international art dealer, a breeder of prize bulls, a distiller, an oilman and a munificent patron of the Prince of Wales's various charitable concerns.

The variety of his interests reflected his remarkable energy (he once spent a sleepless night dealing in silver, making a profit of £85 million) "a knack", as he put it "for sniffing out opportunities"; and a willingness to do a deal with anyone from Lenin to Gaddafi.

"The Doctor" was egotistical, tough and aggressive, a relentless self-publicist and mythomane and a sedulous wooer of the great. To some he seemed a guru, a saintly philanthropist and the *éminence grise* of world politics; to others he was a fraudulent sinister figure, with a manner reminiscent of a James Bond villain.

In any event, his extraordinary career spanned the 20th century, and he was on intimate terms with a number of its leaders – if not quite as intimate as he liked to make out.

Hammer made his first million at the age of 21, during Prohibition in New York, when he cornered the market in tincture of ginger, which made a tolerable highball. But it was nearly 40 years, and many millions, later that he started to build Occidental Petroleum, a run-down company which he acquired as a tax-shelter, into one of the giants of the oil business.

He retained full control of the company to the end, running it as his own private vehicle – sometimes to the detriment of shareholders, and frequently to the frustration of the company's senior management. Despite all his success, Hammer persisted in a need for approval and for the world to know of his doings.

His skills for self-aggrandisement were perhaps over-developed, often tempting him to announce prematurely his increasingly ambitious deals struck on behalf of Occidental, many of which never materialised. While this annoyed some shareholders, most were smoothed into submission by the personality cult he carefully encouraged. Occidental's annual meetings were held on his birthday, and a standing ovation would nearly always accompany the arrival of the birthday cake, each year laden with more candles.

Hammer, however, wanted to be remembered less for his contributions to the Gross National Product than to world peace and to finding a cure for cancer. To both causes he made generous financial contributions, allegedly giving away some 90 per cent of his substantial income. Yet more important than his money may have been his personal intervention.

Claiming among his friends leaders and kings, from Franklin Roosevelt to the Prince of Wales (he recently gave £14 million to charities backed by the Prince), Armand Hammer became in the last two decades of his life one of the most influential businessmen in the world.

His friendship with Lenin, which was established in the early 1920s when he abandoned a career as a doctor in America to attend to famine and sickness in the Soviet Union, won him the confidence of every Soviet leader since Stalin – Hammer described Gorbachev as "very like Lenin in his pragmatism, resourcefulness, sense of humour and ability".

This opened the door of the Kremlin to Hammer at a time when it was closed to the American government, and allowed him to play the part of unofficial arbitrator between the superpowers – a role he adopted with evident relish.

In the mid-1980s, when arms negotiations between the two countries appeared to have broken down completely, Hammer claimed to have played a vital part in bringing together Reagan and Gorbachev in 1985 – a meeting which was a first step towards the agreement on arms control reached two years later.

What is unclear is whether his ability to speak to both sides really made any difference. His much vaunted efforts in 1987 towards a Russian withdrawal from Afghanistan, for example, actually contributed nothing to events.

Despite his close involvement with the Soviet Union – at one point he was singly responsible for all the Soviet trade with the West – Hammer was always a firmly committed capitalist. Never frightened to air his views, in 1921 he discussed freely the failure of Communism with Lenin, and advised him on how to get American capital into the country.

Hammer could not tolerate failure in himself; and his autobiography (the cover of which displayed such unctuous compliments from friends like Gerald Ford that one American magazine made them the subject of a satirical competition) contained not a single example.

An early instance of his refusal to recognise obstacles was displayed in 1932. His first wife, Olga, had threatened not to return to America from the Soviet Union without her illiterate Russian servant, at a time when literacy was a requirement and American officials unbendable. Hammer enjoyed recalling how he boarded their ship in New York, side-tracked the immigration officers, memorised the relevant page of the Russian text, and taught it to the servant.

In most scrapes he also brought his money and influence to bear on a problem which, harnessed to his natural energy and confidence, made him at times seem all-powerful. Well into his eighties, he achieved two of his most impressive international feats.

Within hours of the Chernobyl explosion in 1986 Hammer had flown the best marrow transplant specialists in America to the Soviet Union to help the victims –

though according to the medical journal the *Lancet* the treatment probably did no good and may even have killed two of the patients.

Barely two months later, when it seemed that the Reykjavik summit was on the brink of failure over the imprisonment in the Soviet Union of the American journalist Nicholas Danilov, he suggested a face-saving way in which Danilov could be released, and the summit was saved.

Throughout his life Hammer insisted on getting his own way in matters both large and small. At a party given by Queen Elizabeth the Queen Mother in London in 1984, Hammer found himself in danger of being late for a banquet in Peking with Ronald Reagan and Zhao Ziyang, because his hostess was enjoying herself too much to leave. Unable to leave first, he simply explained his predicament to the Queen Mother, who obligingly departed, leaving Hammer in good time to board his private aircraft.

In 1989 President Bush officially pardoned Hammer for having made illegal contributions to Richard Nixon's 1972 campaign – a crime for which Hammer was fined and given a year on probation – which paved the way for the honorary knighthood of the British Empire which he ardently longed for.

One of three brothers, Armand Hammer was born in New York City on May 21 1898. His father, Julius Hammer, was of Russian-Jewish extraction and a founder of the American Communist party.

Julius combined a flourishing gynaecological practice with a wholesale business selling mouthwash, shampoo and pharmaceutical chemicals; and was later sent to Sing Sing on a manslaughter conviction for performing an illegal abortion which killed his patient. Disagreements with his partners prompted Julius Hammer to buy them out, which brought his venture to the verge of insolvency in 1918.

Young Armand, who was a medical student at the time, salvaged the business with his brothers. He persuaded his family to buy up all the medical supplies they could lay their hands on – the price of drugs had plummeted after the First World War – and the first of many fortunes was made when the market rose again.

In 1921 he went to Russia, where he remained for nine years. When he was offered a manufacturing concession on attractive terms by the Soviet Government in 1925 Hammer opted for pencils.

Within six months he was selling cheap pencils to the Russians, who had until then only been able to buy expensive imported ones, and within a year he was making profits of more than a million dollars.

His involvement in the Occidental Petroleum Corporation began in 1957. Hammer was the last of the big-name oilmen in the age of the corporate committee – as was manifested by his prompt arrival on the scene of the Piper Alpha disaster in 1988 (the North Sea oil platform was owned by Occidental Petroleum).

Despite his involvement in world politics Hammer never lost interest in his business – indeed, the two went hand in hand. It was this combination which transformed Occidental from a loss-making oil explorer worth about $100,000 to one of the largest companies in the world.

The breakthrough occurred in 1961, when Occidental broke the control of the Seven Sisters in the Middle East by winning the concession to drill for oil in Libya. Later, Occidental played an equally important, although less happy part in oil history by being the first company to crumble before the demands of Colonel Gaddafi, a watershed in the establishment of Opec.

Hammer was also celebrated for his art collection which travelled the world on loan to major galleries in both East and West. But his taste for art was never dissociated from his love for business: no aesthete, he saw pictures chiefly as an expression of money and power.

He first became interested in art in the 1920s, when his brother discovered that Tsarist treasures could be bought for almost nothing in the hungry Soviet Union. A huge collection was quickly built, much of which was subsequently sold at large profit to the American public through the imaginative and unlikely channel of department stores.

Hammer continued his phenomenal regimen until his death, working 14 hours a day and making frequent trips around the globe in his private jet: "I don't smoke or drink hard liquor," he declared, "and I swim a quarter of a mile every day."

To his mother and his hardworking but unsuccessful father Hammer was always the loving son; and his memoirs described his father's imprisonment as the most painful episode in his life.

But it was only with his third wife, Frances, that he found matrimonial happiness. His first two marriages, and his relationship with Julian, his only child, were largely sacrificed to his work. But after Frances's death in 1989 he found himself faced with a $400-million lawsuit from the executor of her will, who charged him with systematically cheating her of her share of his fortune.

The executor claimed that Hammer's personal fortune was built on loans from her, which the tycoon acknowledged: "When I married Mrs Hammer I was strapped for cash: Mrs Hammer offered to make loans to me, which I was happy to accept."

December 12 1990

PRINCE JOHANNES VON THURN UND TAXIS

HIS HIGHNESS PRINCE JOHANNES VON THURN UND TAXIS, who has died aged 64, was an aristocrat whose tastes sometimes appeared more questionable than his antecedents.

He was also a successful businessman, who more than recouped the family fortune after the loss of six castles and some 200,000 acres in the wake of the Second World War. The Thurn und Taxis family originated in Lombardy and rose to prominence some 400 years ago when they carried letters all over the Austrian Empire, acquiring the title of Hereditary Grand Postmaster General of the Empire in 1595, and, a century later, the rank of Prince.

Prince Johannes could claim a connection with the Habsburgs, being the great-grandson of Princess Helen of Bavaria, sister of the Empress Elisabeth. But his extravagant way of life rested on his solid modern achievement of increasing the family's assets to more than $1.5 billion, with worldwide interests in banking, breweries, foresty and art.

His first business coup, in the 1950s, was an unglamorous investment in a company called Doduco, which recycled waste from Pforzheim's jewellery industries into electrical equipment. The enterprise prospered with the developing importance of electronics.

The feudal grandeur which the Prince maintained at his 500-room palace – Schloss St Emmeram, a former monastery on the Danube at Regensburg in Bavaria – would have done credit to any of his ancestors. To the end, the Schloss was staffed by servants in livery and powdered wigs.

Five chefs ministered to the caprices of the palate, and a clockmaker was employed full-time to wind and service the various timepieces. In winter there were boar hunts, with beaters in red and blue tabards driving the prey through the forest; and the day would end with game-keepers honouring the slaughtered beasts with ritual salutations upon the horn.

Prince Johannes believed that aristocrats were different from ordinary mortals, and his own behaviour supported this notion. A tall, commanding figure, with the look of an owl and a slow, ceremonial style of speech, he gave the impression that his features had been pickled by years of good living.

His entourage spoke of him as an intelligent, intensely observant man, with a lively sense of humour and an almost psychic awareness of the foibles of those he met. More dispassionate observers noted his outspoken comments on Jews and negroes.

In 1971, on his way to the Shah of Iran's extravagant celebrations in Persepolis, the Prince secreted some cole-slaw in a sickbag on the aircraft; during the flight he feigned sickness, retched violently and proceeded, to the alarm of his fellow passengers, to eat the contents of the sickbag.

Prince Johannes's family had featured on both sides in

the Second World War, and he never lost an opportunity of teasing his "bad German" relations, in whose presence he would finger the lampshades and wonder at the consistency of the fabric.

As a bachelor, the Prince was constantly photographed with the world's most glamorous women. He indulged his reputation as an international playboy to the hilt until, in his fifties, he married Gloria von Schonburg-Glauchau, a vivacious 22-year-old German countess given to dyeing her hair various colours, to riding a powerful motor-bicycle around the German countryside, and to singing at parties.

It was an unconventional marriage. The Princess would throw her arms exuberantly around her husband's neck and declare: *"Oh Johannes! Ich liebe dich!* I love you! I want to cut your throat and drink your blood!"

When Prince Johannes celebrated his sixtieth birthday in 1986, Princess Gloria arranged for the cake to be adorned with 60 chocolate candles sculpted in the form of the male member. The Prince, though, was embarrassed that this tribute to his virility should be paraded before his tenantry, whose children eagerly fell upon the illuminating trophies.

December 16 1990

ALFRED HINDS

ALFRED HINDS, who has died in Jersey aged 73, proved himself, in the course of a prolonged struggle to establish his innocence of a shop-breaking charge, the most successful prison escaper in English history and also one of the shrewdest legal minds never to have been called to the Bar.

His troubles began in September 1953, when, along with four others, he was charged with stealing some £30,000 in jewellery and £4,700 in cash from Maple's store in Tottenham Court Road. That December Hinds, pronounced by Lord Goddard to be "a most dangerous criminal", was jailed for 12 years.

Yet, though it took the jury only half an hour to make up their minds, the evidence against him was essentially circumstantial. The prosecution claimed that traces of a fuse used to blow the safe had been found on Hinds, together with material from the lining of the safe.

One of the other men found guilty of the crime had been at Hinds's house the Sunday after the robbery, and he was carrying watches from the store; Hinds maintained, though, that this visitor had called about a car.

Hinds admitted that he had been near Maple's on the night that the robbery was planned, but said he wanted to buy a carpet – though, as Lord Goddard pointed out, 8 p.m. was an unlikely hour for this purpose.

One of the accused gave evidence against Hinds, the night superintendent at Heals, an "inside" man who later co-operated with the police in their inquiries. He claimed that Hinds had threatened him about giving evidence, and offered him £500 if he failed to pick out his fellow criminal at an identity parade.

Hinds had eight previous convictions, some of them involving safe-breaking. Nevertheless, in recent years it had appeared that he was going straight, living in a house near the Thames at Staines, where he helped his brother in a building and demolition business.

From the very first he protested his innocence, but in

December 1953 the Court of Criminal Appeal dismissed his appeal application. Next year Hinds published a pamphlet in which he demanded an inquiry or a retrial.

This was ignored, and in November 1955 Hinds escaped from Nottingham prison. He took a hacksaw blade out of an electrician's toolbag, made a copy of the prison workshop key from brass after memorising its shape, purloined some planks which he used to climb the prison wall, and made off in a lorry provided by a friend. He was already a seasoned escaper.

Alfred George Hinds had been born at Newington Butts, in south London, in 1917. His father, described variously as a general labourer, a street betting agent and a pugilist, was sentenced to seven years as a consequence of a bank raid at Portsmouth in 1935; he also received 10 strokes of the cat-o'-nine-tails which, Hinds believed, contributed to his early death.

At the age of seven young Alfie found himself in Pentonville remand home, from which he made his first break. Subsequently he was brought up by foster parents in the Midlands, where he acquired his considerable skills at metalwork and machine-turning.

In the Second World War he was in the Royal Tank Corps, until he decided to desert. Subsequently, he arranged for friends to create a disturbance while he was being transported in an army truck at Clapham Junction; with the guards distracted, he made his getaway in a car supplied by another accomplice.

In 1945 Rochester Borstal afforded the next opportunity for Hinds to demonstrate his escaping skills. But the escape from Nottingham prison in 1955 was an altogether more ambitious project, and one that he combined with sustained literary endeavour.

Several papers were bombarded with letters. "I made this escape", he wrote to one, "because it was the only way now left open to me in my fight to obtain justice. I am entirely innocent of the crime for which I was sentenced for 12 years."

The letters were all postmarked SW1, as was the parcel containing the musical boxes which Hinds sent his children for Christmas; nevertheless rumour was endlessly fertile, placing Hinds in Turin, in France, in Ireland, in America.

With fine English logic it was reckoned that his letters were too literate to have been composed by someone of his background. But not long afterwards Hinds's voice was heard on Independent Television setting forth his demands in unimpeachable English.

Scotland Yard announced that it was reconstituting its "ghost squad", credited with more than ordinary powers. This move provoked a letter from Hinds to the *Sunday Dispatch* in which he reflected that public money would be much better spent on an inquiry or a retrial.

Not until he had been free for 245 days, on July 31 1956, was the absconder finally caught, in Dublin: he had been living in a cottage which he had bought for £750 at Greystones, Co. Wicklow.

Hinds was charged with prison-breaking and, acting in his own defence, proved himself more than a match for learned counsel – and also for the judge. "My Lord, I think I can help you there," he would helpfully intervene; and indeed the judge was forced to admit that the accused knew more about some aspects of the law than anyone else in the court.

Hinds managed to get himself acquitted of prison-breaking, and he received only 11 days extra sentence for escaping from custody before returning to serve his longer sentence.

He seemed to have acquired a taste for the law, and in July of that year reappeared before the Queen's Bench Division to argue a point in an action against the prison commissioners for his illegal arrest.

Hinds contacted accomplices who were instructed to smuggle him a padlock into the Law Courts. Once there he asked to go to the lavatory, whither he was accompanied by two guards. When they removed his handcuffs Hinds and a friend succeeded in bundling the guards into the lavatory and padlocking the door.

He was quickly recaptured and R. A. Butler, the Home Secretary, remained deaf to all demands for a retrial. Hinds was sent to Chelmsford prison where, in June 1958, he fashioned a key that gave him entry into the bathhouse and thence escaped by way of a skylight on to the roof and over the wall into a waiting Morris Minor.

This time he eluded his pursuers for almost two years, again in Ireland, where, under the name William Herbert Bishop, he estabished himself as a flourishing second-hand car dealer. It was the customs officials who finally caught him, in January 1960, for possessing cars that had been smuggled across the border, an offence for which he received six months at the Crumlin Road jail in Belfast.

On his return to his native land to continue his sentence for the Maple's robbery – he found time, the while, to sell his life story to the *News of the World* – Hinds settled into a prolonged series of battles with the

English legal establishment. "My Lord, you are not quite with me," he would tell the judge, though he also dispensed praise – "you have summed up very well."

But appeal after appeal was dismissed, and Hinds's legal manoeuvres seemed to have got him nowhere, until in 1964 he successfully sued Superintendent Herbert Sparks for libel, gaining £1,300 in damages and costs. This civil victory forced a reconsideration of the criminal sentence, and Hinds was released.

Even so, in November 1965 the Court of Criminal Appeal decided that the original conviction had been correct, and once again refused him leave to appeal. Hinds, now at large, continued his struggle with a book *Contempt of Court* (1966), and took to lecturing at polytechnics and at the National Council for Civil Liberties. The crying need, he explained, was for a more intelligent police force.

Later he retired to Jersey where he established a property business, and in 1973 reached the semi-finals of a contest to discover the most intelligent person in the island. With an IQ of 150 he made an admirable secretary of the Channel Islands Mensa Society.

January 7 1991

LEE ATWATER

LEE ATWATER, the youngest Chairman of the Republican National Committee, who has died in Washington aged 40, did more than anyone else to ensure that George Bush reached the White House and then took on the even more difficult job of securing the Republican party's grip on power.

Atwater was the first professional political consultant to head either of America's major political parties. Sometimes described as "the Rottweiler of American politics", the wiry, sandy-haired, quick-eyed and tight-mouthed Atwater seemed impervious to accusations of dirty tricks in his notoriously "negative" compaigning.

The leader of a combative new breed of "baby boom" Republicans who believed their party had accepted minority status for too long, Atwater masterminded the successful presidential campaigns of Ronald Reagan in 1984 and of George Bush in 1988. It was the Bush campaign that established him as the master of attacking one's opponent on "values" issues – such as crime, gun-control, taxes, walfare reform, national defence, abortion and school prayers.

Atwater took little interest in the intricacies of government: "My job", he said, "is the politics of politics ... The contest, the winning and losing thing is big for me. I can't stand to lose ... when I lose I get physically sick."

Despite his attempt at a "good-ole-boy" Southern manner, he had an unwavering instinct for the poisoned barb. In the summer of 1989, for example, he was involved in the imbroglio over the attempt to smear Tom Foley, the Democratic Congressman who had just taken over as House Speaker.

A memorandum posted to party officials from the Republican National Committee was entitled "Tom Foley: Out of the Liberal Closet". The document compared his politics to those of Congressman Barney Frank, an avowed liberal and an admitted homosexual. Atwater refused to disavow the memo when it was first released, but apologised to Foley the next day.

The son of an insurance claims adviser of Methodist stock, Harvey Leroy Atwater was born at Atlanta, Georgia, on February 27 1951 and educated at Flora High School – where he formed a white "soul" band called the Upsetter's Review – and Newberry College.

His interest in politics was aroused by a vacation job in the Washington office of South Carolina's conservative Republican senator, J. Strom Thurmond, and he managed his first political campaign while still a student. In 1973 he was appointed executive director of the College Republicans' national office in Washington, where he first made the acquaintance of George Bush, then chairman of the Republican National Committee.

The next year Atwater returned to Columbia, South Carolina, where he established his own political consultancy and began organising campaigns for local Republican office-seekers in the South. In 1980 Atwater was accused of employing "dirty tricks" tactics in a South Carolina congressional race between Republican contender Floyd Spence and Democrat Tom Turnipseed. At a Turnipseed press briefing, a reporter allegedly "planted" by Atwater rose and said that he understood that Turnipseed had formerly undergone psychiatric treatment and electroshock therapy.

Turnipseed protested, but Atwater told reporters he would not respond to someone who, in his words, had once been "hooked up to jumper cables". He later apologised for this comment and insisted that he had not planted the reporter.

Later that year, as manager of Ronald Reagan's 1980

South Carolina primary campaign, Atwater became embroiled in another controversy. On learning that George Bush – also a contender for that year's Republican presidential nomination – had once supported gun-control legislation, Atwater hired Reid Buckley, brother of the influential journalist William F. Buckley, to tape a radio commercial attacking Bush's position.

But the voice on the commercial was identified only as "Mr Buckley", leaving many listeners with the impression that William F. Buckley had branded Bush a moderate.

After the Republicans closed ranks, Atwater became the Southern regional director for the Reagan–Bush ticket, which went on to carry every southern state except Georgia as part of a 44-state landslide.

Following Reagan's inauguration, Atwater, at the age of 29, became special assistant to the President for political affairs. He remained in that post until 1984, when he was appointed director of the Reagan–Bush re-election campaign, steering the incumbents to an easy victory over the Democratic ticket of Walter Mondale and Geraldine Ferraro.

In 1986 Bush asked Atwater to serve as chairman of his political action committee, the $5 million Fund for America's Future – which was used, in part, to get the "Bush-in '88" campaign rolling. After laying the groundwork for that campaign, Atwater was duly asked to become manager of the George Bush for President Committee. The Bush campaign began badly as the candidate finished third in the Iowa caucuses. The nomination battle with Robert Dole became heated and at one point Dole accused Atwater of being behind a series of disclosures about the personal finances of his wife. Atwater responded by calling Dole "a typical schoolyard bully" adding, "he can dish it out but if someone hits him back, he starts whining".

In the general election campaign Atwater masterminded the Republican strategy of depicting Michael Dukakis, the Democratic nominee, as being soft on defence and crime. He fashioned the attacks on Dukakis over Willie Horton, the murderer who raped a woman while on furlough from prison.

"If I can make Willie Horton a household name," Atwater told a Republican audience, "we'll win the election."

It was also Atwater who encouraged Bush to ride out the storm over his running-mate Dan Quayle's questionable military record.

Atwater's key role in Bush's successful bid for the presidency established him as the most prominent political consultant in America, and immediately after the election Bush named him as chairman of the Republican National Committee.

Atwater wasted no time in announcing that the party would attempt to break the Democrats' 35-year hold on the House of Representatives by "targeting" Democratic incumbents. The most ambitious of his strategies was the recruiting into the Republican camp of blacks and other minorities who traditionally supported the Democratic party.

Thus, on the anniversary of Martin Luther King's birthday, Atwater visited the Atlanta church where Dr King had once preached; and he organised an all-star rhythm-and-blues revue to perform at one of George Bush's inaugural parties. The show featured Willie Dixon, Bo Diddley and Sam Moore.

Atwater also sang on this occasion, joining the President himself – who strapped on a white guitar labelled "The Pres" – in a spirited rendition of *High Heel Sneakers*.

Atwater was the proud possessor of six guitars – one of which was a gift from Ronnie Wood of the Rolling Stones – and when in South Carolina, nothing would prevent him from doing a turn at Bullwinkle's, the Columbian nightclub. His own album, *Red, Hot and Blue*, recorded with B. B. King and others, was released in 1990.

But Atwater's attempts to ingratiate himself with blacks as a trustee of Howard University, Washington, ended in ignominy when 200 black students seized the school's main administration building to protest at his appointment. He resigned the next day.

Atwater, who had the disconcerting habit of dousing food in hot pepper sauce, was part-owner of a barbecued-rib restaurant at Arlington, Virginia.

In 1990 he was stricken by an inoperable brain tumour, and during his fight against illness he reiterated his apologies to the targets of his political tactics. In an article in *Life* magazine, for example, he wrote: "In 1988, fighting Dukakis, I said that I 'would strip the bark off the little bastard' and 'make Willie Horton his running mate'. I am sorry for both statements: the first for its naked cruelty, the second because it makes me sound racist, which I am not."

Atwater married, in 1978, Sally Dunbar; they had three children.

March 30 1991

JIANG QING

JIANG QING, the widow of Mao Tse-tung, who has died aged 77, was the leader of the infamous Gang of Four, and probably the most powerful woman in the world during the last decade of the Chairman's rule.

Although she married Mao in 1939, Jiang Qing remained a relatively obscure figure until the late 1950s, when, as a former actress, she began to take a sinister interest in the theatre. In the mid-1960s she emerged as a moving spirit of the Cultural Revolution, and inspired the massacre of innocent civilians as the young Red Guards swept through China enforcing a return to "pure" Maoism.

Her fall was as sudden as her rise had been gradual. After her arrest on October 6 1976, a month after Mao's death, Jiang Qing was denounced by the official Chinese press as a "fascist dictator of the arts" and the "would-be empress of modern China, who sought to squat on the heads of 800 million people".

At her trial four years later Jiang Qing was unrepentant. But despite her defiance, she spoke like a victim: "Everything I did, Mao told me to do. I was his dog. What he said to bite, I bit."

In 1981 she was sentenced to death and dragged screaming from the court-room, but the execution was stayed for two years in the hope that she might show some remorse. She never did, but in 1983 the sentence was changed to life imprisonment. The next year she was released for medical treatment and is said to have been under house arrest ever since.

She was born in Li Jin in Shantung Province in March

1914 (she always refused to divulge the exact date on the grounds that the masses would become too excited) and was brought up in grinding poverty, which she would later describe with a mixture of bitterness and pride. Her father, a carpenter, beat his wife and daughter until they fled him.

By her own account, young Li Jin determined at an early age, to become an actress of modern drama, an avant-garde ambition in the China of the 1920s. Other versions have her running away from home to avoid being sold by her family, or being kidnapped and pressed into service as an entertainer – a practice not uncommon in China at that time.

In 1930 she enrolled at the Shantung Experimental Drama Academy in Tsinan and joined a theatrical troupe in the same city. She became known as "big Miss Li" because of her height, medium by Western standards, enormous by Eastern ones.

She moved to Shanghai where she performed in a wide range of plays. In later life Jiang Qing used to recall with particular pride her portrayal of Nora in *A Doll's House*, claiming that she made more of a rebel out of the character than Ibsen had done.

In 1933 she secretly joined the Chinese Communist party and, between acting jobs, taught female textile workers to read and write. She spent several months in a Guomindang jail as a result of her political activities.

Jiang Qing's film career began in 1934 when she joined the Tien Tung Motion Picture Company in Shanghai as a bit player, using the name Lan Ping ("Blue Apple"). She had a supporting role in *Blood on Wolf Hill* (1936) and went on to play the female lead in *Wang Lao Wu* (1937).

127

She also appeared in several politically contoversial films and became known as something of a heart-breaker – she drove the actor Tang Na, whom she informally married then abandoned, to the brink of suicide.

After the Japanese assault on Shanghai in the summer of 1939, Jiang Qing, along with thousands of other young leftists, patriots and opportunists, made the trek to the Communist headquarters at Yanan, a dusty village in the remote north-west.

She met Mao when he came to give a lecture at the Lu Hsun Art Academy, where she was teaching dramatics. He was captivated and conferred on her the name Jiang Qing ("Azure River").

The marriage of Mao and Jiang, which took place in 1939, was the fourth for him and the third for her – she had previously been married to Yu Chi-wei, a Communist student activist, as well as Tung Na. Mao's comrades in the Communist party hierarchy strongly objected to his cavalier treatment of his third wife, Ho Tzu-chen, a party veteran and a survivor of the Long March.

An agreement was finally reached whereby the union between Mao and Jiang was given party approval provided she abstained from interfering in politics. Shortly after their marriage, Jiang Qing gave birth to her daughter, Li Na, whom she brought up with Mao's other children by previous marriages.

Jiang Qing remained out of the political limelight for the first 10 years of her marriage, although she took great pride in the fact that she was among the few women who made the gruelling two-year march from Yanan to Peking, where Mao established the People's Republic in September 1949.

Shortly before the Communist takeover Mao arranged

with Stalin for his wife, now emaciated and seriously ill, to travel to Moscow, where it was thought she could recuperate with the benefit of superior Soviet medicine.

During this and subsequent forced returns for the treatment of cervical cancer and other ailments, Jiang Qing suffered a bitter isolation in a country whose language she did not speak or understand. She also feared losing Mao as lover and husband, and her foothold among the elite – many of whom resented her mercurial style and envied her intimacy with Mao.

By the late 1950s her vigour was restored – just as Mao's began to ebb – and she returned to her original interest in drama, taking over several opera companies. She built up a body of loyal followers and created a corpus of so-called model plays, designed as classics for the new age.

Jiang Qing decreed that the "emperors, ministers, scholars, beauties and fairies" who had hitherto dominated the stage, were to be seen no more in China. The new heroes and heroines were drawn from the proletariat and acted out trite political fables written by committees.

Jiang Qing's revolutionary ballets, notably *The Red Detachment of Women* and *White Haired Girl*, were a bizarre mixture of traditional Russian ballet, Broadway musical and Maoist madness.

The careers of thousands of seasoned artists were suddenly curtailed as traditional theatre was banned. Writers and actors whom Jiang Qing had known in Shanghai in the 1930s were persecuted for fear they might reveal her Bohemian past.

For Jiang Qing had secret and shameful tastes. It is said that in private she watched Greta Garbo films, wore long chic skirts instead of the regulation Mao suit and cap, and slept between silk sheets. Her favourite novel was *Gone with the Wind*.

When the Great Proletarian Cultural Revolution was launched in earnest in 1965 Jiang Qing became one of its most outspoken champions, and her fiery speeches often signalled the fall from grace of high officials. One of the men she hounded was Deng Xiaoping, who survived and regained power after Mao's death – he is reported to have had the proceedings of her trial piped live to his office.

The country was shaken to its roots. Red Guards swept through the country, setting up "revolutioinary committees" to replace the established power structure in every institution. But members of the old system resisted vigorously and often violently and a civil war resulted which ravaged the economy, cost tens of millions of lives and dashed the formal eduction of the younger generation.

The Cultural Revolution achieved many of its goals: decentralisation of the government, heightened political consciousness, an infusion of new blood into the party leadership, and a change of focus from city to countryside. But it also left China a shambles. At the end of the 1960s a halt was called and a concentrated effort made to mend and rebuild the nation politically and economically.

But Jiang Qing, as head of the Cultural Committee of the State Council, showed little change of direction – in 1972 she staged an unreconstructed version of *The Red Detachment of Women* for President and Mrs Nixon.

After the attempted coup, flight and death of Lin Biao in 1971 the last years of Chairman Mao's rule were dominated by the rivalry between Jiang Qing and the Mandarin-born premier Chou En-lai, whose pragmatic

policies incurred the suspicion of the ideological hard-
liners.

There was a dangerous row between Mao and his wife
after Jiang Qing had told her life story to Roxane Witke,
the American writer, hoping she would produce as favourable account of her life as Edgar Snow had done for Mao.

After their arrest in 1976 the so-called Gang of Four
became the subject of one of the most virulent and
prolonged hate campaigns in history. Jiang Qing was
described as a "wild and shameless witch" and the "devil
risen from a heap of white bones", whose fascist dictator-
ship over the arts was nothing but the means to an
infamous end: that of seizing power in succession to Mao.

Jiang Qing once remarked that "Sex is engaging in
the first round but what sustains interest in the long run
is power."

Her life, even during her period of greatest ascendancy, was grey in the extreme: "The chairman is strict
with me and is a severe teacher to me . . . There are many
things I do not know . . . We live together. He is quiet
and not given to conversation."

Roxane Witke writes: The actualities of Jiang Qing's
life, along with those of most Chinese leaders, have been
rigorously screened from public view. Yet that very
absence of fact served as a stimulus for the "wild histories",
as the Chinese call unorthodox reports, and the plain
gossip that plagued her to the end of her days.

Her own version of her life story she said she told but
once: to myself in the summer of 1972, an account that
was subsequently published as *Comrade Chiang Ch'ing*

(1977). The personality I observed over eight afternoons that continued toward the following dawns was an unstable mix of fragility and toughness; she was at once a lover of beauty, a cherisher of children, and a hater of persons who thwarted her will.

While nimbly fashioning bracelets of fragrant orchid flowers, she lashed out at the renegades, double-dealers and capitalist roaders she had known over the years, many of whose careers she is thought to have ruined in defence of Mao and in the course of her grapple to power.

Considering her ambitions she may have been doomed from the start. In Chinese metaphor she was born feeling crushed by the wheel of history, escaped only to become a crusher and ultimately was crushed herself.

She was also doomed by a deep-seated Confucian prejudice against women who meddle in politics and by the loathing vented by centuries of orthodox historians against the few empresses who briefly reigned, two at least ably. While famous as social equalisers, the Chinese Communists have hardly risen above that aversion to women in power.

A recurring theme in both the hate campaign against Jiang Qing and the trial was that she sought to make herself a 20th-century empress, a charge that seems unreasonable and laughable to me and would have been to her as well, I am sure.

June 5 1991

PETER EASTWOOD

PETER EASTWOOD, who has died aged 77, was the driving force behind *The Daily Telegraph* for more than 20 years.

As night editor and then Managing Editor from 1965 to 1986, he demonstrated unrelenting concern for production standards which made him admired, feared, even hated by colleagues – who nevertheless were bemused by the mild manner of his conversation.

Under the ownership of Lord Hartwell, a system of divided command, with the Editor adopting a reflective, relaxed approach to the pages of opinion, and the Managing Editor exercising rigorous control over the tightly packaged news columns, gave the *Telegraph* an unchanging yet supple formula which only needed to be adjusted in the mid-1980s.

Like other considerable figures in Fleet Street, Eastwood never sought to be all things to all men. He acted single-mindedly in what he saw as the paper's best interests – even where this meant transcending friendships, enmities and wounding tittle-tattle. At the height of his considerable powers as night editor, he ruled the news sub-editing department, where reporters' raw "copy" is selected, corrected and headlined with an unchallengeable strength of mind and character.

He demanded clarity and adherence to innumerable, often obscure, rules – such as that only Malays could be permitted to "run amok" in the paper. From the arrival in the early evening of the galley proofs containing the first printed stories, the subs' room took on the atmosphere of a prep school class ruled by the most testing master, with a steady stream of subs being summoned up to Eastwood's desk under the office clock.

"Who subbed the 'Blackpool Tower'?" he would call out. "Mr Smith, can I have a word. Have you checked that this man's name is right? . . .

"Who subbed 'Cow knocks Bolivian bus over cliff'? You know, you've got the comma in the wrong place, Mr Jones . . . Now, who subbed 'MP's honour'? This used to be our style, Mr Davies, but we gave it up before you were born."

Such was his eminence that if a late change to the front page was needed on deadline, he would exasperate the printers by appearing in the composing room in person and indicating changes to the make-up by the taboo practice of tapping the type with his pen.

Winston Eastwood – known as "Peter" – was born at Manchester on June 11 1913, and educated at Batley Grammar School. He began his career as a reporter on the *Batley News*.

Eastwood later moved to the *Yorkshire Evening News*, where he met his wife Norah, also a journalist (who died in 1989), and switched to sub-editing because, he once confided, "I wanted *power*."

After arriving in Fleet Street in 1936, he spent two years absorbing the craft of dynamic popular journalism as a contract sub on Arthur Christiansen's *Daily Express*, then found a permanent job on the *Daily Mail* until he was called up in 1941.

Two years later Eastwood was serving as a gunnery officer with the 2nd Indian Field Regiment when Lord Louis Mountbatten, the self-styled "Supremo" of South-East Asia Command, told Frank Owen, a former editor of the *Evening Standard*, to form *SEAC Newspaper* for units under his command.

Plucked from the Burmese jungle, Eastwood already had a reputation for intrigue, thanks to his accomplishing the removal from command of a senior officer after he had insisted on breakfasting off mess silver in the sunshine opposite Japanese positions.

Len Jackson of the *Daily Mirror* was appointed editor when the paper began in the *Statesman*'s offices in Calcutta, but Eastwood, the chief sub, soon took over all editorial decisions. With Owen's frequent absences, he was running all aspects of its existence by the time he became editor himself.

When the Allies landed at Singapore, Eastwood – who liked to joke that he was first up the beach with his typewriter – commandeered a rakish Hudson Tourer. He then drove up to the offices of the *Straits Times* and instructed the printers, who had been producing a Japanese paper, to put to bed *SEAC Newspaper*'s first Singapore edition.

Having ensured a supply of newsprint by hijacking a consignment in the docks intended for civilian use, Eastwood started to furnish the finest mess table in the newly relieved colony, despite the order that officers should live on hard rations in accordance with military administration regulations.

He recruited a Chinese cook who purchased the best ingredients on the black market, using profits from smuggling cigarettes to Johore to pay for the choicest items. There was a hiccup, however, when the head of the Military Administration announced that he was coming to lunch.

Regulation bully beef, ships' biscuits and water were

duly served up to the general, who protested "I came to lunch because I heard you kept the best table in Singapore." Immediately Eastwood produced a bottle of Gordon's export gin and set the cook Loy to work on a sumptuous feast.

Shortly afterwards, Eastwood was personally demobbed by Mountbatten to launch the *Singapore Free Press* as an afternoon paper. He ran it for several months, cutting an impressive figure in his black chauffeur-driven Packard, then returned to England where he joined Reuters, the news agency.

After eight months he moved across Fleet Street to the *Telegraph* (where he was nicknamed "The Tunku") and began his steady rise in the sub-editors' department. On becoming night editor and then Managing Editor, he extended his power far beyond that of his predecessors.

With keen awareness of the wear and tear of nightly edition work, he was always ready to encourage colleagues who were unwell to retire early. But such was his dedication that he stayed on himself until he was 72 – and the paper embarked on new technology and a transfer of premises under the proprietorship of Mr Conrad Black.

June 10 1991

RUSSELL 'BIG RUSS' HINZE

RUSSELL "BIG RUSS" HINZE, the Queensland politician, who has died aged 72, became known as "the minister for everything" during the free-booting reign of Sir Joh Bjelke-Petersen.

"Big Russ" was a kind of natural wonder: built on the scale of Ayers Rock, he possessed a hide seemingly impervious to considerations of public propriety. From the time he became a cabinet minister in Bjelke-Petersen's National Government in 1974 until he resigned from politics in 1988, he was continually the target of corruption allegations – although in the tradition of Queensland politics, he laughed them off.

Hinze once described himself as "the roughest, toughest bloody politician you could come across". He gained nationwide notoriety for his keenness to enter beer-belly competitions, his habit of stirring his tea with his finger, and his regular nomination as one of Australia's worst-dressed men.

A large, rumbustious man, grossly overweight in his later years, Hinze pulled no punches. He called for rapists to be castrated, murderers to be executed by firing squad, and "dole bludgers" to wear dog tags.

He was, in fact, the consummate populist, whose larrikin style and amiable nature earned him genuine affection among many of his political foes. Cabinet colleagues respected him not only as an able administrator, but also because he was one of the few figures in the National party prepared to stand up to Bjelke-Petersen. Indeed, he spoke openly of his ambitions to become premier.

Hinze could have flourished nowhere but in Bjelke-Petersen's Queensland, where the dreams of entrepreneurs were endlessly indulged, corruption was a way of life, and civil liberties and social justice received short shrift. As

Minister for Police, Hinze was asked what special qualities he brought to the post. "I've got big feet," he volunteered, "no brains, and I'm 21 stone."

Pulled over once by a young traffic constable, he allegedly opened up a map of Queensland and said, "Right, son, where would you prefer to go, Birdsville or Bedourie?" – referring to two remote townships in the far outback.

As Minister for Local Government, Hinze was also a land developer; as Minister for Main Roads – known as the "Colossus of Roads" – he was a major supplier of gravel for road works; and as Minister for Racing, the proud owner of more than 100 racehorses. Questioned about conflicts of interest, he would insist that his public and private lives were entirely separate. "Say what you like," he would laugh, "I'm a good bloke."

For the inaugural Queensland Beer Belly Championships in 1984 Hinze stood shirtless and laughing, his arms around two men whom he described as "only kids – I'm 24 stone and the biggest of these blokes is only 22 stone." As the crowd cheered he added: "Aren't they the sexiest pair of bastards you've ever seen?"

Hinze's downfall, and that of the National party Government, came a few years later, after the 1987 Fitzgerald report into corruption in the Queensland police force. Hinze was charged with having accepted $A520,000 in bribes from three property developers and an accountant. He was one of seven Queensland cabinet ministers, including Bjelke-Petersen himself, to be charged with a whole range of crimes.

Hinze, who was due to appear in court at the time of his death, had strenuously denied everything from the start. In 1979 he declared his annual income to be

$A360,000, and claimed that he was far too rich to be interested in bribes.

"I've got my sentence," he said in one of his last public appearances. "No matter what they do to me, I've been sentenced by the Lord."

Russell James Hinze was born in Brisbane in 1919, and left school at the age of 12 to help his father to run cows and haul logs behind what is now the surfers' paradise – the Gold Coast strip of southern Queensland.

He milked cows seven days a week for 15 years, but managed in the interim to educate himself in his spare time, and also acted as secretary of the local cricket club.

By 1952 he was a member of the local shire council, and subsequently served for nine years as chairman. He was elected to the Queensland parliament in 1966.

Even in those early years Hinze's frankness disarmed his enemies. Soon after being appointed a cabinet minister he said, with apparent seriousness, "I told the Premier, 'If you want the boundaries rigged, let me do it and we'll stay in office forever. If you don't, people will say you are stupid.'"

As it was, the Nationals stayed in power for 32 years, mostly in coalition with the Liberal party.

Hinze brought a rare light moment to the Fitzgerald inquiry when, during eight days in the witness box, he was asked about allegations that as a minister he had been seen in a brothel. This was impossible, he replied, since his knees had been giving him trouble at that time; he had been on crutches and could not have got up the stairs.

Altogether, the commission was told, Hinze had received millions of dollars in loans and payments. He replied that he borrowed money only from friends and always paid it back.

Hinze appeared in public occasionally after he was forced out of the cabinet. Latterly, suffering from cancer, he was a gaunt shadow of his old self.

Hinze married first, in 1947, Ruth Byth; they had three sons and three daughters. He married secondly, in 1981, Fay McQuillan, his secretary, who appealed to him, he said, "because she never drinks or smokes or swears and, if anyone tells a smutty story, she'll walk out of the room".

July 2 1991

FRANK 'BIG BAMBINO' RIZZO

FRANK "BIG BAMBINO" RIZZO, the former mayor of Philadelphia who has died aged 70, promised on his election to that office: "I'm gonna be so tough as mayor, I gonna make Attila the Hun look like a faggot."

Rizzo did not disappoint his supporters, who were the poor whites of his native "South Philly", disturbed by the racial and student unrest of the 1960s and 1970s, caught between the derision of rich white liberals and the fury of radicalised blacks. It was typical of Rizzo's street-brawler's bravado that soon after he became mayor in 1972 he left a Boys' Club banquet to quell a potential race riot with a billyclub tucked in the cummerbund of his dinner jacket.

In his previous role as Police Commissioner he had vowed to "crush black power", challenged the Black Panthers to a duel and sent his men to raid their headquarters at night, with orders to strip them naked and photograph them. "Imagine the big Black Panthers with their pants down," he was reported to have gloated.

In an earlier incident Rizzo had mobilised the city's entire police force of 7,000 for a minor disturbance in a black area. His declared intention was to stamp out violence before it spread, and during the bicentennial celebrations in 1976 he asked President Gerald Ford for 15,000 federal troops because he feared riots – the request was declined.

Neither the style nor the substance of Rizzo's policies endeared him to civil libertarians, and the allegations against him became so serious that in 1979 the Justice Department filed a suit against the Philadelphia Police Force, citing evidence of beatings with brass knuckledusters, lead pipes and telephone directories. Rizzo dismissed these charges as "hogwash" and told critics that "Philly's Finest" were strong enough to "liberate Cuba with air support".

It was, none the less, a substantial achievement that under his leadership America's fourth largest city avoided the large-scale troubles of its counterparts. Even when the black ghettos exploded over the assassination of Martin Luther King, Rizzo kept things quiet by sending in his men disguised as clergy to pacify the crowds.

The son of Italian immigrants, Frank Rizzo was born on October 23 1920 and educated at South Philadelphia High School. He recalled his upbringing with fondness: "There was no question as to who was right or wrong. There were no democratic formulas. Boom! You got knocked down. It was a good system."

He left school early to enlist in the US Navy, and after joining the Philadelphia Police in 1943 rose through the ranks to become Commissioner in 1967. He never ceased to be a "cop's cop", and this reputation was enough to ensure his election as mayor in 1971, with the support of 90 per cent of voters in South Philadelphia.

Black Northern Philadelphia did not respond with such enthusiasm. But Rizzo counted on the fact that the majority of Italians, Jews and Irish in the city, who traditionally voted Democrat, were moving towards the right. "A conservative," he remarked, "is a liberal who's been mugged."

Richard Nixon knew that Rizzo was disgusted by the sharp leftward trend of the Democratic party, and by George McGovern's successful campaign for the Democratic nomination. The President pumped money into the city and flattered Rizzo ceaselessly; and Nixon's aides were shocked at how easily he slipped into profanity when conversing with the Mayor.

The approach paid off, and Rizzo became one of the traditional working-class Democrats to endorse Nixon, so earning himself the accolade of "the President's favourite Democrat". Rizzo later defected to the Republican side, taking with him 60,000 "Rizzocrats", and became the Philadelphia chairman of George Bush's 1988 campaign.

Rizzo's term of office (which ended in 1978) was dogged by accusations of racism and corruption. A feud over patronage with Peter Camiel, the Democratic city committee chairman, attracted national attention when the two men, at Rizzo's suggestion, took a lie-detector test over charges of political kickbacks in the award of city contracts to architects: Rizzo failed the test.

When the *Philadelphia Inquirer*, the city's leading newspaper, published a satirical interview with Rizzo, Rizzo denounced it as "garbage, filth and treason", and launched a $6m lawsuit.

Rizzo was re-elected in 1975, against the wishes of the local Democratic organisation and two out of three city newspapers. Their preferred candidate in the primary, Senator Louis G. Hill, challenged Rizzo to a debate. Rizzo declined, so Hill appeared with a live chicken on an empty chair. "Lou Hill," countered Rizzo, "is the only politician who can debate with a chicken and lose."

The City Charter debarred anyone from running for a third term, but Rizzo campaigned for its repeal. His forthright appeal to his constituents to "vote white" cost him some support, but won him the Ku Klux Klan's "racist of the month award" in April 1978.

Rizzo failed in two later comeback attempts against Wilson Goode, the first black to be elected mayor of the city. Rizzo called him "the Bomber" in reference to the disastrous battle with the radical MOVE cult that ended with the deaths of 11 people and the destruction of 61 houses when the city police bombed the cult's head-quarters in 1985. "There goes the neighbourhood," observed Rizzo.

Rizzo was the most quotable Philadelphia politician since Benjamin Franklin, and polarised public opinion until the end of his life. But his bark was often worse than his bite.

During his mayoralty more blacks than ever before were appointed to city jobs, and by the time he retired the police force was 25 per cent black. Rizzo inspired fierce loyalty among his friends, to whom he was known as "the Italian John Wayne".

Sporting a slicked-back coiffure, standing at 6ft 2in and weighing 17 stone, he looked a caricature of the Italian-American working man. But he dismissed his reputation as a Lothario.

"The newspapers have made me pure," he declared. "I can't get away with anything. Listen, if I wanted to cut a caper with a promiscuous broad, I'd have to find one who's an eskimo and meet her in an igloo – and I'd probably have to wear a beard for a disguise."

The epitaph he yearned for was "You'd better hope he's really dead."

He married, in 1942, Carmella Silvestri; they had a son and a daughter.

July 18 1991

LAURA RIDING

LAURA RIDING, the American poet who has died aged 90, was as remarkable for the mesmeric force of her personality – and in particular for her influence upon Robert Graves – as for her literary achievement.

Yet she abandoned both Graves and poetry before she was 40. Poetry, if not Graves, was dismissed as "humanly inadequate"; she chose instead to dedicate the remainder of her life to "direct linguistic handling of the truth-problem".

Year after year Riding's *Who's Who* entry proclaimed the imminence of "a book . . . to be entitled *Rational Meaning: A New Foundation for the Definition of Words* (publishing arrangements pending)".

Now, it seems, they will pend perpetually. "History", Riding once declared, had "finished" – for she herself was "Finality". Such claims were advanced without the least tincture of irony or humour, but if, at a distance, it is tempting to snigger, few presumed on such *lèse-majesté* in her presence.

All who encountered Riding attested to her intelligence — a fierce, harsh intelligence, that sought to dominate, never to ingratiate. Once she had pronounced on a subject she never suffered any appeal.

Undeniably there was substance in her self-belief. No less a judge than W. H. Auden described her as "the only living philosophical poet".

But Riding found no pleasure in such praise. Auden, she felt, was a "magpie", who had stolen quite shamelessly from her work. At least, though, he was preferable to Yeats who, in editing the *Oxford Book of Modern Verse*, failed to ask Riding for a single contribution; his death, in 1939, caused her an unholy satisfaction.

As for the public, Riding admitted in the preface to her *Collected Poems* (1938) that it found the greatest difficulty in understanding her work. This, she explained, was because people read her poems for the "wrong" reasons.

Only one person, it seemed, adequately assessed her talent. In 1924 Robert Graves came across Riding's poem *The Quids* in an obscure American literary magazine: "The little quids, the monstrous quids, / The everywhere, everything, always quids", and so on and so forth.

Graves wrote to express his appreciation. Some transatlantic correspondence ensued; and at the end of 1925 Riding was invited to accompany him to Egypt, where he had taken a Chair in English Literature.

The Cairo venture was a fiasco, from which Graves beat a speedy retreat, but his relations with Riding proved more enduring. From the moment of her arrival the newcomer dominated the poet's household.

Graves's confidence at that time was at a low ebb – his poems poorly received, his finances in permanent crisis, his marriage, albeit productive of four children and conducted on the most arduously libertarian principles, heading towards disaster.

Riding's appearance heralded a new and more promising era. The complete intellectual superiority she established – "Laura is sweet to me, and is gradually teaching me to ratiocinate clearly", he wrote in 1926 – had the positive effect of enabling him to maintain a healthy independence *vis-à-vis* the rest of the world.

For a while even his relations with his wife improved. Nancy Graves liked Riding, whose feminist views reflected her own: "Mothering innocents to monsters is / Not of fertility but fascination / In women."

"It is extremely unlikely that Nancy, Laura and I will ever disband," Graves told Siegfried Sassoon in March 1925. Yet by May 1927 he and Riding had moved to a flat at St Peter's Square, Hammersmith, while Nancy and the children were installed nearby in a barge on the Thames.

The year before, through Graves's good offices, the Hogarth Press had published a volume of Riding's poetry. Now, flush with the proceeds from Graves's book, *Lawrence and the Arabs*, the two of them founded a small publishing company of their own, the Seizin Press.

But Graves's dog-like devotion soon diminished his attractions as a lover. Sexual intercourse, Riding explained in her essay *The Damned Thing* (1928), obliged women "to enliven the scene with a few gratuitous falsetto turns", but no one should confuse these noises with any form of pleasure.

But though Graves was now allowed in her bed only to dispense comfort during thunderstorms, Riding had by no means exhausted her interest in the monstrous male. In 1929 she declared that "three-life" had become "four-life" – her way of indicating that an Irish poet called Geoffrey Phibbs, who had been discriminating enough to praise her poetry, had been summoned to the *ménage* in Hammersmith.

Phibbs was received "with open arms"; not so his wife. "Laura," Mrs Phibbs later recorded, "as cold as the cheap sparkling trinkets with which she was covered, accompanied Geoffrey, and they brought me to the Regent Palace Hotel – thrust a bottle of brandy into my hand and said 'Drink this and forget your tears.'"

Yet Phibbs still showed some disposition towards matrimonial loyalty. He fled with his wife to France, and remained recalcitrant even when Riding, Graves and his wife swept across the Channel in pursuit.

In the public lounge of a French hotel Riding threw herself on the floor and screamed – "you seemed to die", Graves tactfully recorded. When a few weeks later, Phibbs sneaked back to London Graves announced that he would "kill Geoffrey if he wouldn't return to Laura".

Riding herself, unable to contemplate life at St Peter's Square without Phibbs, drank a disinfectant called Lysol, and when this tipple failed to bring oblivion, leapt with a "doom-echoing shout" from the fourth-floor window of the flat, landing on the stone below. Graves, sympathetic but cautious, ran downstairs and ejected himself from a window on the third floor.

Amazingly Riding survived – which she appeared to regard as further proof of her divinity. With Phibbs and Nancy Graves (whom the Irish poet unaccountably seemed to prefer) now cast as demons, "four-life" dwindled pretty sharply into "two-life". In October 1929 Graves and

Riding removed themselves to Majorca, where they settled into a life of primitive simplicity, courtesy of an industrious maid.

Their house, Canelluñ, in the fishing village of Deya, and indeed their entire life in Majorca, was financed by the success of Graves's autobiographical *Goodbye to All That* and, later, by *I Claudius* and *Claudius the God*.

But those who visited Canelluñ soon discovered that it was dangerous to offer any praise of Graves's books. When a guest asked Riding whether she would consider writing a historical novel herself, she retorted that she "didn't think she could sink so low" – a statement which would later be borne out by her fictional assault on the Trojan War.

Though such put-downs appeared only to increase Graves's admiration, the sexual strain was beginning to tell; and in 1931 he impregnated a lusty German girl called Elfriede. Riding grandly assured him that the event was insignificant, but insisted on an immediate abortion, standing at the bottom of the bed in order to ensure that the operation was carried out.

Riding's attention turned next to Tom Matthews, an American journalist who had come to Majorca in 1932 with his wife and children in order to work on a novel. For a time she helped Matthews with his work – paring his novel down to the bare conjunctions. Then one day she handed her baffled disciple a letter in which she explained that she perfectly understood the effect that she had on him; but, if he could not control his feelings, he should get up and go; she would quite understand.

Such distractions did not prevent Riding applying herself with grinding industry to her own literary endeavours, until in 1936 a Fascist take-over in Majorca forced her and Graves to flee at short notice on a British destroyer, carrying one suitcase each.

Back in London, they began to develop the idea of a new kind of dictionary, which would give definitions "not only exact but poetic". This was the first seed of the project that came to dominate Riding's life, though it was Graves who did most of the early work.

Meanwhile Riding's attention drifted towards international affairs, which she held to be closely linked with "the woman question". The "outer, predominately male, world", she explained, had become "recklessly disconnected from the world of the personal life and thought".

These reflections found expression in her *Letter on International Affairs* in 1937; and next year Riding called a meeting "to decide on moral action to be taken by inside people: for outside disorders". *The Covenant of Literary Morality* wad duly drawn up, but unfortunately the document never came to Hitler's attention.

In 1938 Riding's *Collected Poems* were published, to a stunning display of critical indifference. In January 1939, however, a poetaster called Schuyler Jackson reviewed the poems in *Time*. Jackson's opinion that the work was "the book of books of the mid-20th century" seemed to Riding to betray an uncommon insight. Plans were now laid for an American visit.

Graves was graciously, if somewhat superfluously, granted his sexual freedom. Shortly before their departure for America, he was summoned to Riding's bedroom to receive her latest revelation: "Love is a beautiful insincerity; and true."

When she and Graves arrived in America at the end of April 1939 they went to live on the Jacksons' farm.

Tom Matthews, who was there, watched in horrified fascination while Riding and Jackson, after their own peculiar fashion, fell in love. Matthews was reminded "of two basilisks, motionless and staring, the rest of us . . . immobilised into cramped stone until the predetermined affair was ready".

It was unfortuante that Jackson was married, but after Laura had subjected Katherine Jackson to a series of "talks" this difficulty was removed. Mrs Jackson, who had initially professed a high regard for her interrogator, now cracked up, became violent and was removed to an asylum.

Poet and critic duly retired, with an absolute minimum of discretion, into a single bedroom – until Riding, as if sensing that this development represented a backsliding of principle, emerged to issue a bulletin: "Schuyler and I do."

Yet, for all the satisfactions which Jackson afforded, Riding had suffered an irreparable loss. Graves's return to England without her did not limit her intellectual ambition; it did, however, portend the end of her literary achievement.

Laura Riding was born in New York on January 16 1901, the daughter of Nathan Reichenthal, a tailor of Austrian extraction, and his second wife Sadie, a native of Manhattan whose parents had been born in Germany.

Nathan Reichenthal's ill-fated business enterprises turned him into a ferocious anti-capitalist, and he dreamed of bringing up his daughter as "an American Rosa Luxembourg".

Young Laura was educated at the Girls' High School in Brooklyn and Cornell University, where she fell in love with Louis Gottschalk, an assistant teacher in ancient history, whom she married in 1920.

Mrs Gottschalk abandoned her own studies to follow her husband to various teaching posts, but by 1923 their marriage was failing, and she was throwing herself with increasing enthusiasm into writing. As Laura Reichenthal Gottschalk seemed a bit of a mouthful to inflict on editors, her middle name was changed to Riding, which she felt carried "a certain identity weight".

Her poems began to appear in various literary journals – notably in *The Fugitive*, a publication produced by an eponymous group of poets centred on Vanderbilt University at Nashville. Riding-Gottschalk was much taken by the Fugitives and determined by hook or by crook to attach herself to their number. But the hectoring manner in which she delivered her tirades about the poet's role – his task was "to take the universe apart . . . and then reintegrate it with his own vitality" – understandably alarmed the Southern *littérateurs*.

Riding removed in disgust to New York, where she gained something of a reptuation as a man-eater, without, however, losing her concern that Americans did not take poetry seriously enough. This was never a fault that could be imputed to Graves. Yet it was Schuyler Jackson who established himself as the strong man who lurked in the shadow of her feminist ideals.

They married in 1941, and went to live in a small house standing on stilts amid the stagnant waters and scraggy Australian pines of Wabasso, in Florida. Jackson bought a grapefruit grove, but the venture failed; indeed, everything that Jackson touched tended to fail, including, fortunately, his attempts to break into the trust fund bequeathed to him by his father. But Riding gratefully fell into the role of fetching his slippers.

She also beavered away at the *Dictionary*, the one

project which she had been determined to salvage from the wreck of her relations with Graves. But in the 29 years of her marriage, Riding, previously such a hive of literary activity, published only a handful of articles in obscure magazines.

Her prose style had always been freakish, but at least, in Matthews's memorable phrase, it had once been "thunderous with unshed meaning ... capable of fierce (and clarifying) lightning flashes". Now, whether in letters she penned to chastise critics for their mistaken views of her work, or in the lectures which she visited upon her acquaintances, her writing became ever more impenetrable.

After Jackson died in 1968, her output of articles increased somewhat; she even, on one occasion, broadcast on the BBC: "I judge my poems to be things of the first water as poetry," she vouchsafed.

No doubt there will be disciples eager to maintain this claim. Yet in the last analysis the life of Laura Riding must serve chiefly as a cautionary tale – of cleverness unsanctified by humility, of power unredeemed by benevolence, and above all of human presumption swallowed up in the vast indifference of eternity.

September 5 1991

CYRIL RAY

CYRIL RAY, the journalist who has died aged 83, was a celebrated wine writer and the archetypal "Bollinger Bolshevik".

His monographs on the evolution of Bollinger and

Lafite are considered by many to be unrivalled, and he wrote the first book in English on Cognac. Yet Ray claimed he could not tell a glass of Lafite from a glass of Latour.

"I'm not really a writer about wine at all. I write about the social history of wine," he demurred. "My reputation is bogus. I am not the World's Greatest Authority. I am simply an old reporter who likes a glass of wine." He claimed that his favourite drink was Guinness.

Nevertheless, he was founder and first president of the Circle of Wine Writers. France made him a Chevalier of the Order of Merit for service to the literature of wine; Italy made him first a Cavaliere and then a Commendatore.

Ray was once described as "a poseur with a muted heroic streak". A colourful and diminutive figure, at times irascible, he was welcomed everywhere he went because of his good stories, usually about his mishaps during the Second World War, and because of his encyclopaedic knowledge of food, wine and gentlemen's clothing.

"The first time I was fired upon by the King's enemies," he would say, "I was wearing a yachting cap, a dark blue blazer, grey flannel Oxford bags and suede shoes." He was one of the first war correspondents to go to war with the Navy and, as he said: "They didn't quite know how to kit us out."

Ray lived in a manor house in Kent, owned a double-set in Albany, rode daily in Rotten Row, sent his son to Eton and smoked large Cuban cigars long before Castro came to power. But, he declared: "The English class system is death and damnation to English life. It is the curse of England."

Similarly, he adored the clubs of St James's ("I love Brooks's and the Athenaeum, in the same way that some people love red-headed girls"), where he would startle his fellow-members with such remarks as: "What's wrong with Stalin?"

Teased for his high living, he would say: "I cannot understand people who say 'How can you be a socialist and drink Lafite?' They don't say: 'How dare you call yourself a socialist and love good books, good painting, and good music?'"

Informed that people nowadays do indeed say that, his reply was: "Well, God knows there's plenty of good cheap wine" – he was himself an advocate of wine in tins.

His shoes, like his suitings, were hand-made and always shined to excessive brilliance, which was much remarked upon. There was a man at New & Lingwood who shined them for him.

For a long time he would send out for an electrician whenever a light bulb needed replacing. "I always try to give employment to craftsmen."

He was born Cyril Rotenberg at Bury, Lancs, on March 16 1908. His Jewish grandparents had emigrated from East Prussia, and his father, an itinerant eye-tester for the Co-Operative Wholesale Society, changed the family name at the beginning of the First World War.

Young Cyril was educated at Manchester Grammar School and won an open scholarship to read history at Jesus College, Oxford, but the family could not afford to keep him there, and after a year he left to teach at what he described as "a very shabby" private school in Westmorland.

He then took a short-service commission in the RAF. He failed to learn how to fly, though, and was sent to Salisbury Plain to look after the balloons, in the baskets of which he read widely.

Ray then worked as an apprentice at Lewis's departmental store in Liverpool. In 1936 he volunteered for the
Republican cause in the Spanish Civil War, but claimed
to have been turned down because he had been in the
RAF, which was looked upon with suspicion by the
recruiting authorities.

Instead he went to Manchester as the manager of a
cinema; he was given the job, he said, because he possessed
a dinner jacket and looked presentable front-of-house.

It was this move that led Ray into journalism. Some
of the reporters of the *Manchester Guardian* were customers
at the cinema, and when Ray showed them some film
reviews he had written they talked him into leaving his
job and joining them in the *Guardian* reporters' room.

"It turned out that all you did was move into the
reporters' room," he recalled, "hang up your coat, and sit
around until there was something to do."

Eventually he was given stories to do on a freelance
basis, and when he started earning more than £5 a week
they decided it would be cheaper to put him on the staff
at five guineas a week.

He found it a priggish organisation, but it suited him
well enough: "We were all prigs on that paper, Crozier
(W. P., the editor) was a teetotal prig, the rest of us were
drunken prigs."

He moved to the *Guardian*'s Fleet Street office as
deputy London editor in 1939, but left for the BBC when
the newspaper refused to let him go on the first bombing
raid of Berlin. Ray claimed this was because the *Guardian*
did not want to pay the life assurance the RAF demanded
for war correspondents, which he thought was typically
parsimonious.

The role of war correspondent was well suited to Ray's

blend of courage, wit and complete self-confidence. He covered the landings in North Africa in 1942 and was with the 8th Army during the Italian campaign, in which he was mentioned in despatches. Once, contrary to the Geneva Convention, he led a group of Canadian infantry who had lost all their officers and had "elected" Ray to get them back to their lines.

He was with the US 82nd Airborne Division at Arnhem, earned a citation at Nijmegen, and was with Patton's 3rd Army at the Ardennes in December 1944 when the front crumbled and the Allies fought "the Battle of the Bulge".

Ray had a bet with Sam White (*qv*), of the Beaverbrook newspapers, that he would be first into the besieged Belgian city of Bastogne. Unfortunately, some American military policeman mistook Ray for a German who had infiltrated the Allied lines.

Ray, who, after Arnhem, wore the red beret of a British parachutist, showed the American MPs his credentials, but one of them said: "If you're British, how come you're wearing a French hat?" He was locked up and not released until the following day, by which time the siege was lifted, with Sam White as witness.

Ray saw out the war with the 3rd Army, and then undertook a series of Unesco missions to Italy, Greece and various parts of Africa. After the war he was Moscow correspondent for the *Sunday Times*, and it was from a chance assignment as a general reporter for that paper that his career as a wine writer began.

In 1958 he joined the *Spectator*, under Brian Inglis, to write about food and wine. On his first day a colleague was heard to remark: "So that is what a gastrognome looks like."

He left the *Spectator* in 1962 ("because it got too Tory") and joined the *Observer*, where he remained until the mid-1970s. He then joined *Punch* as wine correspondent and, under the name Christopher Pym, reviewed crime books.

Ray used to brag that he had never bought a stock or share in his life and that any money he had had been earned with his pen. For 15 years he was editor of *The Compleat Imbiber*, a charming anthology which in 1964 was the first winner of the Wine and Food Society's André Simon Prize.

In 1948 he published *Scenes and Characters from Surtees*, the first of a steady flow of books: as well as military histories, Ray wrote or edited some 30 volumes on wine.

His relationships with his many publishers were fiery. He broke with one because he sent Ray a letter by second-class post. And when Penguin fell foul of him while reissuing two of his wine books he wrote to all the newspapers asking readers not to buy the books.

This behaviour was considered merely eccentric by his many friends and colleagues – just as his ability to list the menus and prices of all the London clubs, pre- and postwar, was thought of as something more sublime than merely boring.

Ray was a liveryman of the Fanmakers Company and a quondam president of the Women's Wine Club, and honorary life member of the Civil Service Riding Club.

He married, in 1953, Elizabeth, daughter of the Reverend H. C. Brocklehurst; they had a son.

September 26 1991

RAYMOND BLACKBURN

RAYMOND BLACKBURN, the former Labour MP, who has died aged 76, seemed destined for high office when he first entered the House of Commons; in the event, his life presented a tale of decline, fall and rehabilitation – as an anti-pornography campaigner.

Returned in 1945 for King's Norton in Birmingham, Blackburn made an immediate impression. His maiden speech, on the UN charter, won the plaudits of Winston Churchill, who emitted several emphatic "Hear, hears", and passed him a note of congratulation.

Blackburn was determined to carve a name for himself. In the columns of the *Daily Herald* he set out his forceful, often original views on the issues of the day; in the Commons he continued to show a penchant for the big occasion, holding forth on the difficulties of demobilisation or on the dangers confronting Britain in the atomic age.

But he continued to attract more approval from Conservative than from Labour benches. When the Austin Motor Factory at Longbridge, in his constituency, was forced to close in 1947 for lack of coal, Blackburn roundly condemned Stafford Cripps's plan for the allocation of fuel.

In the same year Blackburn complained that Labour's Supplies and Services Bill gave the Government "totalitarian powers" over the workforce. He warned that Britain was heading for disaster and called for a new approach, with private enterprise to the fore.

Had he been less independent and less courageous, he

would undoubtedly have been more successful; he might also have been more sober. In 1947 he was charged with being drunk at Piccadilly Circus, the first of a series of such offences.

Although he was re-elected for the new seat of Northfield, Birmingham, in 1950, Blackburn was unable to maintain his allegiance. Within six months he resigned from the Labour party, and called for Winston Churchill – "one of the great men of genius of all time" – to head a coalition government to counter Communist aggression.

Blackburn did not stand in the 1951 election, announcing that he had no desire to enter the lists against old friends, but when he spoke for the Tory candidate in Birmingham, the old friends condemned him as "rat", "blackleg" and "scum".

By now Blackburn was hurtling down the slippery slope, although he never lost his sense of style. When he failed to turn up punctually for an afternoon session of bankruptcy proceedings brought against him in 1954, the Registrar deposed that he had seen him after lunch, "preceded by a larger cigar than most bankrupts wear".

More seriously, in 1954 Blackburn was charged with fraudulently inviting investment in a company set up to lease plots on caravan sites, and notwithstanding a seven-hour speech in his own defence – in which he admitted that, if guilty, he would deserve severe punishment – was sent down for two years.

His panache, however, never left him. On appeal, he sharply rebuked Lord Chief Justice Goddard for "a very wrong remark", adding for good measure that the judge was "determined to dismiss the appeal". "You'd better be careful," Goddard warned, before doing just that.

Blackburn also lost another appeal, against being

struck off the Law Society's lists. And the disastrous pattern seemed bound to continue when, immediately after his release from prison, he embarked upon a disastrous second marriage.

His third marriage, however, brought both salvation and sobriety. Having set himself on an even keel financially through his work as an export salesman, Blackburn re-emerged into the public eye as a social campaigner.

In the late 1960s his target was the gaming clubs – not because he had any great objections to gambling as such (he liked to bet on the horses), but simply because he felt the law against games of uneven chance should be enforced.

His campaign in the courts to make the Metropolitan Commissioner of Police act against illegalities failed, although Lord Denning, in the Court of Appeal, agreed with him that the rule of law must prevail.

In the 1970s Blackburn joined forces with the Earl of Longford to crusade against pornography. The cinema, in particular, engaged his attention; and once more he sought to bring the Metropolitan Chief Commissioner to a proper understanding of his duties.

Blackburn enjoyed a notable success in 1975, when an Old Bailey jury decreed that a film entitled *More About the Language of Love*, which had been licensed by the Greater London Council, was grossly indecent. But the next year a prosecution against the film's predecessor, *The Language of Love*, failed. Blackburn had some harsh words about presiding Judge Neil McKinnon, whose own daughter was a much photographed topless model.

A doctor's son, Albert Raymond Blackburn was born on March 11 1915, and educated at Rugby and London University; he was admitted a solicitor in 1937.

Blackburn volunteered for the Army on the day the Second World War broke out; he fought in France and Belgium as a platoon commander before being evacuated from Dunkirk.

In 1943 he made his first attempt on Parliament at a by-election at Watford, standing for the Common Wealth party. Although he supported Churchill as the national leader, he pointed out that the Conservatives had kept him out of power for as long as they possibly could.

Blackburn's dash and energy won him many friends in theatrical circles. His conversation was at once fluent — unstoppable, some judged — and challenging. "Now here's something you'll agree with," he would tell liberals before launching into some Right-wing diatribe: reactionaries would receive the same treatment in reverse.

But his anger and dismay at injustice were entirely genuine, indeed almost childish in their intensity; no one more keenly relished the process of hunting out the evildoers.

Of his books, *The Erosion of Freedom* (1964) dealt with the dangers presented by the concentration of power into the hands of fewer and fewer people, and by interference with the rights of the individual. *I Am an Alcoholic* (1959) recounted how his political life had been ruined by the demon drink.

Blackburn married three times: first, in 1939 (divorced 1954), Barbara Robeson; they had two sons and a daughter. He married secondly, in 1956 (divorced 1959) Marianne Ferguson (a Brazilian); and thirdly, in 1959, Tessa Hulme: they had three daughters and two sons.

November 5 1991

WILLIAM REES-DAVIES

WILLIAM REES-DAVIES, who has died aged 75, was for 30 years one of the most colourful MPs in the House of Commons, where he sat as Conservative Member for the Isle of Thanet from 1953 to 1974, and thence for Thanet West until 1983.

Affectionately known as the "One-armed Bandit" (he lost an arm in action with the Welsh Guards) "Billy" Rees-Davies was celebrated for his mental agility and wit. A convivial *bon vivant*, he was the subject of many anecdotes, and throughout his career as a barrister and MP was dogged by scrapes and misadventures.

With his black cloak and distinctive gait, he was a familiar figure around the Law Courts. He was more than once suspended from the Bar, and was frequently in trouble for drunken driving and for being a less than satisfactory landlord.

At Westminster he was capable of pungent contributions to debates, although he was apt to act the shy violet when the division bell rang: in one session of 1969, for instance, he was absent from 198 votes.

In 1983 he failed to be reselected as a parliamentary candidate. It was a bitter blow, as three years earlier he had given up his law practice and become a "full-time politician". In that time he had been Conservative leader of the Select Committee on Health and Social Services and chaired the Conservative Committee on Tourism.

A devotee of the Turf, Rees-Davies had also fought a valiant battle, both at Westminster and in the courts, on behalf of gamblers everywhere. At Marylebone Court in

1958 he successfully defended John Aspinall and others from gaming charges, when the prosecution was unable to establish that *chemin de fer* was an unlawful game; later that year he played a hand of "chemmy" in court while defending another three players, and won his case after a speech lasting a day and a half.

The next year Rees-Davies introduced a Private Member's Bill "to tidy up the gambling laws". He knew that his Bill had no chance so late in the session, but wanted to canvass support in the Commons and to test public opinion; his efforts bore fruit in the Gaming Act of 1960.

In 1963 he sponsored a Bill to allow greyhound racing on substitute days (though not on Sundays); and in 1966 he attempted to exclude bets with bookmakers on approved racecourses from the general betting duty.

The son of Sir William Rees-Davies, a former Liberal MP and Chief Justice of Hong Kong, William Rupert Rees-Davies was born on November 19 1916 and educated at Eton (where he acquired a formidable reputation as a bowler, was *Victor Ludorum* and elected to "Pop") and Trinity College, Cambridge, where he won a cricket Blue in 1938.

The next year he was called to the Bar by the Inner Temple and in the course of his career became an expert in the law of Landlord and Tenant, the Town and Country Planning Act, the Factories Act and crime.

At the beginning of the Second World War, Rees-Davies was commissioned into the Welsh Guards; he served until 1943, when he was disabled.

He stood unsuccessfully as a Conservative candidate for South Nottingham in the general elections of 1950 and 1951 before being returned for the Isle of Thanet at a by-election in 1953.

At Westminster he also acquired the sobriquets "Swashbuckling Billy" and (for his cloak) "Count Dracula". Rees-Davies always had a certain sartorial dash and was celebrated for his spectacular waistcoats.

His career at the Bar was somewhat erratic. Suspended for the first time in 1954, he was fined and reprimanded 10 years later by his Benchers for failing to turn up at the Old Bailey to make a speech for his client.

In 1970 he again neglected to appear to make a final speech in mitigation on behalf of his client, who was sentenced to six years. And in 1980 he was suspended from the Bar for six months for professional misconduct – after another absence from court.

Rees-Davies never seemed put out by these setbacks, and he took Silk in 1973.

His legal expertise, though, did not seem to help him where his own property was concerned. In 1982 he was ordered to pay compensation to a family who had rented a "luxury" Corfu house from the MP, only to discover no water, damp beds, mould in the saucepans and fungus in the kettle.

In 1989 he was ordered in the High Court to pay compensation and costs to an American businessman who had rented his house at Monkton, Kent, and on arrival found cobwebs, an unpleasant smell, a dog running loose and fleas in the main bedroom.

But Rees-Davies often brought his legal experience to bear at Westminster. "Juries", he argued in 1976, "often contain people of very little intelligence."

Besides the Turf, Rees-Davies had a passion for collecting pictures and antiques.

His first marriage, to Jane Mander in 1959, was

dissolved in 1981. He married secondly, in 1982, Sharlie Kingsley. He had two daughters by his first marriage.

January 14 1992

THE DUKE OF MONTROSE

THE 7TH DUKE OF MONTROSE, who has died aged 84, was a Rhodesian farmer whose presence in Ian Smith's rebel government gave it a faint whiff of Ruritanian respectability.

A Gaelic-speaking giant of 6ft 5in, of great charm but with opinions noticeably stronger than his executive abilities, Montrose regarded the Beatles, Carnaby Street and long hair as part of a Communist plot to subvert the West.

"It is a common observation that the African is a bright and promising little fellow up to the age of puberty," was his considered opinion submitted to an official inquiry. "He then becomes hopelessly inadequate and disappointing, and it is well known that this is due to his almost total obsession henceforth with matters of sex."

Montrose squared his loyalty to the Queen and support for Smith's Unilateral Declaration of Independence by claiming that the rebels were merely taking power from British ministers which would be returned to her when she reclaimed it personally.

Montrose was refused permission to enter Britain during the rebellion. If he had come he could have been charged with treason, thereby evoking memories of his ancestor, the great Marquess of Montrose, who was executed in 1650 for his brilliant but unsuccessful military campaign in defence of the Stuarts.

The modern Montrose – plain Angus or Lord Graham as he liked to be called in Rhodesia – found himself prevented from attending the weddings of two of his children. It was claimed that he was particularly upset at the Government's veto on his appearance as Chief of the Grahams at a clan gathering in 1977.

The British Government was adamant in refusing him a passport, although his sister Lady Jean Fforde pointed out in a letter to *The Daily Telegraph* that he still received the Queen's command to attend the opening of Parliament.

James Angus Graham was born on May 2 1907, the elder son of the Marquess of Graham, who was in turn heir to the 5th Duke of Montrose.

The Graham family had seen its fair share of fortune, bad luck and eccentricity. The 1st Duke had promoted the Union of Scotland and England; the 3rd Duke was credited with obtaining permission for Highlanders to wear the kilt again after the Jacobite Rising of 1745; and the Duchess of the 4th Duke had publicly booed Queen Victoria for listening to gossip about her husband.

The 6th Duke was the inventor of the aircraft carrier and an early supporter of Scottish nationalism – until he realised that it threatened the Union. Death duties reduced his estates, which consisted largely of uncultivated tracts of land producing no income, from 130,000 acres to some 10,000 in 40 years.

Young Angus Graham was born into straitened circumstances for his rank. He was sent to Eton, where he seemed an impressive figure in the boxing ring – but 40 years on there was rather more interest in a Wall Game where he had bitten Quintin Hogg in the hand. Montrose claimed that the future Conservative Lord Chancellor and fierce political opponent had been cheating.

From Christ Church, Oxford, where he rowed, played rugby and distinguished himself with his fine singing voice, Graham joined a British contingent which travelled around Canada helping with the harvest. His next job was with Imperial Chemicals in Newcastle-upon-Tyne from which he would fly himself home for the weekend to Brodick Castle on the Isle of Arran.

For his wedding in 1930 to Isobel, daughter of Colonel T. B. Sellar, 450 estate workers came by special steamer from Arran to the Edinburgh ceremony, at which he wore the red cloak and carried the sword of the 1st Duke.

Lord Graham's financial position, however, prompted the couple to move first to Johannesburg and then to Salisbury where he worked first as a seed salesman. In his spare time he took boxing lessons from the ex-hevyweight boxing champion and future federal prime minister Roy Welensky who judged him an indifferent pupil.

He then bought a 1,600-acre farm at 16s an acre, and settled down to proving himself as a excellent farmer, rising at 5 a.m. each day to supervise his labourers. After about three years he was forced to sell up by a mining exploration company, which owned the mineral rights. But he began again and successfully built up both a 3,000-acre farm outside Salisbury and a ranch 100 miles away.

Montrose made periodic visits home – on one occasion

giving an address on the wireless in Gaelic – and he also went to Germany several times where he witnessed the Nazi Youth rallies.

It was hardly surprising that Montrose's name should have appeared among the list of supposed members of the German-sympathising Right Club which mysteriously surfaced in 1990, although he later declared that he knew nothing about the organisation.

At the outbreak of war, Montrose immediately rejoined the Royal Naval Volunteer Reserve, in which he had enrolled at 21. He served in destroyers involved in the evacuations of Greece and Crete, and was later given command of *Ludlow*, an American "lend-lease" warship which was on convoy duty first in the Atlantic and then in the North Sea.

Graham, who attained the rank of lieutenant-commander, asked the Admiralty for some Gaelic-speaking crew and adopted as his ship's mascot a jackdaw which would fly unhindered around the upper deck and sit on a man's hand when summoned.

After the war he returned to Rhodesia, where he found the farm growing prosperous but the colony's politics changing. A spirit of retreat had set in at home with Labour's victory in 1945 and he was unimpressed when the Tories launched the last great imperial venture: the Central African Federation of Nyasaland, Northern and Southern Rhodesia.

Graham stood as an unsuccessful Confederate party candidate bent on protecting the white-dominated *status quo* in the 1953 general election.

When he succeeded to the Dukedom of Montrose in 1954 on the death of his father (who left an estate of £802), he saw little reason to come home, preferring to leave the Scottish properties to be run by his 18-year-old son, the Marquess of Graham.

The new Duke's only public gesture was to protest about the Walt Disney film *Rob Roy* which showed the 1st Duke's men murdering the outlaw's mother. His grandfather had made a similar protest about a silent film.

As the Federation's prospects declined, with the growth of an African nationalism fuelled by Westminster funk, Montrose had no doubts about where the blame lay. After being elected an MP in the 1958 federal election, he declared that South Rhodesia's premier, Winston Field, should replace Welensky as federal prime minister in order to ensure that there would be "no miserable compromise with London".

When the Macmillan Government proposed an inquiry into unrest in Nyasaland Montrose joined Viscount Malvern, the former Rhodesian prime minister, and Lord Robins, president of the British South Africa Company, in flying to London for a Lords debate.

Montrose made his mark in a speech calling for the colony to be given the independence of full Dominion status and talked of the 60 to 100 Africans he employed on his farm. Those who lived in Rhodesia "had a great faith in at least 99½ per cent of the African people and are prepared to entrust our wives and children to them and the country far from our nearest European neighbour," he explained.

"If our trust is misplaced, and our families become objects of violence, we feel that is our lookout. But we are not prepared to be made sitting ducks for agitators, egged on by people living 6,000 miles away in safety."

In 1961 he returned to the Lords, where he joined the 5th Marquess of Salisbury in attacking the British

Government's policy on Rhodesia. When Salisbury called Iain Macleod, the Colonial Secretary, unscrupulous, Montrose began by trying to cool the temperature in the House: "Perhaps I may use a term that will bring less odium on him when I say that I have evidence that will persuade you that he at least is a fast worker in his political aims."

Then, with characteristic bluntness, he declared that the Government's proposed constitutional changes were "breakneck and slap-happy" and that Macleod's lack of candour had created "a complete lack of trust".

Although Montrose's style of address involved frequent pauses and references to papers, he commanded a certain respect from his fellow peers that he could not always expect from his fellow legislators in Salisbury when he became Agriculture Minister in Field's Southern Rhodesian Government. Always interested in crop developments, he was at first frustrated that his responsibilities were restricted to white farms, but after independence he was able to bring to bear his experience when dealing with the realities of subsistence farming.

As a conductor of ministerial business, it was remarked, he sometimes seemed rather slower at grasping a point than many of the Africans about whom he had reservations. His manner in answering parliamentary questions would bring cries of despair from his fellow MPs: "No, no, Angus. Not that one . . . Look at the bottom of page 64."

Nevertheless, with his unflinching belief in the leading part to be played by the white man, he became an important factor in the election of Ian Smith as the Rhodesian Front prime minister. As the situation deteriorated and Southern Rhodesia demanded independence –

like the black-dominated Northern Rhodesia (renamed Zambia) and Nyasaland (Malawi) – he was even mooted as a possible Regent.

The suggestion did not appeal to Harold Wilson, whose supple mind was the least likely to appeal to the increasingly exasperated colonists. At a dinner on a visit to Salisbury, Wilson expected the bargaining to continue but Montrose, believing it to be an opportunity to relax from the strain of negotiations, proceeded to sing a "blue" song about a dancer, with illustrative movements. "I now understand", the Labour Prime Minister observed in broadest Yorkshire, "what qualifications you have to be Regent."

When Montrose gave public support for UDI, a Labour MP proposed that the law should be changed to prevent him taking his seat in the Lords. Wilson replied: "You don't use a steamroller to crack a nut; not this nut, anyway."

Although Montrose found little difficulty in agreeing to UDI, he remained concerned that his colleagues might eject his friend the Governor, Sir Humphrey Gibbs, from Government House. "It would be over my dead body," he declared, "that they would put a hand on the representative of the Queen."

Whatever the doubts Smith privately shared with Wilson about the ducal intellect, he recognised Montrose's public relations value by making him External Affairs Minister. When Montrose rather than Smith greeted Herbert Bowden, the Colonial Secretary, at the airport, it indicated that the colony now considered itself an independent country.

Montrose's reputation also played an important part in attracting what Ken Flower, head of Rhodesian Intelligence, called the "Nuts in May". Among the visitors were an armorist styling himself The Gayre of Gayre and Nigg, who believed the Zimbabwe ruins were too sophisticated to have been produced by Africans; Captain Henry Kerby, an eccentric Tory MP with many Intelligence connections; and L. Ron Hubbard, leader of the Scientology cult.

The trouble was that, as the consequences of the constitutional act of madness became apparent to Smith, the Rhodesian leader found Montrose still in no mood to compromise. Montrose played a key role in the Cabinet rejection of the offers made by the Wilson Government on HMS *Tiger* and HMS *Fearless*.

One Salisbury joke had it that Smith took half an hour to explain the British offer to colleagues and they then took 12 hours to explain it to Montrose.

After the *Fearless* talks failed Montrose was involved in an attempt by Cabinet right-wingers to introduce formal apartheid. It failed; two colleagues resigned, but Montrose continued in office several more months.

In the 12 years of independence, Montrose was an increasingly ignored figure. An attempt to persuade the party to drop Smith as its president in 1972 failed, and he was defeated when he stood for the new Senate.

When the Rhodesian rebellion ended in 1980, Montrose moved to Natal and paid a visit home to Scotland, where he attended a retirement party on the family estates for a gardener, a gamekeeper and a shepherd which had been put off until he could attend.

"I did all I could for Rhodesia. I cannot do any more. I did my best for my country," he told a reporter. Later he took the oath of allegiance again by taking his seat in the Lords.

As the sands of time began to run out for South

Africa, Montrose finally returned home in 1988 after 57 years in which he had witnessed the full sweep of Britain's imperial decline. The Duke, who spent his last years in Kinross, was Hereditary Sheriff of Dunbartonshire.

His first marriage was dissolved in 1950; they had a son and a daughter. He married secondly, in 1952, Susan, widow of Michael Gibbs and daughter of Dr J. M. Semple, of Kenya; they had two sons and two daughters.

The heir to the dukedom and subsidiary titles is his eldest son, James Graham, Marquess of Graham, born 1935.

February 12 1992

LORD BRIGINSHAW

THE LORD BRIGINSHAW, the former general secretary of the National Society of Operative Printers, Graphical and Media Personnel (NATSOPA) who has died aged 83, began his career as a Communist and ended it in the House of Lords.

En route he created much disruption in the newspaper industry. His Left-wing credentials were eventually tarnished by charges of corruption, but during his period as general secretary, from 1951 to 1975, "Dick" Briginshaw succeeded in negotiating for his members some of the highest wages of any group of workers.

If it was usually the National Graphical Association that set the pace in the interminable internecine disputes between the print unions, a settlement with this union would invariably be followed by a secondary dispute with NATSOPA, as Briginshaw sought to ensure parity, or better, for his men.

Briginshaw conducted union affairs with a flamboyance which was also reflected in his physical appearance. Tall, tanned and lean, with wavy silver hair and a froggish face adorned with heavy, horn-rimmed spectacles, "the ageing Tarzan", as he was known, meant to make his presence felt. Indeed, he was once described as "unstable with a marked tendency towards megalomania".

His unpopularity with other printers' unions, especially those associated with the Printing and Kindred Trades Federation, was marked. In 1956, when he stood for election to the printing and paper group of the Trades Union Congress General Council he received 901,000 against 7.3 million for his rival from the National Graphical Association. Not until 1965 did he secure a place on the General Council.

Briginshaw, always an enthusiastic supporter of the application of union power for political ends, advocated a wholesale reorganisation of the trade union movement in order to maximise its clout. In his own field of printing he argued for a single comprehensive union to cover the entire industry.

He did succeed, in 1966, in bringing about a merger between NATSOPA and the National Union of Printing, Bookbinding and Paper Workers, but the comrades proved unable to maintain the spirit of unity; and within four years the two sections had gone their separate ways.

During Briginshaw's reign the administration of NATSOPA put observers in mind of Tammany Hall politics. But not until the Inland Revenue queried some minor discrepancy in the accounts did the shady manoeuvring begin to come out into the open. *Private Eye*, which nicknamed the union "Notsober", played an eager part in the process.

Slowly and painfully it emerged that two union premises, one of them an office in Blackfriars Road, had been secretly sold *twice* in the same afternoon. In 1982 Briginshaw and three colleagues were accused by NATSOPA of misapplying £78,000 raised from these properties.

The money appeared to have been laundered in a number of nefarious ways, one of them involving the acquisition of some £8,000 worth of Krugerrands, the South African investment coins that were anathema to the Left. In addition Briginshaw was accused of retaining funds placed in a Swiss bank account between 1968 and 1972.

Briginshaw insisted that he had merely been setting up a secret union "slush fund" in order to protect his members against the Conservatives' anti-union legislation, which threatened the expropriation of assets. After four days of the trial the union and its former officials agreed to settle out of court.

Richard William Briginshaw was born at Lambeth on May 15 1908, and educated at Stuart School. He began his printing apprenticeship while still a boy, and soon became involved in union actitivies. By 1938 he had been elected assistant secretary of the London Machine Branch of the Union.

By his own admission he was a Communist at this stage of his career, an allegiance which later, in 1952, gave rise to a curious interchange during an inquiry into a printing dispute.

"Are you a Communist?" asked Mr Gilbert Beyfus QC. "No," returned Briginshaw. "Have you ever been to Russia?" persisted counsel. "Not to my knowledge," the union leader cannily replied. When questioned further he agreed he had been to Moscow, and had meant "not to my *immediate* knowledge".

During the Second World War Briginshaw served with the Army and on demobilisation returned to the printing trade. He claimed to have abandoned Communism before the war; certainly he did not martyr himself for the creed in the later 1940s, when George Isaacs, the NATSOPA leader, banned party members from holding office in the union.

Briginshaw joined the Labour party and became closely associated with its Left wing – though he also worked for Catholic Action. For a time he ran the Printers' Anti-Fascist Movement, and acted as a sponsor of Amnesty for Spain, a non-party body which raised funds for dependants of Franco's victims.

Later, he spoke of starting a new political party, though the aims he envisaged remained nebulous. There was no doubt, however, that he was viscerally anti-European, and he played an active role as president of the Forward Britain Movement, which campaigned against the Common Market.

Briginshaw did not take kindly to the Wilson Government's attempt to enact a Prices and Incomes policy in 1968; and the next year he staged a dramatic walk-out from Downing Street during the discussions on *In Place of Strife*, Barbara Castle's attempt to curb the unions.

It was a surprise, therefore, when Harold Wilson created him a life peer as Baron Briginshaw in 1974.

Lord Briginshaw is survived by five sons and a daughter.

March 28 1992

LORD HAVERS

THE LORD HAVERS, who has died aged 69, had the dual distinction of holding office as Attorney-General for the longest period since the 18th century and as Lord Chancellor for the shortest time since the 19th century – a mere five months.

For better or worse Michael Havers had an uncomplicated view of life and the law, and a shallow understanding of political and public feeling. He was not regarded as – nor ever laid claim to be – a great lawyer, but he was hard-working, conscientious and an able advocate. Later in his career he often found himself at the centre of fierce controversy, and his years in the courtroom were never without colour.

Perhaps his most spectacular case came when he prosecuted the Canadian economist Professor Hugh Hambleton on charges of passing Nato secrets to the Russians. After hours of relentless questioning by Havers, Hambleton suddenly threw up his hands and confessed.

Things were rarely completed with such ease, however, during his successive periods of office as Attorney-General, when law and order entered the highest political priority and the teething problems of the Crown Prosecution Service imposed unprecedented burdens upon him. Havers admitted that he had little interest in politics and was often criticised for his lack of political skill as the Government's senior law officer – a traditionally ambiguous constitutional role requiring a delicate balance of the two crafts.

None the less he was staunch in defence of the political

independence of the Law Officers – and never more so than during the Westland crisis in 1986, when a leak from the Prime Minister's office revealed a highly selective quotation from a legal opinion by the Solicitor-General, Sir Patrick Mayhew. Both men threatened to resign. Havers asked Mrs Thatcher to order an official inquiry into the source of the leak and threatened to send the police into No 10 Downing Street to investigate a clear breach of the Official Secrets Act.

He was later most indignant when accused by the Commons Defence Select Committee of having asked for an inquiry when he already knew that Mr Leon Brittan, then Trade and Industry Secretary, had authorised the leak by Miss Colette Bowe, his director of information. Havers stoutly denied that he knew the author of the leak. Far from being complicit in it, he had forced the facts out into the open.

A few months later he was at the centre of another extraordinary episode when he compelled the Cabinet Secretary, Sir Robert Armstrong, publicly to withdraw evidence he had given in the New South Wales hearings of the Government's attempts to ban publication of Peter Wright's *Spycatcher*. The *Spycatcher* case cast the gravest doubts on Havers's wisdom as Attorney-General – and, some would allege, his impartiality. It exposed the Government to ridicule, made the book a worldwide bestseller and led to clashes between the Government and the press over its freedom to publish what was already common knowledge throughout the world.

The Prime Minister constantly argued that the Government had an obligation to seek to enforce the oath of lifelong confidentiality given by servants of the Crown – a view Havers shared. On the other hand, no action was taken against those who had leaked information with what looked like tacit official approval to such authors as Chapman Pincher and Nigel West.

Havers's role in both this case and the Westland affair rapidly became public knowledge, much to Mrs Thatcher's anger and embarrassment. This was compounded when it later emerged that a conversation between the Attorney-General and a fellow diner in the lavatory at the Garrick Club had been overheard and passed on as vital information for the defence lawyers in the trial.

Discretion, however, was never one of Havers's strong points, least of all at the Garrick, where, with cigar in one hand and glass in the other, he regularly delighted fellow members over expansive lunches. On one occasion, when he was considering, as Attorney-General, legal action against the *Observer*, Havers injudiciously proclaimed the pleasure it would give him to make "that bugger [the paper's editor Donald Trelford] squeal in the witness box".

The Garrick was also the setting for a lunch which nearly ended Havers's career. At the height of the storm over the Government's attempts to ban the BBC's televising of the Zircon revelations, a Labour MP revealed that Havers had entertained the programme's author, Duncan Campbell.

Although Havers was on the Right of his party on issues of law and order — he voted for the restoration of capital punishment for terrorist offences, for example — he was a traditional Tory with little taste for Thatcherism. Such was the lack of sympathy between him and the Prime Minister that many doubted whether he would gain the succession to Lord Halisham of St Marylebone as Lord Chancellor.

In the event he was appointed to the Woolsack, only to resign in October 1987. Havers cited the reason as ill-health, but the brevity of his office evidently provided rewards all round: he earned his right to a handsome annual pension; while Mrs Thatcher was able to replace him with Lord Mackay of Clashfern, and so pave the way for her dramatic reforms of the legal profession.

Robert Michael Oldfield Havers was born on March 19 1923 into an East Anglian family and educated at Westminster in the generation of Peter Ustinov and Anthony Wedgwood Benn.

During the Second World War he spent five years in the Mediterranean, Normandy and the Far East as a lieutenant in the RNVR, before going up to Corpus Christi College, Cambridge.

Called to the Bar by Inner Temple in 1948, he joined the predominantly criminal law chambers of Fred Lawton (later Lord Justice Lawton) and Gerald Howard, MP, his pupil master, before being appointed to the High Court bench.

Havers soon progressed on his chosen South-Eastern circuit. His part-time judicial appointments as a pre-Beeching Recorder – first of Dover, and then nearer home, at Norwich – were followed by a period as deputy chairman of West Suffolk Quarter Sessions and Chancellor of the Dioceses first of St Edmundsbury and Ipswich, then of Ely. Havers took Silk in 1964, and became Master of the Bench in 1971.

During this century the Havers family established something of a legal dynasty: his grandfather had been an East Anglian solicitor; his father, Sir Cecil Havers, became a popular High Court judge (and a Wimbledon tennis player); and his sister Elizabeth is Lord Justice Butler-Sloss, the only woman to have been elevated to the Court of Appeal. One of his sons, Philip, has followed him to the Bar, while his other son, Nigel Havers, has flourished on stage and screen – a career which has an affinity with the Bar, and with Michael Havers's own predilections and sense of theatre in his court performances.

A good deal of his practice at the Bar, too, was on behalf of film and stage clients. He first came to national prominence defending two of the Rolling Stones, Mick Jagger and Keith Richard, on minor drug charges, which would probably not be brought today; but such was the climate of the time that no defence was likely to succeed.

Havers did not enter politics until 1970, when he succeeded the late Sir Cyril Black in the safe Conservative seat of Wimbledon. He readily admitted to doing so with an eye on one of the legal appointments rather than a political one, and in 1972 Mr Edward Heath duly appointed him Solicitor-General under Sir Peter Rawlinson as Attorney-General.

Havers's popularity as a constituency MP was not increased when he took his landlady, the widow of a local schoolmaster, to the Rent Tribunal when she requested a small increase in his modest rent. At subsequent elections disaffected Wimbledonians adopted the ironic slogan "Vote for Havers, the Widow's Friend"; and after the unfortunate widow's house was bombed by the IRA the MP ceased to keep a *pied à terre* in his constituency.

When the Heath Government fell in February 1974 Havers returned to practise at the Bar. He succeeded Sir Peter Rawlinson (later Lord Rawlinson of Ewell) as

Shadow Law Officer under first Heath and then Mrs Thatcher, and was thus poised to return to office as Attorney-General in 1979.

Besides the *Spycatcher* case, during the ensuing years he was involved in a series of other prosecutions under the Official Secrets Act. Havers was directly concerned in advising Mrs Thatcher to expose Sir Anthony Blunt as a Soviet spy under the umbrella of Parliamentary privilege, to frustrate the possibilities of libel proceedings against Andrew Boyle for disclosures, confirmed by the Prime Minister, in *The Climate of Treason*.

He also advised proceedings against the civil servants Clive Ponting and Sarah Tisdall, who had leaked Government secrets (respectively, about the sinking of the *Belgrano* and cruise missile deployment). But the imprisonment of the latter for a breach of confidence and the refusal of a jury to convict the former brought the Official Secrets Act into more disrepute.

Whether a more subtle Attorney-General would have pursued a different course in such cases is a matter for speculation, and Havers's dilemma was a real one. He had been among the many to advocate a reform of the Act; but since it had not been reformed – and as Attorney he made no efforts to do so – it had to be enforced.

In defence of his position Havers once remarked: "Those who obey the law and who are honourable and discreet would become very fed up if they found that those who broke the law could do so without anything happening to them. I think it is very important that we should encourage those who keep the trust we place in them." This rationale, however, evidently did not disallow a high degree of selectivity.

Another miscalculation that led to much criticism of

him – many felt unfairly – was over the trial of Peter Sutcliffe, the "Yorkshire Ripper", on charges of murdering women. Havers concluded that Sutcliffe was insane, and that lifelong confinement could be achieved by accepting a plea of guilty to manslaughter rather than exposing relations of the victims to the ordeal of giving evidence at a long and gruesome murder trial.

This humane suggestion provoked bitter comment from the public and the popular press – who were eager to see Sutcliffe arraigned for his crimes – and was finally rejected by the trial judge.

But besides the many highly publicised cases he handled, Havers had a heavy workload in advising the Government on such novel legislation as that for the sale of council houses, the reform of the trade unions and privatisation. During the Falklands War there were also complex questions of international law and Britain's rights under it. His department was responsible, too, for the massive administrative changes occasioned by the introduction of the Crown Prosecution Service.

In 1989 another shadow darkened Havers's legal reputation, when the Court of Appeal decided that the Guildford Four had been wrongly imprisoned 14 years previously. Mr Chris Mullin, the Labour MP, claimed that top legal officers – including Lord Havers – had known that the four were innocent years ago, and that Havers (then Crown Prosecutor) had chosen to ignore the fact that the wrong people had been arrested.

After the quashing of the convictions Mr Douglas Hurd set up a judicial inquiry into the case, headed by Sir John May, and this in turn led to investigations into the conviction of the Maguire Seven for running an IRA bomb factory. The Maguire family had first come under suspicion after being implicated in confessions by two of the Guildford Four, and they were convicted in 1976 on the basis of scientific tests – used to detect nitro-glycerine on their hands and gloves – which were later discredited. Havers had again been the prosecuting counsel in the case.

Earlier in 1989 Havers had found himself once more embroiled in a political row: this time over the Lord Chancellor Lord Mackay's proposals for the legal profession. Havers had always urged the need for evolutionary change rather than a radical breaking down of the very features which identified the legal profession, and he said on *Panorama* that he would vote against the Government for the first time in his political career if the Green Paper proposals – an attempt to bring the profession more under the control of market forces – were put forward in a Bill.

In 1988 Havers took on the chairmanships of R. H. M. Outhwaite, the Lloyd's underwriters, of the Solicitors Law Stationery Society and of the Playhouse Theatre. He had previously been a member of the Privileges Committee and chairman of the Lakenheath Anglo-American Community Relations Committee.

By way of recreation he enjoyed shooting, photography and writing. He co-wrote books on two Victorian *cases célèbres*, *The Poisoned Life of Mrs Maybrick* and *The Royal Baccarat Scandal*, both published in 1977.

The *Baccarat* book, subsequently adapted for the stage, told of an alleged cheating at cards in the presence of the then Prince of Wales, later King Edward VII. He also co-wrote *Tragedy in Three Voices: the Rattenbury Murder* (1980).

Havers was knighted in 1972, created a Life Peer as Baron Havers in 1987 and elected an honorary Fellow of Corpus Christi College, Cambridge, in 1988.

He married, in 1949, Carol Elizabeth Lay; they had two sons.

April 2 1992

SIR PETER HAYMAN

SIR PETER HAYMAN, who has died aged 77, had an eminent career in the Diplomatic Service, which culminated in his appointment as High Commissioner in Canada from 1970 to 1974; but after his retirement, and years of blandly shepherding the press at news conferences in various parts of the world, Hayman fell into dark disgrace and himself became their quarry.

In 1978 a package of obscene printed matter was found on a bus; it was addressed to a "Mr Henderson" at a flat in Notting Hill, which the police then raided and found to belong to Hayman. The flat contained 45 volumes of diaries recounting his sexual adventures and fantasies, and a mass of pornographic material.

It emerged that Hayman had for some years been connected with the Paedophile Information Exchange (PIE), and had received their contact magazine – carrying advertisements from men seeking sex with children – through the post.

Police interviewed Hayman and various other people identified by the material found in the flat, and a file was submitted to the Director of Public Prosecutions. A decision was made not to prosecute, ostensibly on the grounds that there was no evidence of any offence, except possibly one of receiving indecent material through the post, and Hayman escaped with a caution.

But the police continued their inquiries into the activities of the PIE, and in 1980 two other members of the group were brought to trial at the Old Bailey. In the course of the trial Hayman was referred to only as "a senior civil servant", but his name was leaked by the police, surfacing in *Private Eye*.

"Humpty Dumpty Hayman" as Hayman was known by his colleagues, on account of his naked domed head, at once resigned his directorships, from the South Oxford-shire Conservative Association and from various charity committees – though he remained a member of the Travellers' Club in Pall Mall and of MCC. The next year Hayman was named in the House of Commons by Mr Geoffrey Dickens, the Conservative MP, in a Parliamen-tary question addressed to the Attorney-General, Sir Michael Havers (*qv*).

Havers strenuously denied that there had been a cover-up, and Mr Douglas Hurd, then a Minister of State at the Foreign Office, maintained that a full inquiry into the affair had revealed nothing to suggest that national security had been prejudiced. Nevertheless, the discrep-ancy between the treatment of Hayman and his fellow paedophiles inevitably aroused indignation.

Peter Telford Hayman was born on June 14 1914 and educated at Stowe and Worcester College, Oxford, before joining the Home Civil Service in 1937. From 1939 to 1941 he worked in the Ministry of Home Security; he served in the Rifle Brigade until 1945, rising to the rank of major. In 1949, on the strength of his military experience, he was appointed to the Ministry of Defence; and three years later he was seconded to the UK Delega-tion to Nato. The head of the delegation was Sir Frederick

Hoyer-Millar (later Lord Inchyra), who was impressed by Hayman's abilities and recommended his permanent transfer to overseas service.

Although Hayman was over age for recruitment, he was taken into the Diplomatic Service as a first secretary in 1954 and posted the next year to Belgrade. Rapid promotion to counsellor followed, and in 1958 he was sent to Malta as adviser on press and public relations to the governor, who had had trouble with Mintoff. From 1959 to 1961 Hayman served as Counsellor in Baghdad, and was then assigned to another public relations post as director-general of British Information Services, New York.

Hayman was appointed CMG in 1963, and the next year became Minister in Berlin, where he was also Deputy Commandant of British Military Government. He was appointed CVO in 1965. The next year he returned to the Foreign Office as Deputy Under-Secretary, with special responsibility for relations with the USSR and Eastern Europe.

A useful initiative taken at this time was the establishment of the Great Britain–East Europe Centre, designed to take cultural relations out of the hands of the "Friendship Societies" which had restricted visitors from the "People's Democracies" to contact with groups of fellow-travellers in this country.

Hayman concluded his career as High Commissioner in Canada, and was appointed KCMG in 1971.

With his dome, bushy eyebrows and wide if not always convincing smile, he was a commanding figure. He had always seemed a solid family man, and until his exposure there had been no hint of scandal about him.

But in 1984 he suffered further humiliation when he was fined £100 for an act of gross indecency with a lorry driver in a public lavatory in Reading.

He married, in 1942, Rosemary Blomefield; they had a son and a daughter.

April 10 1992

WILBUR MILLS

WILBUR MILLS, who has died at Kensett, Arkansas, aged 82, exercised, as former chairman of the Ways and Means Committee of the US House of Representatives, an authority over tax, social security and trade policy comparable with that of any president. But he came spectacularly to grief, however, over his liaison with a striptease *artiste* known as "the Argentinian Firecracker".

The origins of his decline lay in his failure to gain the Democratic nomination for the Presidency in 1972 – a disappointment compounded when George McGovern, the candidate selected, rejected Edward Kennedy's suggestion that Mills should be his running mate.

Mills took to the bottle. In October 1974 his motor car was stopped by the Washington police for speeding near the Jefferson Memorial: Mills's female passenger then jumped from the car and waded into the nearby tidal basin. It emerged that the fugitive was the stripper Fanne Foxe. The next month Mills – whose amusements had previously been confined to reading the tax code in bed – proceeded to join "the Argentinian Firecracker" on stage at a strip joint in Boston's "Combat Zone".

In December 1974 Mills resigned the chairmanship

of the Ways and Means Committee (although he remained in Congress for another two years) and entered Bethesda Naval Hospital for treatment for alcoholism.

Wilbur Daigh Mills was born at Kensett, Arkansas, on May 24 1909 and educated at Hendrix College and Harvard Law School. He was admitted to the Arkansas Bar in 1933.

The next year he was elected judge for White County and in 1938 he became the second youngest member of Congress, where he was a protégé of the Majority Leader, Sam Rayburn of Texas. In 1943 Mills was rewarded for his loyalty with promotion to the Ways and Means Committee – and but for his Southern base he might eventually have become Speaker of the House.

He lost the support of liberal northern Democrats when, with other members of the Arkansas delegation, he signed the "Southern Manifesto" pledging to fight desegregation.

In 1958 Mills became chairman of the Ways and Means. Acquainted with every comma of the tax code, he was perfectly suited to the office, and proved adept at forging a bi-partisan agreement before tax bills were reported to the full House. Within a short time he seemed irreplaceable. "Wilbur Mills knows that he was chairman of Ways and Means before I got here and that he'll still be chairman after I've gone – and he knows I know it," observed President Kennedy. "I don't have any hold on him."

Mills denied Kennedy the Medicare Bill, which would have allowed ordinary Americans to contribute to their old age health insurance under social security. But after Lyndon Johnson's landslide victory in 1964 Mills recognised that the administration had the votes in Congress for a more radical approach. By the time the Bill became law in 1965 his legislative mastery had secured provisions far more expensive than those envisaged by the administration.

By 1966, however, the mood had turned against Johnson's "Great Society". The mid-term elections in that year brought in more than 40 new Republicans, including George Bush, who became the first freshman congressman to be nominated to the Ways and Means Committee in almost half a century.

So enthusiastic was the neophyte's advocacy of birth control for the Third World, that Mills nicknamed him "Rubbers" Bush – a sobriquet that did not endure.

In 1967, when Johnson sought to close the deficit with a six per cent tax surcharge, Mills, sensitive as ever to the shifting moods in the House, informed the President that he could not secure support for such a measure without cuts in the Great Society programmes.

Johnson was furious. "I saw Wilbur holding my Bill up there and I knew why he was doing it," he raged. "Not because he didn't believe in it but because that prissy, prim and proper man was worrying more about saving his face than about saving his country . . . But when you run around saving your face at day, you end up losing your ass at night."

Mills did not "lose his ass". He extracted $6 billion in cuts and passed a 10 per cent tax surchange; but his relations with Johnson never recovered.

President Nixon was too shrewd not to appreciate the necessity of currying Mills's favour. Indeed, by this time Mills's reputation was such that the Japanese Textile Federation negotiated an agreement on voluntary import quotas with him rather than with the government.

Mills became increasingly eccentric, however, and decided to run for President without any kind of national political base. To further his chances in the run-up to the New Hampshire primary he suddenly came out in favour of automatic upward adjustments in social security payments – a total reversal of his previous pronouncements on the subject.

Since the Nixon administration was unwilling to oppose this measure in an election year, the legislation passed.

Wilbur Mills married, in 1934, Clarine Billingsley: they had two daughters.

May 9 1992

SIR JOHN GALSWORTHY

SIR JOHN GALSWORTHY, the former Ambassador to Mexico who has died aged 72, in many ways enjoyed a conventional Foreign Office career. At its outset, however, he was embroiled in the shameful episode of the return of Russian prisoners of war to Stalin.

At Yalta in February 1945 the Americans and British acceded to Stalin's demand that all Soviet PoWs in the West should be repatriated, notwithstanding fears (which proved all too well justified) that this would condemn them either to instant execution or to a slower death in the labour camps.

To some extent, the Allies' hands were tied by the need to secure the return of British and American prisoners who had fallen into the hands of the Red Army in its sweep towards Berlin. But the policy which the

191

Foreign Office pursued under Anthony Eden was succinctly described by General Martell, head of the Military Mission in Moscow, as "licking the Bolshies' boots until we were black in the face".

Galsworthy was 26 in 1945. As a civil servant he had no hand in the formulation of policy. As a mere Third Secretary he did not even determine the guidelines under which that policy was administered. Yet he shared to the full his department's eagerness not merely to implement the Yalta agreement, but even to go beyond its terms in the repatriation of prisoners.

What, for instance, was to become of those Russians who, having joined the German Army (generally to save their skins rather than out of enthusiasm for Hitler), tried to resist repatriation by pleading that they were German PoWs, protected under the Geneva Convention? While the Americans showed themselves sympathetic to such claims, the British Foreign Office appeared positively eager to shut the gates of mercy.

"As far as I know", minuted Galsworthy, "the basis of our interpretation [of the treaty] is one of expediency." The Foreign Office, he explained, had had enough trouble with the Russians without adding to its difficulties by espousing doubtful causes.

Nevertheless, he was compelled to admit, "Some of the people whom we are obliged to hand over are persons who have suffered under the Soviet regime through no fault of their own, have not fought against it, and are merely trying to escape it."

A particular case concerned 43 Russians who were held at a camp at Bexhill. A neighbour there befriended some of them, and wrote to the Home Office to enquire if there were any procedure by which these men might avoid repatriation by becoming British. He himself was prepared to put two of them up until they were properly established in this country.

It fell to Galsworthy to reply. "As Soviet nationals, these men must, of course, be repatriated to the USSR when opportunity arises, irrespective of their wishes. Moreover, they admit to having gone over to the enemy to fight against the Allies and we have presumably no proof that their statement that they gave themselves up voluntarily is true. They seem to us to deserve no sympathy and we think our principal aim where they are concerned should be to ensure that they cause no trouble between us and the Soviet authorities over here."

Galsworthy also bent his mind to the means used to deal with Russians who seemed recalcitrant about returning to their native land. "It was, I thought, agreed that when a Soviet deserter came into the hands of the civil police the latter should more or less assume, or pretend, that the man in question was willing to return voluntarily to his camp, and hand him over to the local military authority accordingly. Any misunderstanding about the man's real wishes, was, I thought, to be attributed to 'language difficulties', etc.

"Once back in a Soviet camp, the unfortunate individual will have no access to any civil authorities, and will not, therefore, be in a position to protest against this rather rough injustice."

Galsworthy's intransigent approach did not inhibit promotion in the Foreign Office.

John Edgar Galsworthy was born in London on June 19 1919 and educated at Emanuel School, Wandsworth, and Corpus Christi, Cambridge. He joined the Army at the beginning of the Second World War, only to be invalided out after losing his right eye during a training exercise. He then went to the Government Communications Headquarters at Bletchley as a temporary administrative assistant.

In 1944 Galsworthy moved to the Foreign Office as a temporary Third Secretary in Northern Department. A gifted linguist, in 1946 he went to Madrid, where he was promoted Second Secretary. Three years later he was sent to Vienna.

In 1951 he became Head of Chancery at Athens, and in 1954 assistant in the economic relations department of the Foreign Office. Two years later he was appointed assistant in Southern Department, and in 1958 he went to Bangkok as Head of Chancery.

From 1962 he was concerned with Britain's application to join the Common Market, first as counsellor with the UK Delegation to the EEC, then from 1964 to 1967 as economic counsellor at Bonn, finally as Minister under Christopher Soames, the British Ambassador in Paris.

Galsworthy's period as Ambassador to Mexico from 1972 to 1977 was notable for two state visits. In 1972 President Echeverria came to Britain, and three years later the Queen and Prince Philip made a notably successful return visit to Mexico.

After retirement Galsworthy worked as a business consultant, helping the Davey Corporation to gain a contract in Mexico. And in 1982 his fluent Spanish made him a natural choice as an official observer of the elections in El Salvador.

Galsworthy was appointed CMG in 1968 and KCVO in 1975.

He married, in 1942, Jennifer Ruth Johnstone. They had a son and three daughters.

May 22 1992

JEFFREY HAMM

JEFFREY HAMM, who has died aged 76, was one of Sir Oswald Mosley's most dedicated followers, a footsoldier sweating in the heat of the day while the leader of British Fascism dreamed his dreams in his Temple de la Gloire in the Paris suburbs.

Hamm claimed that he joined the British Union in 1935 because he believed that Mosley's Keynesian policies afforded the best hope of deliverance from the unemployment and poverty he had seen in his youth. Others have endorsed this conclusion: A. J. P. Taylor wrote in his *English History 1914–45* (1965) that Mosley "offered a blueprint for most of the constructive advances in economic policy to the present day".

But that, of course, was only part of the story. Nicholas Mosley has written of his father that, "while the right hand dealt with grandiose ideas and glory, the left hand let the rat out of the sewer".

The same dichotomy was observable in Hamm. Journalists who took the trouble to interview him were invariably obliged to admit his courtesy and his honesty. "He had the suggestion of a stutter," wrote one scribe in 1958, "and a quiet serious manner that you felt may well have concealed strong and complex feelings. He has a sudden, rather disarming smile. His collar was not terribly clean."

As a mob orator, however, Hamm was transformed into a ranting, racialist demagogue. Like Mosley in the 1930s, he denied anti-Semitism, but he appeared to be under the same compulsion as his master to lead the public to the opposite conclusion.

"The pale, pink, palpitating pansies with long toenails have been chanting 'We don't want Fascism!'" he cried at a meeting at Dalston in 1947. "I say, 'We don't want Jewish Communism!'" The crowd was driven into a frenzy by these sallies, and Hamm was arrested.

No doubt he was correct in claiming, on such occasions, that the Communist opposition was looking for a fight. But it is also true that he appeared to relish the sterile and squalid thuggery of street combat.

Driven to Mosley's banner by some ineradicable psychological quirk, he enthusiastically embraced his position beyond the pale of society – an outcast for landladies, an unacceptable risk for employers, a universal target for brickbats, and a constant source of concern to the police. Directed to a worthier cause, such loyalty, courage and sacrifice might have been called heroic.

Of Somerset farming stock, Edward Jeffrey Hamm was born at Ebbw Vale on September 15 1915, and educated at West Monmouth School, where he showed an early penchant for debating. Before the Second World War he earned his living as a teacher – in Wales, at Lewes and at the King's School, Harrow.

But the crucial event in his life occurred in 1934 when he came across a Blackshirt meeting and immediately felt the call. Another formative experience was a holiday in 1937 in Germany, where he was particularly impressed by Nazi social policies. Hitler "certainly did a certain amount of good and he certainly made a number of mistakes", was his even judgement of the Führer.

Soon after the outbreak of war, which Mosley opposed, Hamm obtained a teaching post in the Falkland Islands. But within a few months he was arrested in his cottage (50 miles from Port Stanley) under Defence Regulation 18b, on grounds of promoting Fascist views to the islanders and the children under his care – a charge which he strongly denied, even when the Government released his file in 1986.

After being held for four months in the hull of a ship in Port Stanley harbour, Hamm was transported to Leuwkop internment camp in South Africa, where he was not dissatisfied to find himself in the company of German internees. On his release in April 1941, the new-found comrades touched him to the core with a performance of *Ich hatt' einen Kameraden*.

Back in England, Hamm joined the Royal Armoured Corps, though he was informed, before the end of the war, that "His Majesty has no further use for your services". Only in the Roman Catholic Church, however, into which he was received in 1944, did the pariah at last discover an institution which welcomed all comers.

In 1946 Hamm organised a British League of Ex-Servicemen and Women in the East End of London. This became the main active force in the new Union Movement, of which Mosley became leader in 1948.

Sir Oswald soon discovered that West Indian immigration, rather than the Jewish conspiracy, had become the principal threat to high wages for British workers. But he now rejected narrow nationalism in favour of a united Europe, which would use Africa as a source of raw materials and as a market for manufactured goods.

Hamm, to whom Mosley's authority was absolute, duly accepted the new policies. He was given various dogsbody editorial tasks for the Mosleys, for which he was rewarded in 1956 by his appointment as Secretary of the Union Movement.

In his autobiography, *Action Replay* (1983), Hamm related how Mosley once told him to appear "about lunchtime" at a French hotel. In the event the leader arrived at 3 p.m., dictated for some hours and then summarily departed, leaving the exhausted and still unfed acolyte to reflect admiringly on his hero's supreme dedication to the great purpose.

Hamm organised Mosley's disastrous attempt to win North Kensington in the 1959 election, and stood himself for Middlesbrough in a 1962 by-election, when he received a derisory vote. Four years later, though, when he stood for Birmingham Handsworth in the General Election, his candidacy helped to render Sir Edward Boyle's majority paper-thin.

Despite Hamm's devotion to the cause, he found no place in the copious index of Mosley's *My Life* (1968). But even after Sir Oswald's death in 1981, he did not relinquish the struggle.

He had no regrets: "If I were on my deathbed I would not say that I had wasted my life, but that I had had a hard life, but an interesting and exciting one. I had tried, I had 'had a go'." Hamm also had a son and a daughter.

May 22 1992

CHARLES ST GEORGE

CHARLES ST GEORGE, the racehorse owner and businessman, who has died aged 66, had a colourful reputation
which won him admiration on the Turf, although less
favourable opinions in the City of London.

In the world of racing he was regarded as an expansive,
knowledgeable figure, passionately committed to the
welfare of the sport. He formed one of a small and
disparate group – Robert Sangster, Louis Freedman and
Lord Howard de Walden being others – whose horses
provided effective resistance to the ever-increasing ascendancy of the Arab owners. He was associated with top
trainers but was probably best known for his long
association with Lester Piggott, who rode numerous
winners clad in St George's familiar black jacket adorned
with white chevrons.

St George stood loyally by Piggott during the great
jockey's troubles – he was one of his sureties when Piggott
was awaiting trial on tax charges – and gave him his first
ride on his return to the saddle.

Among St George's best horses were Ardross (the
1982 "Horse of the Year"), Ginevra (winner of the 1972
Oaks), Bruni (1975 St Leger), Michelozzo (1989 St Leger)
and Lorenzaccio (which beat Nijinsky in the 1970 Champion Stakes). St George's 56 victories in Group races – 11
of them gained with Ardross – placed him fourth in the
list of the most successful pattern race-winning owners
since the system was introduced in 1971.

After his Giacometti won the Gimcrack Stakes at
York, St George made a stimulating Gimcrack Club

speech in 1973, setting out a seven-point formula for better racing in Britain. His proposals included more prize money, which could come from closed circuit television in betting shops, and adequate insurance of jockeys and stable lads.

St George himself set an excellent example to his fellow owners by insuring every jockey who rode for him against permanent and temporary injury. He also made a spirited defence of the "much maligned" owner. "Without the owners and the money they put back into the industry," he said, "racing would grind to a halt."

In the Lloyd's insurance market, however, St George was a highly controversial figure. He was for some years chairman and managing director of the Oakley Vaughan underwriting agency, which was the subject of an investigation in 1981 when it was revealed that the Oakley Vaughan syndicates had been taking on substantially more business than their capital base allowed.

This resulted in the suspension of three underwriters and a reprimand for St George from the Lloyd's committee – kept private on condition that he gave up executive responsibility. Oakley Vaughan went on to suffer three disastrous underwriting years, resulting in a suit against St George himself in which it was claimed that he had offered to guarantee one syndicate member's losses personally in order to dissuade him from resigning. The case was settled on undisclosed terms.

Although underwriting activities ceased in 1983, the firm's losses eventually mounted to £2.5 million and in 1988 it was forced into receivership, becoming the first such firm in the history of Lloyd's to do so. At the hearing it was stated that St George had not been a director of the company for some years; and he denied in the press that he was any longer involved in its affairs.

Of Maltese extraction, Charles Anthony Barbaro St George was born on June 21 1925. During the Second World War he served with the Coldstream Guards. Afterwards a brother officer launched his career in insurance by finding him a place as a "half-commission man" with Tufnell Satterthwaite.

He soon attracted business through his racing contacts, and went on to buy the Oakley Vaughan agency from the widowed Lady Oakley. He built it up both on the bloodstock insurance side and in the management of Lloyd's underwriting syndicates. He introduced a number of celebrated sporting figures as new Lloyd's "names". But the major source of his fortune remained bloodstock dealing itself.

St George was a shrewd backer of horses. At Royal Ascot in 1975, for instance, he won £69,000 for an outlay of £275 on mixed trebles and an accumulator.

Latterly he experienced mixed fortunes with his horses. His horse Kneller won the Ebor impressively in 1988 but subsequently had to be put down because of injury; and in 1990 St George sold Saumarez, only for the horse to go on to win the Prix de L'Arc de Triomphe.

In 1991 St George cut back his string of horses after heavy losses at Lloyd's. He was briefly the owner of Fort Belvedere near Windsor, formerly the retreat of King Edward VIII, and in 1984 he bought the Sefton Lodge stables at Newmarket from the late Jim Joel. Unlike Joel, St George was not a breeder; he bought all his horses, mostly on the basis of an idiosyncratic but seemingly very effective analysis of their heartbeat.

St George was closely involved in several charitable concerns, including the Stable Lads Welfare Trust.

He was twice married and had four sons.

Jeffrey Bernard writes: Charles St George was one of the best friends I have ever had – and best friends are not easy to come by. Although he was a solid and tough character, he was an amazingly good sport.

I first met him, when I was working on the *Sporting Life*, through Lester Piggott. Charles's relationship with Lester amounted to a legendary friendship.

I remember that when Charles heard I was in the Middlesex Hospital he transformed my room there into a combination of flower-shop, fruit-shop, tobacconist and newsagent. When he left after visiting me, he put £200 under my pillow, saying: "You'll need some money for toothpaste."

He might have been the kindest man I have ever met.

May 29 1992

ANTHONY 'FAT TONY' SALERNO

ANTHONY "FAT TONY" SALERNO, who has died at a prison hospital in Missouri aged 80, was once regarded as the top Mafia boss in America.

Jowly and scowling, with his cane, his fedora and his shirt buttoned at the neck, "Fat Tony" (a sobriquet sparingly used) seemed the epitome of the old-time *mafioso*. In 1986 *Fortune* magazine, in an article on the nation's top 50 Mafia bosses, rated Salerno No 1 on the basis of "wealth, power and influence".

The cigar-chomping mobster, said to be the former "Godfather" of the infamous New York-based Genovese crime "family", was serving two long sentences at the time of his death. In 1986 – notwithstanding his lawyer's pleas that "bells are going off in his head" – the ailing Salerno was sentenced to 100 years for his role on the New York Mafia's ruling "commission of *La Cosa Nostra*" – a group of bosses that met regularly to sort out demarcation disputes and authorise executions, or "hits".

"You have spent your lives feeding on this community," pronounced Federal Judge Richard Owen, "through murders and violence and threats of murders and violence."

And in 1988 Salerno was sentenced to 70 years in connection with an organised crime bid-rigging scheme which affected virtually every high-rise building in Manhattan that used more than $2 million worth of concrete.

The trial afforded several diverting vignettes. At one stage Salerno turned to the prosecutor, Alan Cohen, and said menacingly: "I want to live to see the day *you're* in the Mafia." The startled Cohen replied: "They don't let Jews in."

"For you", growled Salerno, "they'll make an exception."

Later the judge questioned whether Salerno's new lawyer might experience a conflict of interest as he was representing another gangland client. "I don't think that will happen your honour," rasped Fat Tony. "But if it does, I'll have to shoot him."

Antonio Salerno was born in 1912 and rose steadily in the Genovese hierarchy.

For years, investigators claimed at his trials, Salerno presided over a multimillion-dollar gambling and loan shark operation. But he was shrewd enough to move his organisation into "legitimate" businesses such as music, construction and concrete.

In 1978 Fat Tony was convicted on gambling and tax evasion charges, but his lawyer Roy Cohn (celebrated as a McCarthyite investigator) said Salerno was not a gangster, merely a "sports gambler".

Salerno finally became boss of the Genovese family sometime in the early 1980s after the retirement of Philip Lombardo. He supervised an organised crime network that stretched across the north-east, and used his control of powerful Teamsters Union locals to influence elections.

In the mid-1980s the FBI planted an electronic listening device in Salerno's social club and captured conversations in which Salerno met other mobsters. In one exchange, he and another New York boss bemoaned the lack of respect among younger members – one of whom had presumed to call him "Fat Tony" to his face.

Evidence gathered for the "commission" trial showed that Salerno even benefited from hot dogs sold at the Bronx Zoo with a "mob tax" of one cent added to the cost of each frankfurter.

His 1988 conviction was overturned on appeal, but the Supreme Court reversed the lower court's ruling shortly before he died.

He is survived by his wife, Peggy.

July 30 1992

DOCKER HUGHES

DOCKER HUGHES, who has died aged 38, was a former Portsmouth shipyard labourer, who came to public attention in the 1987 General Election, when he stood as the 657 Party candidate in Portsmouth South.

His party was named after the 6.57 a.m. train which Portsmouth football club's notorious hooligan group would take to away matches. "Docker's" manifesto included pledges to establish an Orange Order at Portsmouth and to introduce duty-free goods on the five-minute Portsmouth–Gosport ferry crossing; he also campaigned against beards.

His 455 votes were thought by some to have swung the seat to the Tories, whose margin of victory was only 205 over the sitting SDP MP. At the count "Docker" was so drunk he had to be supported by his agent. He is thought to have died of natural causes.

August 8 1992

JOHN CAGE

JOHN CAGE, the composer, who has died in New York aged 79, was the most iconoclastic and influential representative of that radical, saltishly independent strain in American music.

As the heir of such eccentric loners as Charles Ives, Carl Ruggles and Henry Cowell, Cage showed a willingness to take chances, to strike out fearlessly into uncharted territory, and a refusal to be bound by any traditionally accepted, textbook notion of what music might or might not be.

As early as 1937 Cage had foreseen a future in which, he believed, "the use of noise to make music will continue and increase until we reach a music produced through the aid of electrical instruments and which will make available for musical purposes any and all sounds that can be heard".

Cage spurned classical models and, above all, everything inherited from the still-dominant European tradition. Few composers pursued more rigorously the goal of an art of collage based on non-musical sounds – what one of Cage's severest critics, the composer Virgil Thomson, defined as an homogenised chaos that "would carry no programme, no plot, no reminders of the history of beauty, no personal statement".

Whether revered as an icon of the avant-garde and the father of modern experimental music, or reviled as a hateful and bizarre excrescence, Cage undeniably made a significant impact on the evolution of musical thought in the second half of the 20th century. During that time his own musical creations underwent many startling changes of style and method; what never changed, however, was their unquenchable sense of adventure.

A Californian, John Milton Cage, Jnr, was born in Los Angeles on September 5 1912. His mother was a journalist and his father an engineer and inventor, whose patents included a revolutionary steering and propulsion system for submarines, the first radio powered by alternating current and a cold-cure inhaler that combined menthol and thymol in an alcohol suspension.

Young John was praised at school – where he excelled

in oratory and Latin – for his scholarship and his leadership. He spent the spring of 1930 in Europe, studying music and architecture in Spain, France and Germany.

On his return to America he continued his studies with, among others, Henry Cowell and Arnold Schoenberg. Cage then worked briefly in Seattle (where he began his lifelong collaboration with the innovative choreographer Merce Cunningham), San Francisco and Chicago, before he settled permanently in New York in 1942.

Cage's preoccupation at that time was with the rigours of rhythm, rather than harmony or melody, and his music of those years was written almost exclusively for percussion. These pieces displayed an exuberant racket and a feathery delicacy, inspired by the ensembles that he directed in all four cities.

He also began experimenting with the "prepared piano", a notion which involves the insertion of various objects between the strings to create a quirkily diverse repertoire of percussive effects.

By the late 1940s Cage's reputation was sufficiently established for a complete performance of his major work for prepared piano, *Sonatas and Interludes*, to be mounted at Carnegie Hall. Legend has it that a horrified janitor in a concert hall once removed tacks from a "prepared piano" the night before a Cage concert. The performers had to "vandalise" the instrument in a hurry the next day.

Outwardly Cage's life during the 1950s appeared to proceed much as before – teaching at American colleges, or touring in Europe and America with Merce Cunningham and the pianist-composer David Tudor. It was at that time, however, that his thinking about the process of music underwent its most dramatic change.

Stimulated by his avid study of Zen and other oriental philosophies, Cage began producing his first works using chance procedures based on the Chinese classic *I Ching*, in which the throw of a coin determines attack, duration, the length of the notes and so on. He also made liberal use of electronics, computers, graphic notation and even the unpredictable sounds created by the random turning of the dials of a chrous of 12 and more radios.

At one extreme was the notorious *4' 33"* in which the performer sits silently in front of an instrument playing nothing; at the other, the cacophonous free-for-all of the *Atlas Eclipticalis*, which was intended for any ensemble of more than 86 unspecified instruments. Then there were the *Variations IV* for any number of players and any means; and the grandiose, multi-media pieces, such as *HPSCHD* or *Roaratorio*, based on James Joyce's *Finnegans Wake*.

All Cage's creative activities were underpinned by his frequently declared aim to "bring about a music which is like furniture – a music, that is, which will be part of the noises of the environment". Cage expounded this philosophy not only in his music, but also in the lectures that he delivered throughout the world – collected in a steady stream of publications, from *Silence* (1961) onwards. Essential to his aim was the breaking down of the distinctions between life and art: "There is no noise," he used to say, "only sound."

Whereas for many of his eager young disciples Cage represented liberation and the freedom to do exactly what they liked, for others he quickly became the object of ridicule and the most aggressive hostility. It was hardly surprising that the sight of Cage in his *0' 00"* preparing and slicing vegetables, putting them into a blender and then drinking the results, with the actions amplified around the hall, should have seemed like the work of a self-promoting charlatan.

Yet from about the mid-1950s onwards he was increasingly sought after as a lecturer and performer.

A tall, lanky figure with a mesmeric personality, John Cage was a dedicated walker, woodsman, mycologist and player of such games as cribbage, poker, scrabble, bridge and backgammon.

At the height of his fame he appeared on the Italian television quiz show *Lascia o raddoppia* over a five-week period, answering questions on mushrooms.

Cage married, in 1935, Xenia Andreeva Kashevaroff, daughter of a Russian Orthodox priest who was the librarian of the Alaska Territorial Library. The marriage was dissolved in 1945.

August 14 1992

JOHN POULSON

JOHN POULSON, who has died aged 82, was the architect at the centre of one of Britain's most notorious postwar corruption cases.

In the 1960s Poulson controlled the biggest architectural practice in Europe, but by the end of that decade his empire was in difficulty. In 1972 he filed for bankruptcy, and so precipitated a major political scandal.

Reginald Maudling, the Conservative Home Secretary, was soon forced to resign because he had accepted the chairmanship of one of Poulson's companies. His resignation became necessary when the Metropolitan

Police, for which the Home Secretary has responsibility, was asked to investigate matters arising from the bankruptcy hearings.

In 1973 Poulson and George Pottinger, a Permanent Under-Secretary for Agriculture at the Scottish Office, were arrested on conspiracy and corruption charges (Poulson had paid Pottinger £30,000 in return for public contracts). The scandal soon spread to Teesside. Among those subsequently arrested were Andrew Cunningham and T. Dan Smith (both leading members of the Labour party in the north-east), two ex-mayors, an NUM official and a journalist. It emerged that other MPs had also accepted money from Poulson.

At Leeds Crown Court in January 1974 Pottinger was sentenced to five years (cut on appeal to four), Smith to six and Poulson to seven. In the event he served a little more than three years. He left prison in poor health in 1977, after the Earl of Longford had declared that his continued incarceration was an "indefensible cruelty".

Poulson maintained that he was not a criminal, but rather the scapegoat of what he called "the British Watergate that has never really been exposed". He threatened to do so in his memoirs, for which he was paid £20,000. But although a 200-page book was printed (entitled *The Price*) its publication was prevented by the fear of libel writs.

John Garlick Llewellyn Poulson was born in 1910. His father ran a pottery business in Ferrybridge, Yorkshire. He left his Methodist public school without gaining his school certificate, joined a firm of architects, failed his architectural exams and was sacked in 1932.

That year, with capital of £50, he set up his own practice in Pontefract, designing private houses and carrying out improvements to public ones. The Poulson practice took off during the Second World War, when a friendship with a senior official at the Ministry of Works led to a string of government contracts. Poulson began to seek out men in public life, offering cash and gifts in return for their putting contracts his way.

He became a licentiate member of RIBA in 1942, and by 1954 was rich enough to design himself a house – which he named "Manasseh" (Hebrew for "relaxation") – where he and his wife gave parties which became the high point of Pontefract social life.

Poulson went on to open offices in London, Middlesbrough, Edinburgh, Lagos and Beirut. By the mid-1960s he had a staff of 750, handling some 450 projects a year; he also had a fleet of luxurious motor cars and a permanent suite at the Dorchester Hotel.

In effect, Poulson ran a kind of architectural supermarket, maintaining profits by paring margins to the bone and increasing the volume of business to the highest possible level. He was good at choosing able staff, and gradually brought every professional service he needed into his company – interior designers, structural engineers and so on. He was a dictatorial master, apt to berate his executives in public and fire them abruptly.

He was involved in the design of numerous council houses and flats, a £1 million swimming pool in Leeds, the Cannon Street station redevelopment in London and the £3 million Aviemore tourist centre in Scotland. In 1967 he designed the £1.5 million Victoria Hospital at Gozo, Malta, and was presented to the Queen.

Poulson became involved in politics, as chairman of the National Liberal Party of Great Britain and of the Goole Conservative and Liberal Association. He also became a leading figure in the Methodist Church and the Freemasons. He held strong moral views, and once dismissed a married man for having an affair.

By 1969 his business was suffering acute cash-flow problems. Poulson turned to his brother-in-law, Mr John King (later Lord King of Wartnaby, chairman of British Airways), to rescue the practice, but it was too late.

In 1980 he was discharged from bankruptcy, when the court was told that just over £300,000 of his £900,000 liabilities had been recovered.

Poulson was a devoted fan of Leeds United Football Club.

He married, in 1939, Cynthia, and had two daughters.

February 4 1993

IAN MIKARDO

IAN MIKARDO, who has died aged 84, was the driving force behind the Left-wing Bevanite movement that tore the Labour party apart in the 1950s and 1960s.

Aneurin Bevan was the movement's leader, with Richard Crossman and Michael Foot providing the intellectual dimension, but it was Mikardo's relentless energy and organising skill that moulded a disparate group of prima donnas into a national force.

A quondam chairman of the party and for many years a member of the National Executive, Mikardo was MP for Reading from 1945 to 1959, for Poplar from 1964 to 1974, for Tower Hamlets, Bethnal Green and Bow from 1974 to 1983 and for Bow and Poplar from 1983 to 1987.

He was an uncompromising ideologue and a some-what enigmatic figure. His heavy jowls and thick black-rimmed spectacles gave him a rather sinister appear-ance, particularly on television. In Mikardo's younger days Winston Churchill had once asked "Is he as nice as he looks?"

The answer from the many who disliked or mistrusted him was an emphatic "No". But "Mik" had his devotees.

He had a talent for succinct expression, both from the platform and in print, which he combined with a robust Jewish sense of humour. Although he represented Dock-lands seats for many years he was not an Eastender by birth, but had many of the earthy qualities of that breed.

Something else that endeared him to MPs of all parties was his self-appointed role as Westminster's unofficial "bookie", always willing to lay odds on any contentious issue. He prided himself on keeping a "clean book" (never making a loss) by applying a shrewd brain to politics rather than horses. He did particularly well out of Tory loyalists over the downfall of Edward Heath.

Mikardo's Left-wing sympathies sometimes led to his loyalty being questioned, and he was certainly much courted by East European diplomats during the Cold War years. But whatever his underlying sympathies with Communism may have been, he was first and foremost a passionate Zionist who never forgave Stalin's pogroms against the Jews.

The son of East European immigrants, who found work in Britain in the tailoring trade, Ian Mikardo was born at Portsmouth on July 9 1908 and educated at secondary school and Portsmouth Municipal College.

His parents wanted him to become a rabbi, and his first earnings were from teaching Hebrew and translating

Yiddish; his mother was appalled when young Ian's headmaster suggested he might become an MP.

On leaving school he learned accountancy and went into industrial management. He joined the Labour Party in 1930 and soon became a regular delegate to its annual conferences.

He first came to prominence in 1944 when he led a revolt against Herbert Morrison on a motion demanding a programme of sweeping nationalisation for the postwar election manifesto.

During the war Mikardo had worked in the aviation industry as a management consultant. He applied this experience in a book, *Centralised Control of Industry* (1942), and to the art of mobilising the maximum vote in elections.

In the early postwar days, canvassing of voters and "knocking up" by party workers on election day being rather hit-and-miss affairs, Mikardo evolved what became known as the "Reading system", which helped him to retain his highly marginal seat.

At Westminster he soon found scope for his destructive energies and organising talents in mobilising the Left against his own Government. In 1947 he contributed to *Keep Left*, the pamphlet that became the bible for rebellions against the leaderships first of Attlee and then of Gaitskell.

He had a gift for the telling phrase. When Harold Wilson launched his grandiose "National Plan" for economic recovery in the 1960s, Mikardo described it as "an engineering drawing without the operation schedule and kit of tools". He was instrumental in securing Labour's reduction of the voting age from 21 to 18.

In his diaries for 1965 Richard Crossman noted a

meeting of the Party's National Executive: "Suddenly Mikardo said we had to make a decision on votes for 18-year-olds and pointed out that if we didn't do it that very morning the Speakers' Conference would reach the item without Labour Members having a view . . . it was carried unanimously."

In spite of his contempt for capitalism and profit making, Mikardo developed a lucrative but often controversial trade as a middleman between Communist bloc trading corporations and British businessmen. He discovered that the lot of the socialist trader is not always easy, nor Communist importers any less demanding than capitalists. There was much amusement at Westminster when the Russians rejected one shipment of his clothing as "shoddy".

Although his trading with Soviet bloc countries was perfectly legal – he also acted on behalf of major British companies – it was diplomatically awkward to deal with East Germany at a time when that regime was seeking Western acceptance after the erection of the Berlin Wall.

Mikardo's Left-wing credentials gave him an entrée, and to the Communists he seemed worth cultivating for political as well as for business reasons. Whether he gave away any sensitive political information may never be known – but the suspicion was certainly there.

It would be tedious to recite the causes Mikardo espoused. He did suffer two notable humiliations, however. The first of these was when he lost his seat on the executive of his trade union, ASTMS, for advocating the nationalisation of banks and insurance companies. It was a cause that might have appealed to an otherwise Left-wing union, but as many of its members worked in both industries, the union prudently decided to drop him.

The second was when he attacked Enoch Powell for racialism after Powell's "Rivers of Blood" speech at Birmingham. Dockworkers in his solid Labour constituency then marched the streets chanting "Mikardo – a Japanese Jew!" (confusing "Mikardo" with "Mikado"). It was, for him, a salutary insight into the vagaries of human nature.

His books included *The Labour Case* (1950), *It's a Mug's Game* (1951), *Socialism or Slump* (1959) and an autobiography, *Back-Bencher* (1988).

Mikardo married, in 1932, Mary Rosette; they had two daughters.

May 7 1993

ALADENA FRATIANNO

ALADENA FRATIANNO, who has died in an undisclosed American city aged 79, was a former Mafia hitman known as "Jimmy The Weasel".

Fratianno, who had been in hiding since becoming an FBI informant in 1977, was one of the longest-serving claimants under the federal witness programme, which offers protection and financial support in return for regular testimony in cases of organised crime.

"The Weasel" signed on to the programme and turned informer after learning that there was a Mafia contract out on his life. For the first 10 years of enforced isolation he enjoyed a $100,000 annual allowance and a permanent armed guard.

Then, in 1987, the US Justice Department struck

Fratianno off its payroll. "We've squeezed the lemon dry," said an official.

"The Weasel" was furious: "They just threw me out on the street. I put 30 guys away, six of them *capos*, and now the whole world is looking for me. I tell you, I am a dead man." Few were prepared to stake much on his chances of survival. "The Weasel is now 74," said one police officer, "and I wouldn't bet a dime on him reaching 75."

But he survived five years before succumbing to Alzheimer's disease.

Fratianno earned his notoriety as a key witness during the trials of *mafiosi* throughout the late 1970s and early 1980s. It was on his testimony that such characters as Carmine "The Snake" Persico, "Fat Tony" Salerno (*qv*) and Johnny "The Rope" Roselli went to prison.

In the course of the trials Fratianno admitted that he had directly committed five murders and participated in six others.

He painted a vivid picture of life in "The Mob", describing how, at his initiation in 1947, he was escorted into a room where 40 Mafia members sat around a table on which were arranged a gun and a sword.

"All the guys stood up," recalled Fratianno. "My finger was pricked with the sword to draw blood. Then I was introduced to each member and we kissed on each cheek."

"The Weasel" also alleged that Frank Sinatra had enjoyed close relations with a number of senior *mafiosi*. For a time it appeared that the allegations threatened Sinatra's chances of regaining his Nevada gaming licence, which he had lost after Sam Giancana, the Chicago Mafia boss, had visited a casino in which he had an interest.

Sinatra vehemently denied the charges, and dismissed Fratianno as "a fink".

After being discarded by the witness protection programme, Fratianno appeared on television, pleading to be allowed to leave the country. But permission was denied, and he spent the rest of his life in a remote, Mid-Western town under an assumed identity.

Fratianno eked out a living on social security and the royalties of his two books of memoirs – *Vengeance Is Mine* and *The Last Mafioso*.

He was married.

July 3 1993

MARGARET
DUCHESS OF ARGYLL

MARGARET DUCHESS OF ARGYLL, who has died aged 80, was one of the most photographed and publicised beauties of the 20th century and a seemingly indomitable social figure.

But between 1959 and 1963 she was involved in a sensational and sordid divorce case, when her second husband, the 11th Duke of Argyll, Chief of the Clan Campbell and Hereditary Master of the Royal Household in Scotland, sued her for divorce on grounds of adultery. The court case lasted 11 days, and its piquant details included the theft of a racy diary, in which the Duchess listed the accoutrements of a number of lovers as though she was running them at Newmarket.

The 50,000-word judgment, in which the Duke was

granted a decree, was one of the longest in the history of the Edinburgh court. The Duchess was found to have committed adultery with three men named in her husband's petition and with a fourth, unidentified figure. A pair of photographs was produced in court showing the Duchess, naked save for three strings of pearls, engaged in a sexual act with a man whose face was not shown and who passed into folklore as "the Headless Man".

Lord Wheatley, who tried the case, described the Duchess as "a completely promiscuous woman. . . . Her attitude towards marriage was what moderns would call enlightened, but which in plain language was wholly immoral".

Nor were the Duke's morals found to be above rebuke. The judge found his fondness for pornographic postcards especially deplorable.

A host of other legal actions delighted the press before and after the actual divorce hearing. Accusations about trust finds, libel and conspiracy to defraud were played out, at an estimated cost to the Duchess of more than £200,000.

One particularly juicy action concerned the Duchess's outrageous suggestion that her recently widowed stepmother was having an affair with her estranged husband.

Margaret Argyll continued to be a favourite subject of gossip columnists long after the furore about her divorce had died down. Her feuds with her family, her landlords, her bankers and her biographers were all lovingly documented, usually with her own connivance.

As recently as 1989 she was involved in a highly public prosecution of her Moroccan maid, who had run up a telephone bill of thousands of pounds. The maid said that the Duchess had given her permission to call her family in North Africa but was unable to remember having done so because of her inordinate consumption of whisky.

The maid's stories were dismissed and she was given a suspended sentence, but the case sparked off a debate about the servant problem. The Duchess was herself an old hand with recalcitrant maids, suffering a series of unhappy arrangements after she dispensed with the services of the redoubtable Edith Springett, who looked after her for more than a decade.

Springett fell out with the Duchess after being found unconscious on the floor of Her Grace's bedroom, with an empty bottle of her whisky lying close by. The Duchess dispatched solicitor's letters instructing Springett to desist from calling her a "Mayfair whore" and a "silly old bitch" in front of guests.

In her later years the Duchess fell on hard times, although she still retained the shadow of her remarkable beauty – melting green eyes and pale magnolia skin.

At one point her debts were gallantly paid off by her first husband, the American golfer Charles Sweeny. The Duchess later recalled of that marriage that she had felt "like a bird in a not-so-gilded cage".

She reserved her virulence for her second husband. "Ian Argyll," she would announce at regular intervals, "was a fiend and a sadist."

Ultimately Margaret Argyll became a figure of pathos, the harder to help for lingering vestiges of arrogance.

The daughter of George Whigham, a self-made businessman from Glasgow who founded the British and Canadian Celanese Corporations, she was born on December 1 1912 and christened Ethel Margaret.

She was educated at Miss Hewitt's Classes in New York, at Miss Wolff's in London, at Heathfield and with

Mlle Ozanne in Paris. Miss Whigham was launched as a debutante in London with an extravagant coming-out ball in 1931.

Her striking looks and perfectly formed figure immediately made her the toast of numberless hopeful swains. In later years she would look back on this period of her life with rage in her heart, claiming to have grown up in a world where innocence marched hand in hand with ignorance, in which money and a title were the only goal for wayward Cinderellas.

She was briefly betrothed to the 7th Earl of Warwick, but shied away from matrimony after the invitations for the wedding had been sent out, on the grounds that she "did not love him sufficiently".

Instead she married, in 1933, Charles Sweeny, a tall, dashing American. Their wedding at Brompton Oratory drew a crowd of 3,000 onlookers.

A son and a daughter followed in quick succession, and Margaret Sweeny appeared to carry all before her. Cole Porter immortalised her in his hit song "You're The Top" from the musical *Anything Goes*:

> *You're the nimble tread*
> *of the feet of Fred Astaire*
> *You're Mussolini*
> *You're Mrs Sweeny*
> *You're Camembert . . .*

But the Sweenys were divorced in 1947, and four years later she became the third and penultimate wife of the 11th Duke of Argyll.

Margaret Argyll continued to throw lavish parties at her Grosvenor House apartment throughout the 1970s and 1980s, although as time went on it was less easy to detect any particular merit in her guests. She favoured Americans for their natural courtesy and their dollars.

Although she was not a witty woman – "She don't make many jokes" was the pithy conclusion of one peer who sat next to her at dinner – Margaret Argyll was the mistress of boring banter, delivered with a drink in one hand and a cigarette-holder in the other.

Her memoirs, *Forget Not* (1975), were generally judged a disappointment. No clues were offered as to the identity of the "Headless Man", and no mention made of her much-publicised estrangement from her daughter, the Duchess of Rutland.

Reviewing the book, Alastair Forbes observed: "Her father may have been able to give her some fine earrings but *nothing* to put between them."

The Duchess was interviewed about the book on a literary programme on television, and was asked why she had not employed a ghost. She seemed flummoxed by the question, since she had obviously not written a word of the book, and directed her melting green eyes with memorable ferocity towards her interlocutor.

In 1979 she was given a gossip column in *Tatler* magazine ("Stepping Out with Margaret Argyll"), but was defeated by the difficulties of spelling names correctly. By 1981 her soporific social jottings had been reduced from two pages to a small corner of one, and the connection was severed entirely the following year.

Although Margaret Arygll may not have been accepted in the "Establishment", she enjoyed star status in the world of show business and money. She presided over a lavish party for Paul Getty's 80th birthday at the Dorchester, attended by King Umberto of Italy and Tricia Nixon, daughter of the American President.

Nor was her life devoid of good deeds. She adopted two boys, Jamie and Richard Gardner, whom she put through school, and also espoused a campaign to save the Argyll and Sutherland Highlanders from disbandment, energetically assisted by Lieutenant-Colonel Colin "Mad Mitch" Mitchell.

The Duchess also delighted in dogs. She kept a series of miniature French poodles – 14 altogether, most of them black. She was an inveterate campaigner for animal rights and served for many years as president of the Bleakholt Animal Sanctuary in Lancashire.

In 1990 Margaret Argyll was evicted from her suite at Grosvenor House over unpaid rent; she later took up residence in a nursing home in Pimlico.

"I do not forget," she concluded. "Neither the good years, in which I laughed and danced and lived upon a cloud of happiness; nor the bad years of near despair, when I learned what life and people and friendship really were. . . . Unfortunately I am only too aware that I am still the same gullible, impulsive, over-optimistic 'Dumb Bunny', and I have given up hopes of any improvement."

July 28 1993

T. DAN SMITH

T. DAN SMITH, who has died aged 78, was a Labour party chieftain in the North-East in the 1960s and 1970s and a key figure in the Poulson scandal.

Known as "Mr Newcastle", Smith was the nearest Britain has had to a Chicago-style city mayor. He controlled all the key committees on the city council, which he used to further the interests of John Poulson (*qv*) a corrupt architect and developer who was the chief client of Smith's public relations firm.

In the municipal euphoria of the 1960s Smith boasted that when he had finished with it Newcastle would be transformed into the "Venice of the North". He cleared the Scotswood Road slums of the city, cleaned up the polluted River Tyne, built a civic centre and was instrumental in creating Newcastle University, which awarded him an honorary degree. With his tower blocks and dual carriageways he also did grave damage to some of the glories of Newcastle's 19th-century architecture.

The scandal broke when bankruptcy proceedings against Poulson exposed a web of bribery over the allocation of publicly financed building contracts in Britain and abroad. Smith and Poulson, George Pottinger (a senior civil servant) and several leading Labour councillors from the North-East were jailed. The scandal also touched Reginald Maudling, the Conservative Home Secretary and former Chancellor of the Exchequer, who escaped prosecution but was nevertheless ruined.

Smith told Leeds Crown Court that he had not set out to be corrupt but that his public relations firm had been so from the moment Poulson made him an offer in 1963. From then on its basic objective was to secure work for Poulson's companies, which became its main source of income, paying some £156,000 in seven years. It was impossible, Smith explained, to accept money from an architect and declare an interest at council meetings, because the architect would then have been struck off.

Before Smith was sentenced the Labour politician George Brown testified to the court that Smith was "one of the most outstandingly forthright, courageous, solid and loyal men I have met". Donald Herrod, QC, on the other hand, described Smith as "a wicked and cunning man", who had given a nauseating performance in the witness box. "At least Maurice Byrne [former mayor of Pontefract] was a straightforward crook. One could not say that about Dan Smith."

Thomas Dan Smith was born on May 11 1915, the son of a Durham miner much addicted to drink and gambling, and a mother who worked as a charwoman to keep the family going. He left school at 14 to become a painter's apprentice.

In the Depression of the 1930s young Dan (he later affected the style of "T" after a confused episode at an airport) suffered long spells of unemployment, and joined the Independent Labour party and Trotskyites, only to be expelled from both for refusing to toe the line.

In the early 1940s, as a founder member of the Peace Pledge Union, he tried to build a war resistance movement on Tyneside. Smith then joined the Labour party and in 1950 was elected to Newcastle city council. He soon grew disillusioned with the incompetence with which it was run and determined to introduce business methods and "professionalism". Newcastle was the first authority to appoint a city manager with outside business experience.

Smith campaigned for local government reform and was a persuasive advocate of city and regional planning. He was appointed to the Buchanan Committee on traffic in town and the Maud Commission on local government reorganisation. But rumours spread about his business ethics, and an air of mystery surrounded his work for the Labour party. He hoped for a Cabinet post when Harold Wilson formed his 1964 government, but he was kept at arm's length. He later claimed that he had declined the offer of a peerage from Wilson.

In 1965 George Brown appointed him chairman of the Northern Development Council, a body which never fulfilled Brown's grandiose ambitions. In 1970 Smith was at his apogee when he was charged with corruption over contracts with Wandsworth borough council. He was acquitted, but the case hung over him for 18 months and damaged his standing in Newcastle, where the rumours surrounding him seemed confirmed.

Worse was to come with Poulson's bankruptcy in 1972, which sparked off Labour's equivalent of the Conservative Profumo scandal, with money rather than sex as the motivating force.

Smith was jailed for six years, but released on parole after three. He served his time in a total of 18 prisons, in one of which be befriended a young man convicted of a killing, whom he encouraged to take up acting. The young man was Leslie Grantham, who went on to become "Dirty Den" in BBC Television's *EastEnders*.

On Smith's release in 1977 from Leyhill Open Prison, near Gloucester, the governor said of him: "You might call him a model prisoner."

He dreamed of returning to public life, but the next year his application to join the Moorside, Newcastle-upon-Tyne, branch of the Labour party was rejected: "I'm disappointed that a party to which I have given my life can take such an illiberal view," he said.

In 1987 he successfully applied to rejoin the Newcastle Central constituency party.

While Profumo found rehabilitation doing social work at Toynbee Hall, Smith sought it by working for the

Haldane Society for Penal Reform. His purpose was both to improve prison conditions and to encourage employers to give ex-offenders a chance.

He also campaigned for a better deal for pensioners, urging people to "unite to create pensioner-power today – tomorrow is too late".

He found a job as an electrician, and lived a simple life in Newcastle, where he occupied one of the Cruddas Park council flats he had helped to build.

Smith married, in 1939, and had a son and two daughters.

July 28 1993

H. R. HALDEMAN

H. R. HALDEMAN, who has died at Santa Barbara, California, aged 67, was the hard man in Richard Nixon's White House – which meant that he was very hard indeed.

"Every President has to have his S.O.B.," Eisenhower had told Nixon. "Bob" Haldeman played the part to perfection.

If the grubbiest work was allotted to "Chuck" Colson, and the more subtle insinuations were left to John Ehrlichman, Haldeman had no rival in administering the face-to-face humiliation. Whie Nixon disliked confrontation, Haldeman proclaimed his talent for "chewing people out". Theirs, as Ehrlichman remarked, was a "true marriage".

In his book, *The Ends of Power* (1978), Haldeman

suggested that his iron man image was cultivated; that in earlier manifestations he had been a particularly easygoing executive. If so, the transformation was perfectly realised.

"He sits 100 gold-carpeted feet down the hall from the Oval Office," noted *Newsweek*, "glowering out at the world from under a crewcut that would flatter a drill instructor, with eyes that would freeze Medusa." He impressed on his staff that he was a "zero defects" man.

"I rode them hard," Haldeman boasted, "made heavy demands on them for flawless work with no mistakes or excuses. I drummed into them the concept that anything can be done if you just figure how to do it and don't give up. I wouldn't take No for an answer."

Together with Ehrlichman he formed "the Berlin Wall" which controlled access to Nixon. This was not just a matter of shielding the President from the superfluous meetings and encounters; it also involved protecting the President against himself.

Nixon's visceral reaction to adversity was to issue a vindictive order: "*All* press is barred from Air Force One," he would bark; or "Put a 24-hour surveillance on that bastard!" Haldeman, unlike Colson, knew when to ignore such imperatives.

He denied keeping Nixon isolated; his purpose, he claimed, was to ensure that the President *did* see the people whom he needed to meet. Nor was he a sycophant. He was both conscientious and adept in conveying to the President accurate summaries of opponents' views. Yet Haldeman's dedication to Nixon's cause was too absolute to permit objective judgement.

In 1972, as he recalled, he "believed Nixon could accomplish almost anything. In the past six months he had not only begun the disarmament talks with the Soviet

Union, he had dramatically reopened diplomatic relations with China and – finally – he was about to end the crippling, suicidal Vietnam war."

To combat the foes of such a paragon, any means appeared justified. Thus Haldeman employed the muck-raking Donald Segretti to smear the Democrats, and he himself helped to draw up lists of "enemies".

In return Nixon came to depend totally upon his chief of staff – though Pat Nixon, jealous of the *apparatchik*'s influence, forbade any purely social contacts.

Haldeman also made an enemy of Rosemary Woods, Nixon's loyal secretary, whom he banished to basement office at the White House. But Miss Woods knew that Haldeman, as always, was carrying out orders from above. "Go fuck yourself," she told the President-elect.

It was not to be expected, then, that the news of the break-in at the Democratic National Committee head-quarters at the Watergate building in Washington on June 17 1972 would provoke a moral crisis in Haldeman, any more than in his master.

Haldeman had no part in the planning of the break-in, which he believed had been ordered by Colson. But in his book he was quite clear that "the President was involved in the cover-up from Day One". That was akin to admitting his own involvement – "though neither he [Nixon] nor we considered it a cover-up at the time".

Haldeman conceded in his book that he had been party to the plan to instruct the CIA to prevent the FBI's investigation of the case, and that he had used a presidential fund to stop the burglars from talking. He insisted that up until the spring of 1973 only a tiny percentage of his time had been spent on the Watergate affair.

Nevertheless when John Dean began to blab, the

game was up. On April 29 1973 – six months before the tapes were published – a tearful and religiose Nixon demanded Haldeman's and Ehrlichman's resignations.

Sentiment had been less in evidence a few days previously: "Is there any way you can use *cash?*" the President had wondered.

On television Nixon referred to Haldeman and Ehrlichman as "two of the finest public servants it has been my privilege to know". In private he was hardly less distraught: "There ain't anybody around here to do this son-of-a-bitching thing," he bemoaned.

Harry Robbins Haldeman was born on October 28 1926 into what Nixon described as "one of the finest families in Los Angeles". His grandfather had helped to found the Hollywood Bowl, and had been a member of the Better America Federation, an early anti-Communist organisation. His mother had been named "Woman of the Year" by the *Los Angeles Times* in the 1950s.

Having performed unremarkably in the state system of education, the young Haldeman was sent to a private military school for "straightening out". Here he imbibed "a zest for regimen and rigid command structure" that found further outlet when he was enrolled in the American Navy's wartime V-12 officer training programme at Redlands, part of the University of California at Los Angeles.

Haldeman led the campus Christian Science Organisation and was president of Scabbard and Blade, the military fraternity. But he later denied that he had any political or ideological commitment when he moved on to the university proper: "I was a rah-rah college type."

After leaving UCLA, he joined the advertising agency J. Walter Thompson in New York. Before long he was transferred to San Francisco, and then to Los Angeles, where he was promoted to vice-president.

At J. Walter Thompson Haldeman hired several young men who would later serve Nixon's administration, including Ronald Ziegler and Lawrence Higby. Meanwhile, he had been "fascinated" by the case of Alger Hiss (*qv*), in which Nixon made his name.

He was also attracted to the young politician's espousal of *laissez-faire* economics, while the notorious "Checkers" speech filled him with admiration for the candidate's fighting spirit. As far as Nixon was concerned, it helped that Haldeman was not one of "those Harvard bastards".

Haldeman worked on Nixon's vice-presidential campaign in 1956, and was chief advance man in his drive for the presidency four years later. In 1962 he counselled Nixon against running for the governorship of California – although he loyally supported the doomed campaign.

He stayed in contact with Nixon during the ensuing wilderness years, and in 1968 the former "assistant" was appointed chief of staff for Nixon's second presidential campaign. His technique of presenting a studiously relaxed Nixon and of carefully limiting public appearances succeeded in securing a narrow victory.

After Haldeman's resignation in 1972 he tried to persuade Nixon to grant pardons to the Watergate offenders – to no avail. In 1975 he was found guilty of perjury, conspiracy and obstruction of justice, and was imprisoned from June 1977 to December 1978.

Although he remained loyal to Nixon and unrepentant about having served him, Haldeman was piqued into publishing his book after seeing Nixon's 1977 interviews with David Frost. The former President seemed to suggest that his main fault had been his kindness in not sacking Haldeman and Ehrlichman earlier.

After leaving prison, Haldeman became a business consultant, dabbled in property and held the franchises on eight Sizzler Family Steak Houses in Florida.

He married, in 1949, Jo Horton; they had two sons and two daughters.

November 15 1993

JAMES RUSBRIDGER

JAMES RUSBRIDGER, who has died aged 65, was a self-styled expert on the Intelligence Services and an indefatigable writer of letters to newspapers, notably *The Daily Telegraph*.

He reckoned to see about 60 of these in print each year. They were always vigorous, often controversial and sometimes inaccurate. His forte was poking fun at the Official Secrets Act and explaining the niceties of telephone-tapping, but he would happily write about almost anything. By one post he might attack the ill-effects of tourism on his beloved Cornwall, by the next supply a vignette about Butlin's free holidays for curates in the 1940s.

At the height of his powers he wrote at least four letters a week for publication to this newspaper alone, and once had letters published in three national papers in one day. But he accepted rejection with equanimity: "Well, that's the way it is, my dear, I know."

Rusbridger was less successful with his books. His prose tended to limp, and he was too fond of conspiracy theories. His wide-ranging survey *The Intelligence Game* (1989) was beset by many of the illusions and delusions he was trying to expose. With *Betrayal at Pearl Harbor* (1992), written with the Australian codebreaker Captain Eric Nave, he showed that the Japanese codes had been broken before America joined the war, but could offer no firm evidence that Churchill had deliberately withheld information. The book, however, did contain valuable insights into the nature of wartime code-breaking.

James Rusbridger was a tireless researcher, a "snapper up of unconsidered trifles" which often led him into the realms of fantasy.

A man of ostentatious mystery, James Ernest Stuart Rusbridger was born in 1928 in Jamaica, where his father, a lieutenant-colonel in the Duke of Wellington's Regiment, was on staff duties. He would later claim, erroneously, that Peter Wright, the author of *Spycatcher*, was his first cousin.

He had a varied schooling, going to Dover College and Tenbury School before National Service. He then became a management trainee with Vickers Armstrong.

According to his unreliable account of his career, Rusbridger then answered an advertisement in *The Daily Telegraph* and found himself building a sugar refinery. He had considerable success selling produce in the Far East during the Suez crisis. As managing director for a commodity broker he sold some cut-price sugar to Eastern Europe – to the delight, he claimed, of the CIA, which congratulated him for undermining Fidel Castro.

No one within the Secret Service ever supported Rusbridger's claim to be an MI6 courier in Eastern Europe. But he was certainly arrested in Bulgaria – for taking photographs of a fishing village that was banned to foreigners during a visit by Khrushchev. Supplied with a form confessing to espionage he scrawled "I do not understand" across it, and he was eventually freed with an apology.

After a spell in the silver business in the early 1970s, Rusbridger retired and devoted himself to his letter-writing, which brought him an invitation to write about intelligence work in *Encounter*; some reviewing of spy books led to appearances on television.

Tall and dignified, with something about him of the actor Dennis Price, Rusbridger always seemed well briefed and became a master of the emerging art of the "sound-bite". He enjoyed controversy and was delighted to be moved on by police when filming for Italian television outside the Mirabelle, a favourite intelligence officers' restaurant in Mayfair.

Rusbridger claimed to have written the article which prompted Paul Keating to attack the British for letting down the Australian troops in Singapore. When invited to tea with the Queen in Cornwall he casually observed that a brother of his had once slept with Prince Philip – explaining that as young naval officers they had shared a bedroom *chez* Rusbridger.

As an open-handed bachelor (he once hired a helicopter to see the sights of Sydney), Rusbridger was generous to writers, proffering material and advice that often went unacknowledged and unpaid.

His body was discovered attired in a frogman's outfit.

February 8 1994

BOB CRISP

BOB CRISP, who has died aged 82, was a cricketer, soldier and journalist – blending, it was once said, 50 per cent genius, 40 per cent guts and 10 per cent glorious irresponsibility.

Tall, with film star good looks which rarely failed to turn female heads, Crisp was a natural athlete. He still has a place in the *Guinness Book of Records* for twice taking four wickets in four balls in first-class cricket: playing for Western Province in the Currie Cup against Griqualand West in 1931, and against Natal in 1933.

Crisp's greatest triumph was as a medium-fast bowler in the successful 1935 South African Test side; he took five for 99 at Old Trafford and achieved 107 wickets during the tour, for an average of 19.58 runs. He also turned out for Rhodesia to play the All Blacks in 1928, and as a 110-yard hurdler beat the American world champion H. Q. Davis at a Johannesburg athletics meeting in 1935.

To such talents, however, the gods added a notoriously short fuse. In the Western Desert during the Second World War Crisp's senior officers appreciated his competence and bravery in battle but were often exasperated by his riotous behaviour behind the lines.

After the war he held several enviable journalistic jobs – although rarely for long – and as old age approached he abandoned England for a wanderer's life in Greece.

A railway engineer's son, Robert James Crisp was born in Calcutta on May 28 1911 and educated at Prince Edward's School, Salisbury, Rhodesia.

235

Shortly after joining the *Bulawayo Chronicle* at 16 he wrote a report of an athletics meeting which featured a full account of his own successes in several events. "Bit immodest, aren't you?" said the news editor. "Not at all," replied the cub reporter. "My job was to report the meeting, giving the most important items first."

Crisp made his mark on the wider world by appearing for a Northern Rhodesian side against MCC in one match and then for the tourists in another when some of their men fell ill.

After hitchhiking 1,000 miles to Cape Town he worked for the *Cape Times*, but gave up the job to act as driver for a Swiss botanist on a four-month trip to Central Africa. He climbed 19,710ft Kilimanjaro twice in a fortnight and on his second descent he was met with a cable inviting him to try for a place on the England tour.

Fascinated by the young bowler, Fleet Street reported that he wore plus-fours in the nets because his kit was lost; there was even an erroneous suggestion that he had spent a Sunday with the film star Myrna Loy.

After the tour Crisp found a job on the *Nottingham Journal* but spent part of the next year as a member of the team raised by the millionaire Sir Julien Cahn to tour Malaya. After the inevitable falling out with Sir Julien, Crisp joined the *Daily Express*.

In 1938 he played for Worcestershire, taking 42 wickets in eight matches, and also worked as secretary to the novelist Francis Brett Young (who was working on his African novel *The City of Gold*), before returning to South Africa for an England tour. Crisp was not picked for the host team, and he had to compensate himself with filing for the *Daily Mail* and the *Natal Mercury*.

But he was caught out when he persuaded an *Express*

colleague to file to the *Mercury* for him. The following day the report with his byline appeared in the same edition as a picture of him at a dance 300 miles away.

On the outbreak of the Second World War in 1939, Crisp worked his passage to England on a tramp steamer, and joined the Westminster Dragoons before being transferred to the 3rd Battalion, Royal Tank Regiment. This was despatched to North Africa, but on the way its troopship stopped briefly at Durban, and Crisp failed to return from a party on time. He had to be taken out to his ship by a cruiser, and was temporarily reduced from captain to second lieutenant.

When the regiment was transferred to Greece, Crisp proved himself as good a soldier in the front line as he was a liability out of it. With three A-10 tanks under his command nicknamed "Cool", "Calm" and "Collected" he played a conspicuous role in the retreat from the Monastir Gap to the sea, being the last of 60 commanders to abandon his vehicle.

After extricating themselves, 3 RTR returned to North Africa where at first he amused himself eyeing the local bathing beauties at the Heliopolis Club and then drinking John Collins's cocktails and bowling out the England captain Wally Hammond in a match at the Gezira Sporting Club.

3 RTR switched to American "Honey" tanks, but these were markedly inferior to the Mark III Panzers confronting them. So Crisp devised a system by which his tank halted its zigzagging path to fire accurately at a target before driving off within four seconds. In a 28-day period of action, he had six tanks knocked out from under him and was awarded an immediate DSO in the field for leading an attack on 10 Panzers.

But Crisp had a reputation for ignoring orders. He was given a severe reprimand for risking his own vehicle in order to rescue the crew of another, though another RTR officer, Colonel "Pip" Gardner, was awarded a VC for an almost identical action outside Tobruk at the same time.

Back in Cairo, Crisp was court martialled for selling a German staff car he had captured, but he was acquitted because he said that the proceeds were to go to mess funds. On his return to the front, a brother officer had to intervene to prevent him shooting his driver with a pistol for refusing to drive on.

When Crisp was recommended for a Bar to his DSO for supervising his troop on foot while under heavy fire at Mitariyat Ridge, Montgomery personally reduced the recommendation to an MC.

Crisp was mentioned in despatches four times and finally invalided out after being wounded in Normandy. "Has your bowling been affected?" King George VI asked when Crisp went to receive his MC at Buckingham Palace. "No, Sire," came Crisp's reply. "I was hit in the head."

Nevertheless Crisp's playing days were over. He covered the Victory Tests against Australia for the *Daily Express* and became a sports columnist for the *Sunday Express*. But he walked out after a story of his about corruption in greyhound racing was "spiked".

He and his wife, the former Barbara Davies, returned to South Africa, where they had two sons. Crisp founded *Drum*, the pioneering black magazine, but his backer disliked his romantic view of tribal life, and they parted company.

Crisp was unable to find a job in Fleet Stret on his

return to England so he ran a mink farm in Suffolk then was offered a leader-writer's job on the *East Anglian Daily Times*. Obliged to turn out two leading articles six days a week, he was given *carte blanche* apart from being told to stop attacking farmers so vigorously because he was costing the paper five readers a week.

While at Ipswich Crisp wrote two excellent books: *Brazen Chariots* (1957), a vivid account of his desert war which the Israeli Army used as a manual; and *The Gods were Neutral* (1960), about the Greek campaign. An account of the founding of Johannesburg, *The Outlanders* (1964), was less successful.

But he had never spent so long in one place before. The day his second son found a job, he left a note explaining that he had a call he could not refuse.

With only a £10 disability pension, he settled in a Greek hut without water or electricity. But when he was told that he had cancer he cured himself by walking around Crete with a donkey, recounting his experiences in the *Sunday Express* under the pseudonym Peter White.

In later years, Crisp mellowed to become a mainstay of the British community at Stopa, the Peloponnesian birthplace of Zorba the Greek. He died in England at the house of a son. A copy of *Sporting Life* was on his knee, and he had just lost a £20 bet.

March 25 1994

JIMMY O'BRIEN

JIMMY O'BRIEN, who has died in the South of France aged 74, was the proprietor of the legendary Eve night club, which opened in an alley off Regent Street in 1953 and ran for 39 years.

In its Cold War heyday the Eve was the most discreetly *risqué* establishment in London. It counted among its habitués Earl Jellicoe, Errol Flynn and Judy Garland. In a setting of velvet opulence, maharajahs, shipping magnates, spies and politicians drank vintage champagne with scantily clad showgirls, who performed erotic floorshows.

Watched by MI5 and KGB agents, sitting at their favourite tables with their backs to the wall, the hostesses would chat up the Eastern-bloc spies and diplomats who frequented the club, gleaning information which they would then pass on, sometimes unwittingly. This arrangement was initiated by O'Brien's Romanian wife Helen (née Elena Constaninescu), who ran the club with him. Approached by the Romanian secret service, she instead struck a deal with an MI5 officer.

The club was celebrated for the beauty of its girls, and the O'Briens would interview a hundred hopefuls to find one who was "just perfect". Christine Keeler failed the Eye test. "She wasn't suitable," explained Mrs O'Brien. "I felt she was an easily led girl – and I was proved right." Keeler ended up, like Mandy Rice-Davies, at Murray's Club nearby.

James Tector O'Brien was born on July 5 1920 at Clonroche, Co. Wexford, where his parents ran the local pub. As a boy he entertained visions of entering the priesthood. Finances were strained, though, and at 18 he moved to London with a £1 note in his pocket and found a job with Joe Lyons.

He then became a cloakroom attendant at Murray's Cabaret Club in Beak Street, where he was promoted general manager and met Elena, who was working as a dancer and whom he hired as a cigarette girl. They were married in 1953.

O'Brien had for some time thought about running his own club. Hearing that there were premises available in a large Regent Street basement, modelled on the first-class passenger deck of a transatlantic liner, he secured a bank loan as down payment, and the Eve Club opened on St Valentine's Night 1953.

It was an immediate success. The O'Brien formula was to have stunning showgirls wearing fig-leaves and outrageous headdresses performing slow routines on the first-ever illuminated rising glass floor. In its day, it was the most daring show in the West End.

O'Brien attributed the success of the club to its policy of discretion. Regulars included the late Marquess of Milford Haven, the newspaper magnate Sir Max Aitken and the shipping tycoon Aristotle Onassis; film stars such as Jack Hawkins would swap stories with the Sultan of Jaipur or Sir Billy Butlin; several Dukes were members, and the late Bishop David Savage married an Eve Club showgirl.

The rules were clear. A man could invite a girl to sit with him or to dance, but an Eve girl must not leave the premises with a male customer. The 1962 brochure, when membership was a guinea a year and there were 100 dishes on the menu, said of its star performer: "Her attractions are stunning, her talent is extraordinary and her telephone number, sir, is none of your business".

O'Brien's club enjoyed great success until the mid-1960s, when the "permissive society" rendered its floorshows somewhat *passé*. The golden years were over, but O'Brien and his wife carried on until they were forced to admit defeat in 1981, when they changed their cabaret formula to guest acts in place of the big 30-girl extravaganzas.

During the 1970s O'Brien owned Le Connoisseur restaurant in Golders Green, which within a year of opening received a Michelin star.

O'Brien had far-ranging interests outside the club, including iconography, fine wines and skiing. It had always been his intention to retire to Ireland, which he managed to do in 1993, when he sold his London house and moved to Dublin. He also bought a house at Valbonne, having fallen in love with the town in 1954 after a month's booking at the Juan-les-Pins casino. He had hoped to write his memoirs and a book about Marian icons.

He had two daughters.

July 13 1994

ROBIN COOK

ROBIN COOK, the novelist who has died aged 63, was a devotee of the low life and wrote chiefly about the milieu in which the upper and criminal classes meet.

He did so first under his own name in the 1960s, with such satires as *The Crust on Its Uppers*, and secondly as "Derek Raymond" in the 1980s, with a series of brutally explicit detective novels.

An Old Etonian, employed at various times as a pornographer, organiser of illegal gambling, money launderer, roofer, pig-slaughterer, mini-cab driver and agricultural labourer, Cook spent much of his early career among criminals. This gave him an original perspective on his upbringing. "The act of becoming a gentleman," he wrote in *The Legacy of the Stiff Upper Lip* (1966), "is one of murder . . . You can treat everyone badly if you have treated yourself badly, if you're not *there* any more."

Cook was fiercely dismissive of the genteel style of detective fiction perfected by Agatha Christie. "Who Killed Roger Ackroyd?" he would ask. "Who fucking cares?"

He complained that the details of homicide were often ignored by the "body in the library" school. His own work demonstrated a tolerance for the sordid which surpassed that of many of his readers. A publisher to whom he submitted his most outrageously nauseating book, *I Was Dora Suarez* (1984), claimed to have vomited when he read the manuscript.

Cook claimed that *I Was Dora Suarez* "struggles after the same message as Christ. *Suarez* was my atonement for 50 years' indifference to the miserable state of this world. It was a terrible journey through my own guilt."

In later years he was inclined to exaggerate his own criminal career, but his underworld connections were real enough. "My involvement," he explained, "was largely a protest against society. But in fact I was indirectly working for the Kray brothers. You see, I've always been ready to do anything – a weak character who'll always say yes. Because it's much easier to say yes than to say no. If you say no, it means you have to spend a lot of time arguing. If you say yes, you've already bought time and you can argue about it later."

Cook was jailed only once – in Spain, for voicing anti-Fascist opinions in a bar in the late 1950s. In the 1960s, as a subordinate of the notorious conman Charles de Silva, he was interviewed on several occasions by the police.

In the summer of 1960 Robin Cook's name was on the front pages of Sunday newspapers after he was taken in for questioning after the disappearance of a Rubens, a Renoir and works by 17th-century Dutch masters. These had been in Cook's possession but, according to the author, had been stolen from his flat.

"It was a scam," he confessed 30 years later. "The insurance company was in the sights – a company of which my father was, rather conveniently, a director". The paintings were never recovered.

"I have wandered between two very different worlds," Cook once said, "and I am a contradiction in terms. This is a very useful thing for a writer, because it means you can hold as many opinions as possible, all of them opposite."

Robert William Arthur Cook was born at Marylebone, London, in 1931. His father was chairman of a City textile firm and a director of the Royal Exchange insurance company.

He was educated at Eton, which he left after three years. "An absolute hot-bed of buggery," he recalled. "*Terrible* bloody place. They were trying to make you into a good all-rounder: a future banker; a cabinet minister, a bastard. The physical suffering was bad enough, the beatings. Worse was the mental torture. I have never worn an Old Etonian tie, except when out on a scam, in which case it can be quite handy. An Eton background is a terrific help, if you are into vice at all."

Having completed his National Service, Cook went to Spain, where he was involved in smuggling tape recorders and cars. After a period in North America he returned to England, broke, in 1960.

As a result of a chance encounter in Soho he began "fronting" for property companies run by Charles de Silva

("The Colonel"). "The villains needed people like me," Cook recalled, "because we were plausible and didn't have any form."

In the days before the 1961 Gaming Act he helped to run illegal gambling tables in Chelsea, and at one stage peddled pornography in Soho. "We had to pay protection to the police," he recalled. "Prominent public figures used to come in, trying to get something for nothing. Eventually we put a sign up saying: 'The following MPs will not be served'."

Although he became gaunt, almost cadaverous, in later life, Robin Cook was thin and dandyish in his prime. A friend from those days remembered him as "really very beautiful, but always dirty – never, never clean".

In the 1960s Cook published a number of novels based on his experience of Soho and Chelsea, *The Crust on Its Uppers*, his debut, lovingly chronicled the slang and mores of the London underworld. Like its successors it attracted a cult following but earned him little money.

Cook was not bothered by the lack of income or mainstream literary kudos. "I've watched people like Kingsley Amis struggling to get on the up-escalator while I had the down-escalator all to myself," he said. "I was moving downwards because that's where I wanted to be . . . I've no time for those who use writing as a means of social advancement."

In 1966 Cook moved to Italy, where he struggled to combine a literary career with wine-making. By the time he settled in France, in 1973, his muse seemed to have deserted him, and he earned his living as a farm labourer, living in a 15th-century tower in Aveyron in the Gorge du Tarn.

"I've always thought you can never see your own

country properly unless you see it from another place," he argued. "It's like artillery, where you actually sight your gun backwards from the target you want to hit."

Cook was taken much more seriously as a writer in France than he ever was in Britain, and in 1991 he was made a Chevalier des Arts et des Lettres.

In the 1980s, still based in Aveyron, he began turning out such thrillers as *How the Dead Live* and *He Died With His Eyes Open*, which concerned the exploits of a maverick detective working for a unit called "Unexplained Deaths", who quotes liberally from *The Faerie Queen*. Cook called them his "Factory" novels (after the slang term for a police station).

He published his memoirs, *Hidden Files*, to considerable acclaim. One of his detective novels, *How the Dead Live*, was filmed by Claude Chabrol, and the rights to his "Factory" novels were bought by the BBC.

As well as his home in France, Cook maintained a flat at Willesden in London, and often revisited his old Soho haunts.

The instability of his professional life was reflected in his marital career. He married five times: Dora ("a terrible sixty-three days . . . I knew things were going wrong by day 20, when I put the shopping on the table and the table coughed"); Eugenie ("Fourteen months. A nice girl from Clerkenwell; I took a powder there"); Rose ("nine years with a year's sabbatical"); Fiona ("twelve months"); and Agnès ("French. Fourteen months").

August 1 1994

LAWRENCE DURDIN-ROBERTSON

LAWRENCE DURDIN-ROBERTSON, who has died aged 74, was a clergyman of the Church of Ireland until 1972, when he became a priest of the Egyptian goddess Isis.

He was subsequently a founder and elder of the Fellowship of Isis, which attracted some 12,000 followers devoted to reviving the worship of the "Divine Feminine".

The head of an Irish Ascendancy family, "Derry" Durdin-Robertson lived with his sister Olivia at their ancestral home, Huntington Castle, a 17th-century tower house in Co. Carlow said to be haunted by a number of ghosts.

Olivia immersed herself in psychic and spiritualist studies from an early age, and in 1966 had a revelation that God was a woman. Derry, then still a clergyman, was himself growing increasingly interested in alternative religions, and became convinced that his sister was right. The two founded a movement to worship "Isis of the 10,000 names", the representative of goddesses of all faiths.

The basement of Huntington Castle was coverted into a temple, complete with 12 shrines (one for each sign of the zodiac) and five chapels (each consecrated to a different goddess). To perform the rites of Isis, Durdin-Robertson would don blue robes, a crook and a tall blue hat of ancient Egyptian style.

Several times a year bands of followers converged on the castle to pray, meditate and perform in pagan dramas and musical processions. The movement was in no way secretive – Olivia Robertson described it as "fun and jolly" – and tourists and people from the neighbouring village were welcome to watch or participate in its rituals. The Durdin-Robertsons also held annual conventions in London, and established a College of Isis, with a Magi Degree Course taught by a priestess-hierophant.

Derry Durdin-Robertson believed he lost his psychic powers on the death of his wife in 1987, but he continued to worship Isis until his death.

He was born Lawrence Alexander Robertson in London on May 6 1920. His father, Manning Durdin Robertson, was an architect; he carried out various alterations to Huntington Castle, the seat of his mother's family, the Durdins. In 1979 Derry Robertson laid claim to the Robertson Scottish feudal barony of Strathloch.

His mother was Nora, daughter of Lieutenant-General Sir Lawrence Parsons, a cadet of the family of the Earls of Rosse; she shot big game, invented the fishing fly known as the Black Maria, and wrote a delightful book of memoirs, *Crowned Harp*.

Young Lawrence was educated at St Columba's College in the Dublin Mountains, and at Trinity College Dublin. He served in the Irish Army in 1940, and then worked at the Admiralty Research Laboratory for five years.

In 1948 he was ordained in the Church of Ireland, serving as assistant curate of the Maryborough Union until 1951, and for the next year as rector of Aghold and Mullinacuff.

After a spell in England, as rector of East Bilney with Bettley in Norfolk from 1952 to 1957, he returned to

Huntington Castle, and carried on his duties as a clergy-man of the Church of Ireland.

After leaving the Church of Ireland he relinquished the style of Reverend. In 1972 he assumed the additional surname of Durdin by deed poll.

He was the author of *The Cult of the Goddess*, *The Goddesses of Chaldaea, Syria and Egypt* and *The Goddesses of India, Tibet, China and Japan*.

Durdin-Robertson was an imposing figure, rather gaunt, quiet and pensive.

He married, in 1949, Pamela, the cheerful extrovert daughter of Major Maurice Barclay, of Brent Pelham Hall, Hertfordshire, a celebrated Master of Foxhounds. She died in 1987. They had a son and three daughters.

August 8 1994

FRANCO MOSCHINO

FRANCO MOSCHINO, who has died in Italy aged 44, was the *enfant terrible* of the fashion world.

Moschino loved jokes, English puns and *trompe l'œil* effects, and the clothes he designed invariably brought a smile to the habitually scowling faces of catwalk audiences. Slogans such as "WAIST OF MONEY" were woven into his couture pieces. Buttons spelt out "FASHION VICTIM" or "BORN TO SHOP".

Glamorous bustiers were revealed, on closer inspection, to have pretty little teacups embroidered on the breasts. Jackets had absurd, albeit accurate, price-tags emblazoned on the back. Moschino made hats from teddybears, skirts from ties, belts from tape measures and a ball-gown from dustbin bags. (The gown's message he explained, was that "fashion is trash".)

His shows were predictably surprising. On one celebrated occasion, in Milan in 1988, he shooed the models off the catwalk and showed instead a video full of statements such as "Fashion is full of *chic*" (uttered in a strong Italian accent).

Moschino teased the label-conscious with endless spoofs of the Chanel suit – trimming it, for example, with colourful plastic ruffles. Although he claimed that he could never cut a pattern, his clothes were always beautifully made, and his tailoring revealed him as a master of the classic as well as the ridiculous. The more he mocked, the more successful he became.

Beginning with a small collection under his own name in 1983, he built up a company worth millions. By 1991 Moschino was designing 29 collections each season, under the umbrella of his Milan-based parent company Moonshadow. Besides his couture range he turned out the Cheap & Chic line, Moschino Jeans, hosiery, shoes, handbags and so on.

He had a great talent for publicity, emblazoning his mainly black accessories with his name in gold capitals. He knew that post-modern fashion was largely a question of communication, and his "victims" from Tokyo to Stockholm happily acquiesced in carrying his name across their bodies.

After Italy, his clothes sold best in Britain. Moschino was full of praise for his British customers, whom he called much more discerning and fun-loving than their counterparts in France and America. He was himself a frequent visitor to London, where he had his suits made in Savile Row and his shoes at Lobb. He was also fond of marmalade, which he took back to Milan by the suitcase, and Lloyd Webber musicals: he had been to *Evita* 10 times, and to *The Phantom of the Opera* 12 times.

The son of a foundry proprietor, Franco Moschino was born on February 27 1950 at Abbiategrasso, a small town near Milan. From the age of 14 he was made to work at the foundry in the holidays, an experience he remembered with a shudder: "Dante *thought* his inferno; I *lived* mine."

Young Franco took refuge in the steel-cooling room, where he would inscribe the dust-blackened walls with huge frescoes of human bodies. At 18 he ran away from home and found work as a model and waiter, while enrolling for night classes at the Academia delle Belle Arti at Brera.

He was employed as an illustrator by advertising agencies, theatres and magazines, before some of his sketches of the Milan collections caught the eye of the designer Gianni Versace, who invited him to work on a publicity campaign.

Versace persuaded the young artist that he had an eye for fashion, and in 1977 Moschino became a designer for the Italian label Cadette.

He remained at Cadette's until 1982, when he left to launch his own line. Cheap & Chic was introduced six years later, with a show which opened with a few characteristic stanzas on the state of the art: "As we told you once before, fashion shows are now a bore."

In recent years Moschino poked particular fun at the notorious importance attached by the Milanese to their food. Gold knives, forks and spoons decorated a little black jacket and matching bustier dress.

A retrospective of his work, *Ten Years of Chaos*, was

shown last year in Milan. One exhibit was a vampire's face covered by the slogan "STOP THE FASHION SYSTEM".

Like most clowns, Moschino had a deeply serious side. He loved fashion but wanted it to show greater social conscience. An ecologist and pacifist, he made some dresses according to natural methods. He used advertisements to subvert the form – "Beware!" read one. "Advertising can seriously damage your brain and wallet."

At the time of his death he was collaborating on a project called "Smile", dedicated to a holiday home for children with Aids. He died of cancer.

September 21 1994

JAMES FRERE

JAMES FRERE, who has died aged 74, was a picaresque and eccentric character on the fringes of the old Establishment.

As Bluemantle Pursuivant of Arms and Chester Herald, he played an important ceremonial role in many great State occasions, and at the Coronation in 1953 was stationed closer to the throne than all but the Great Officers of State. He later claimed that he had stocked a nearby oak chest with cold duck, Perigord pie and black cherries in port wine, but could not gain access to them during the long ceremony.

At the Opening of Parliament the previous autumn the young herald had caught the eye of Cecil Beaton, who wrote in his diary: "The procession of the Heralds, in complete silence, brought vivid touches of scarlet, blue and gold. There was something quite haunting about one, a young man whose name I discovered to be Frere. His hair was sand-coloured, his complexion colourless, his eyes tired. With his pale, lovelorn face he seemed to be burnt out by some romantic passion. Nothing was left to him but to materialise – as he did – a perfect work of art, in his quartered tunic and sombre stockings, as he held the two Sceptres in pale ivory hands."

Frere's medieval looks, love of dressing up and taste for ceremony were underlined by a somewhat contemptuous attitude. As Earl Marshal's press secretary during Coronation Year he frustrated reporters with his standard reply, "I really couldn't say"; and his haughty attitude to colleagues at the College of Arms and irresponsibility over money led to his resignation as Chester Herald in 1960.

He then turned to authorship. His first book, *The British Monarchy at Home* (1963) contained an unflattering portrait of the Queen and was attacked by *The Daily Telegraph* for its misuse of English.

It was followed the next year by *Now, the Duchesses*, written with the Duchess of Bedford, which described the lives of various ducal consorts. A third book, *Margaret Argyll and the Whigham Family*, was never written, though this title appeared against Frere's name in *Burke's Landed Gentry*.

James Arnold Frere was born on April 20 1920, the elder son of John Geoffrey Frere of Southern Rhodesia, scion of an East Anglian family. He was educated at Eton and Trinity College, Cambridge, and served as a lieutenant in the Intelligence Corps during the Second World War.

In 1948 Frere's extensive knowledge of heraldry led to his appointment as Bluemantle, and he was promoted Chester Herald in 1956.

Two years later he had the first of several brushes with the law when he was fined £5 for walking across a zebra crossing at Boston, Lincs, against the express orders of the police constable on duty. Asked for his age and occupation the Chester Herald responded: "I'll see you damned first."

Frere's love of grandeur found expression in his occupation – albeit short-lived – of various large country houses. In 1956 he acquired the 14th-century Assington Hall in Suffolk (along with the lordships of the manor of Assington, Shimplingfold, Levenya Stratton and Searles). His attempts to revive a feudal manorial court at the Hall – with himself in a purely ceremonial role – were thwarted when the house burned down the next year.

After his departure from the College of Arms in 1960 Frere moved briefly to the Villa Frere in Malta, palatial home of his great-great-great-uncle John Hookham Frere, a diplomatist.

Back in England a few months later he began a remarkable ramble through the English shires, living beyond his means in a series of unheated and unfurnished castles and stately ruins. In 1962 Frere's heraldic banner – featuring two lions' heads – fluttered briefly over Dacre Castle in Cumberland, which he had leased from the Hasells of Dalmain. Major "Teddy" Hasell later pronounced his tenant to be "a man of straw".

Frere moved on to Mynde Park in Herefordshire, an enormous rambling house belonging to the Twiston-Davies family. In 1964 Frere resurfaced at Orleigh Court, Buckland Brewer, Devon, which was described in Sir Nikolaus Pevsner's *Buildings of Britain* as "in a bad state of repair and recently rather slummified".

A few years later he moved to Doddington Hall, Somerset, a house described by Pevsner as "a ruin", and in

1975 he was found at Stogursey Castle in the same county, a stately pile said to have been destroyed in the Middle Ages.

Frere caused considerable interest among his rural neighbours, walking the country lanes dressed in belted tweeds and occasionally casting an approving glance at the flag flying over his current country seat.

His love of ceremony also drew him into the Roman Catholic Church, and he was appointed a Knight of Malta in 1959.

Eight years later, he left the church and resigned his knighthood, but other more obscure titles and positions were soon acquired.

Frere's bulging and ever-changing entry in *Who's Who* pronounced him to be, among other things, a Liveryman of the Worshipful Company of Scriveners, Marchese de le Unión, a Knight Grand Cross of the Supreme Military Order of the Temple of Jerusalem and a Knight Grand Cross of the Military Order of the Collar of St Agatha of Paterno.

In later years Frere lived more happily in a cottage at Llanymynoch, Powys.

He was unmarried.

December 8 1994

FANNY CRADOCK

FANNY CRADOCK, the irascible *grande dame* of the kitchen who has died aged 85, rejoiced in her singular combination of *haute couture* and *haute cuisine*.

In her various television series in the 1950s and 1960s

Mrs Cradock eschewed aprons and appeared in Hartnell ballgowns while roaring gravel-throated orders – "more *wine*, Johnnie! More *butter*! Don't *stint*" – at her forbearing companion, a kindly looking cove sporting a monocle.

She also wrote children's fiction and romantic novels, and was a prolific journalist – principally for *The Daily Telegraph*. With the late Johnnie Cradock (her third husband) she wrote articles about restaurants, food and wine under the pseudonym "Bon Viveur".

It was easy to make fun of Fanny Cradock and the much-put-upon Johnnie – she was, for instance, guyed as "Fanny Haddock", the husky-voiced harridan in the wireless comedy shows *Beyond Our Ken* and *Round the Horne* – but she did much to awaken British regard for cooking after the war and to improve the standards of commercial catering.

Her aim was to make good cookery easy and fun for the postwar generation of housewives, who had grown up during the years of food shortages. But she was dedicated to classical cookery, and refused to cut corners.

She was particularly proud of the fact that in 1956, before an audience of 6,500 *Daily Telegraph* readers in the Royal Albert Hall, Queen Elizabeth the Queen Mother said that she believed the Cradocks had been largely responsible for the improvement in British catering.

The Cook's Book and *The Sociable Cook's Book*, which the Cradocks wrote for the *Telegraph* at the request of readers, were both extremely popular.

Yet latterly Mrs Cradock became as celebrated for her bad temper as for her cooking. "I have always been extremely rude," she boasted, "and I have always got exactly what I wanted."

Her broadcasting career finally came to an end in

1987 when she was sacked by the BBC for attacking the mild-mannered presenter Pamela Armstrong in front of a studio audience. "Nobody, but *nobody* goes on my set!" she shouted at the bemused Miss Armstrong. "I've never seen such a *bloody shambles* in all my life!"

The BBC discontinued her spot on the show. "It's obvious she's not feeling too well," a spokesman said, "we think it better if she doesn't appear."

She was born Phyllis Pechey in the Channel Islands on February 26 1909. Her father, Archibald Pechey (alias Valentine or Mark Cross), was a butterfly collector and a writer of novels, pantomimes and plays; his greatest success in the theatre was the Aldwych farce *Tons of Money* (1922). Fanny's mother, Bijou, was an actress and a singer.

At the age of one, the infant Fanny was given to her grandmother ("the Belle of Leicester") as "a birthday present", and remained with her until she was 10. She later claimed to have learnt almost everything about food and wine from grandmother.

"All the food was pink," she recalled of one of their elegant *soirées*, "pink mousse on pink glass plates chilled in pink ice into which pink moss rosebuds had been frozen."

Away from the table, young Fanny spent her early childhood dress-making and communing with the dead: "I was on intimate terms with the court of Louis XIV," she recalled.

She was sent to board at the Downs, which she described as "the hell pit", "prison" and "that awful hole". At 15 she was expelled for encouraging other girls to contact "the spirit world".

Although her parents wanted to send her to a finishing

school Fanny was determined to stay with her grand-mother. She earned her keep by cooking dinner each evening: "They insisted I was in evening dress and in my place by the time the fish was served," she claimed. "To save time I wore my Schiaparelli beaded frock and slave bangles in the kitchen – that's how I learned to cook in ballgowns."

At 17 she eloped with her first husband to Brighton, but he died a few months later in an accident, leaving Fanny a pregnant widow. After her father went bankrupt in 1928 she was reduced to earning a living by washing up at a Roman Catholic canteen.

She pawned some clothes in order to place an advert-isement for a dressmaking service in a local newsagent's window. Another source of income was demonstrating a Swiss roll mix, and selling vacuum cleaners door-to-door.

She made a second marriage, though it is not mentioned in her highly unreliable memoirs, *Something's Burning*.

In 1939 she met Johnnie Cradock, an amiable Old Harrovian, and began an association which lasted until his death in 1987; they did not marry until 1977.

Initially they lived in a house which was celebrated for both its ghosts and its hospitality. "Our cooking used to amaze our friends," Fanny Cradock recalled. "They thought we had black market supplies from Fortnum's."

Locally available food would be ingeniously disguised: "Bracken shoots were asparagus and I used liquid paraffin for my pastry. We caught and cooked sparrows from the garden and often ate baked hedgehogs (rather like frog's legs)."

While Johnnie Cradock served in the Army during the Second World War, Fanny spent her time writing novels. She had some success with such bodice-rippers as *The Lormes of Castle Rising* and *Storm Over Castle Rising*, under the name Frances Dale.

After the war she turned to cookery writing, publishing *The Practical Cook* (1949) and *The Ambitious Cook* (1950).

Fanny Cradock also wrote a "Hair and Beauty" column for *The Daily Telegraph* (as Elsa Frances); a cookery column for the *Daily Mail* (as Frances Dale); a series of articles on the lost city of Atlantis (as Philip Essex); and two more columns for *The Daily Telegraph* (as Nan Sortain and Bon Viveur).

Mrs Cradock liked to savour the memory of numerous "run-ins" with hoteliers, restaurateurs and members of the public. She recalled one *contretemps* with some youths outside a hotel who refused to move their car: "I went in kicking low. I can still remember how exhilarating was the slosh of handbag on fleshy nose." The youths fled.

In 1954 the Cradocks toured Britain lecturing on cookery for the Brains Trust. Two years later they gave the first live televised cookery demonstration.

Before the show Mrs Cradock was so nervous that she had to leave the set, run to the nearest church and pray for 20 minutes before she could face the cameras. Johnnie Cradock's encouragement was more prosaic. He froze and was pushed on to the set by a technician who whispered: "Get a move on, you silly sod, you're on."

Fanny Cradock went to enormous lengths in the service of television. She dieted rigorously and even had plastic surgery on her nose when technicians told her it was "too big" and was "casting shadows over the food".

As the years advanced she became increasingly

eccentric and temperamental. In 1964 she was charged with careless driving, and fined £5; the arresting officer described her as "abusive and excited".

When he asked her to move her Rolls-Royce (parked across the stream of traffic) she called him a "uniformed delinquent" and told him to wait while she finished her conversation. When he insisted she move her car, she reversed into the car behind.

"You told me to back up," she said in court. "I was just doing as I was told."

In 1968 the Cradocks published a plan to produce a "second Fanny and Johnnie". The couple searched for two teenagers: "We want to groom them so that in the future they can continue to educate people towards decent standards of *cuisine*," announced Mrs Cradock.

Later that year a film crew visited *chez* Cradock, where they found that one cupboard contained 60 wholesale-sized packets of cornflakes, and another was packed with cases of sardines.

Mrs Cradock claimed that the cornflakes were eaten entirely by her "houseboy" – "sometimes as many as three packets at a time."

She ate the sardines herself. Her speciality was a dish called "Dog's Dinner": mashed sardines and boiled egg, squashed on to brown bread.

By the 1970s her memory for detail – always somewhat variable – seemed to be failing. When, in 1977, she finally married Johnnie Cradock at a register office there was confusion over both her age and her name.

Mrs Cradock claimed she was 55, even though her elder son was then 50 and her second son 48. She thought her family name was de Peche rather than Pechey, and, when pressed, claimed it was Valentine.

In 1983 Mrs Cradock was again prosecuted for dangerous driving. She had swerved across her lane (perhaps following her grandmother's advice to chauffeurs to "stick to the middle of the road") and caused a collision. When the other driver tried to talk to her she shouted, "How dare you hit my car!" and drove off.

The other driver followed her for 15 miles, "honking and signalling". He finally overtook her and stood in front of the car, waving her down. Mrs Cradock proceeded to run him over. In court she told the judge that the other driver's "threatening behaviour" had made her afraid to stop.

Country neighbours of the Cradocks used to complain of Mrs Cradock's erratic behaviour, especially of her distressing tendency "to lash out with her walking stick at those who got in her way".

In 1987 Mrs Cradock went missing for seven days during a court case involving jewellery stolen from her home. She eventually appeared, claiming that the police search had not been very thorough: "I was at home all the time."

The Cradocks received numerous gastronomic awards, including the *Grand Mousquetaire d'Armagnac*, and were appointed *Chevalier et Grande Dame de la Tripiere d'Or*.

December 29 1994

LORD KAGAN

THE LORD KAGAN, who has died aged 79, arrived in Britain as a refugee in 1946 and went on to become a multi-millionaire, an acolyte of Harold Wilson, a life peer, and an inmate of Rudgate open prison.

Kagan made his fortune with Gannex cloth, in which air was sealed between nylon and wool linings to create a lightweight, waterproof and warm fabric for jackets and coats.

Kagan partly owed his business success to Wilson, who first wore a Gannex raincoat on a visit to Russia in 1956, the year the fabric was patented. By the time Wilson became Prime Minister, in 1964, his Gannex mac was as much a part of his persona as the celebrated pipe. Other world leaders, including Chairman Mao, soon took up the style.

Kagan's greatest promotional coup was to persuade the Duke of Edinburgh's valet to order a Gannex coat from Harrods, which immediately placed a large order. The police and armed forces followed suit. Gannex coats were even tailored as winter wear for the royal corgis.

A short, plump man with a slight limp, "Joe" Kagan had an uncanny ability to charm his way into the highest circles. To capitalise on Wilson's patronage he became a major contributor to Labour Party funds, and helped to finance Wilson's private office. The friendship with Wilson – and his *entrée* to the Downing Street kitchen cabinet – stemmed in part from the Prime Minister's admiration for Jewish immigrants who had triumphed over misfortune.

At times Kagan seemed a sinister figure, and this impression was reinforced by his friendship with Richard Vaigauskas, who was expelled for espionage in 1971. Vaigauskas was said to have been the head of the Soviet spy network in Britain, and went on to command the KGB in Moscow.

Kagan claimed that the association sprang from a

mutual love of chess, and Wilson denied that Kagan ever had access to official secrets. But the security services were naturally alarmed at the possibility of a Soviet contact in the Downing Street entourage. Kagan was created a life peer in the Wilson resignation honours list of 1976.

When sales of Gannex began to dwindle Kagan tried to carve a niche in the growing market for denim. But his business acumen inclined to short cuts rather than steady endeavour, and in 1978 he was charged with the theft of indigo dye and with defrauding the public revenue.

After two years on the run Kagan was tried and convicted in 1980.

He claimed at the trial that the stolen funds were intended to help Jewish refugees from the Soviet Union. But he never revealed the contents of the Swiss bank accounts where the money was held, and most was never recovered. Subsequent investigations suggested that the ill-gotten fortune may have amounted to as much as £750,000.

A textile manufacturer's son, Joseph Kagan was born in Lithuania on June 6 1915. In 1933 his father sent him to Leeds University to study textiles. He took a degree in Commerce.

The Second World War broke out when Kagan was visiting Lithuania, and his father's factory was taken over by the Russians under the Nazi–Soviet pact. The textile mill was "liberated from bourgeois control" and the former family chauffeur was put in charge. After three months, however, the ever-plausible Kagan persuaded the local commissar that he would run the business better.

When the Nazis invaded in 1941 Kagan was interned in the Jewish ghetto at Vilijampole, where in 1943 he married Margaret Stromas. Kagan managed to escape with his wife and mother, and they hid in a factory until the Nazis retreated in 1944.

At the end of the war Kagan travelled to Bucharest and persuaded the British mission to allow him in to England. Kagan later claimed to have been penniless on his arrival; in fact his father had transferred part of the family business to Elland, Yorkshire. Kagan took a job there as a salesman.

He then tried his hand in the motor trade and set up a blanket-weaving firm. None of his projects was particularly successful, until Gannex.

So intimate was Kagan's involvement with the Wilson entourage that he often acted as intermediary in the complex private life of Wilson's confidante and political secretary, Mrs Marcia Williams. In 1967 he helped her to buy a flat close to Downing Street, paying the deposit and personally guaranteeing the mortgage.

Kagan's own domestic arrangements were far from straightforward; he claimed to have had 40 mistresses by the age of 60. "My wife is not interested in fidelity," he explained. "But no one has ever taken her place in my life. Marriage is for keeps."

His longest affair was a five-year relationship with the journalist Judy Innes, then fashion editor of the *Daily Mail*, whom he met at a Downing Street party; they had a son.

When Kagan's business affairs came under suspicion he fled the country and abandoned his wife and elder son, both directors of his company, to the prospect of prison (they were later exculpated by his admissions at the trial).

He took with him into exile his 22-year-old secretary. He first sought asylum in Israel, pleading for citizenship as a victim of Nazi persecution and insinuating that he had been the victim of "silken-gloved" anti-Semitism in Britain. The Israeli authorities refused his request.

He then went to Spain, which had no extradition treaty with Britain. But on a trip to Paris he was "shopped" by a disaffected mistress.

Back in Britain he insisted that customs inspectors interview him in the ante-room of the House of Lords. "My full title is Baron Kagan of Elland," he announced. "You may call me Lord Kagan for short."

He served 202 days of a 10-month sentence, which he described as a "fascinating experience" he was glad not to have missed.

Although Kagan was stripped of the knighthood conferred on him in 1970, annulling his life peerage proved too complicated. On his release from jail in 1980 he immediately returned to the House of Lords.

"I certainly do not feel discredited or disgraced," he declared. But – to use a term Wilson had coined in another context – Kagan was a "parliamentary leper".

Kagan and his wife had two sons and a daughter.

January 19 1995

SIR NICHOLAS FAIRBAIRN

SIR NICHOLAS FAIRBAIRN, the Conservative MP for Perth and Kinross who has died aged 61, brought a dash of roguish colour to the House of Commons.

Many found him too much of a good thing, but behind the frivolous façade, the rather petulant expression and the ridiculous clothes (Fairbairn prided himself on designing and making his own outfits, usually in tartan), there was a serious lawyer and a courageous politician.

Fairbairn made his name as a defence counsel at the Scottish Bar, where his most dramatic case was as defence counsel to Patrick Meehan, charged with murder. He pursued the case long after losing it, and seven years later his judgment and tenacity were vindicated when the conviction was quashed and Meehan was granted a Royal Pardon.

There was a measure of outrage among the Scottish legal establishment when the maverick Fairbairn was appointed Solicitor-General for Scotland in 1979; and no little gloating when he was dismissed by Margaret Thatcher in 1982 after a Commons row over his decision not to prosecute in an alleged rape case. Fairbairn, who subscribed to the theory that women often say "no" to sex when they mean "yes", once called women who made rape allegations "tauntresses".

Sex and alcohol played a large part in "Nicky" Fairbairn's life, the influence of the latter often provoking ribaldry from the Opposition benches and embarrassment on his own. He once riveted the House with an account of how Mrs Thatcher had rebuffed the amorous advances of a well-known Scottish drunk (thought by some to be himself) with the cutting observation: "You are not up to it!"

Fairbairn's own erotic career included an incident when one of his girlfriends, Pamela Milne, was reported to have tried to hang herself from a lamppost outside his London house after discovering he was to marry another woman (whose husband had cited Fairbairn as co-respondent).

The anguished Miss Milne later claimed that Fairbairn

had begged her to be "the Mistress of Fordell" (his castle in Scotland), and given her an engagement ring. "Sometimes he would ring saying how much he loved me," she recalled. "Other times he would shout demanding his ring back, because he was broke."

Fairbairn's own account of his relationships tended to be more romantic. He recalled that his attraction to women had begun at the age of eight when he became infatuated with his prep-school matron. "Any relationship I have with a woman is essentially sensuous and romantic rather than lustful," he explained. "I go to great lengths to please. I design clothes for the woman I am in love with, write poems and paint pictures for her, send flowers and adorn her with jewels."

Fairbairn thought harems and polygamy preferable to monogamy and fidelity, and deprecated what he saw as a lack of style in women MPs (excepting the Speaker, Miss Betty Boothroyd). "They lack fragrance on the whole," he said. "They're definitely not desert island material ... They all look as though they are from the 5th Kiev Stalinist machine-gun-parade."

He was once admonished by the BBC for choosing as his luxury on the radio programme *Desert Island Discs* a photograph of Mrs Khrushchev, whose ugliness he thought would prevent him from fantasising about sex.

The lamppost episode occurred while Fairbairn was in the Government and led to speculation that he might have to resign. Mrs Thatcher and Willie Whitelaw interviewed him and, according to Fairbairn, proved understanding and sympathetic. But when the storm broke over the alleged rape case he was peremptorily sacked.

During the campaign for the 1992 general election

Fairbairn embarrassed his party by warning of the dangers of uncontrolled immigration: "Under Labour," he said, "the country would be swamped with immigrants of every colour and race." Other Tories were quick to distance themselves from this outburst, over which Fairbairn was typically unrepentant.

The furore did not seem to damage him in the eyes of his constituency, which returned him with an increased majority, but in April 1994 Fairbairn announced that he would not stand at the next election. "My sole reason for entering politics was to destroy socialism," he said. "I never thought I'd see it in my day, but all over the world the dragon seems to be dead and my motivation is gone."

Nicholas Hardwick Fairbairn was born in Edinburgh on Christmas Eve 1933, the son of a distinguished psychiatrist who was convinced of the necessity of frequent involuntary releases of tension through sneezing and orgasm. As an adult Fairbairn would claim to have been permanently scarred by his parents' incessant quarrelling.

Educated at Loretto and Edinburgh University, he was called to the Scottish Bar in 1957; he took Silk 15 years later.

With not wholly unwarranted bombast – for he really was a man of parts – Fairbairn described his occupations as "author, forester, painter, poet, TV and radio broadcaster, journalist, dress designer, landscape gardener, *bon viveur*, raconteur and wit".

He made his entry into politics as the Conservative candidate for Central Edinburgh at the 1964 general election; he again fought that seat with no success in 1966. But in 1974 he succeeded Sir Alec Douglas-Home at Kinross and Perthshire West (later renamed Perth and Kinross).

For all his exhibitionist posturing, Fairbairn was an effective champion of the arts. As a council member of the Edinburgh Festival, chairman of the Traverse Theatre and of the Scottish Society for the Defence of Literature and the Arts, he proved a doughty opponent of the city fathers. He was also an effective chairman of Scottish Heritage.

In the 1960s and early 1970s he was director of Ledlanet Nights, an enjoyable if somewhat chaotic attempt to create a sort of Scots Glyndebourne at the Kinross-shire pile of his quondam political opponent, the publisher John Calder.

Another of Fairbairn's favourite, if unlikely, causes was birth control: he was a member of the council of World Population Crisis and chairman of the Edinburgh Brook Advisory Centre.

He was knighted in 1988. After 1960 (when he purchased Fordell, a ruined Fifeshire castle, for £100) he had adopted the feudal style of "Baron of Fordell", and it gave him great pleasure to be addressed as such. He did much of the restoration work on the castle himself.

His memoirs (*A Life is Too Short*) were notable chiefly for their bizarre and recondite vocabulary. Each year, in an effort to amuse, Fairbairn would list different recreations in *Who's Who*. His most celebrated entry read: "making love, ends meet and people laugh". The latest – "languishing and sandwiching" – suggests a sad falling off.

He married first, in 1962, Elizabeth Mackay, elder daughter of the 13th Lord Reay; they had four daughters (one of whom died in infancy) and a son (who also died in infancy). The marriage was dissolved in 1979 and in 1983 he married Suzanne Mary Wheeler.

February 20 1995

BERNIE CORNFELD

BERNIE CORNFELD, who has died aged 67, was the founder of Investors Overseas Services (IOS) and precipitated one of the most spectacular financial scandals of modern times.

In the 1960s IOS grew at a breathtaking rate. Through aggressive pyramid-selling of mutual fund (unit trust) investments the company attracted more than a million investors in 95 countries, amassing some $2.4 billion of savings, much of it held in Cornfeld's notorious Fund of Funds, which provided him with cover for years of reckless mismanagement and sharp practice.

Cornfeld was ousted in 1970, after market confidence in his empire collapsed. Though his investors suffered massive losses, he was eventually acquitted of fraud charges.

On his way down no less than on his way up, Cornfeld advertised the benefits of self-enrichment by maintaining a wildly flamboyant way of life. "I deliberately went out and created an image I thought most people wanted to emulate," he explained. "I had mansions all over the world. I threw extravagant parties. And I lived with 10 or 12 girls at a time. I know the average man couldn't carry it off, living with a harem. But I could. For me it was a lot less complicated to have a lot of pretty girls around than having just one ... I wanted casual, playful relationships."

The many women who shared Cornfeld's mansion in Beverly Hills, his house in Belgravia and his chateaux in France and Switzerland included the actress Victoria Principal (later a star of *Dallas*), who was Cornfeld's "backgammon teacher".

He also claimed to have "discovered" Heidi Fleiss, the Hollywood madam, as a 19-year-old; she left him because "he was not monogamous".

Cornfeld was stocky and unprepossessing, and his success with women, as with investors, was achieved by his silken powers of persuasion. He was occasionally accused of beating his girlfriends, and his views were unreconstructedly sexist: "A beautiful woman with a brain is like a beautiful woman with a club foot."

Bernard Cornfeld was born in Istanbul on August 17 1927. His father was a Romanian actor, impresario and film producer; his mother was of Russian Jewish origins. The family migrated to America in 1931, settling first in Providence, Rhode Island, and later in Brooklyn, where young Bernie attended Abraham Lincoln High School.

After a two-year stint in the Merchant Navy, Cornfeld completed his education with a degree in psychology at Brooklyn College. There he developed Left-wing opinions and was much influenced by the theories of Alfred Adler (Freud's great rival), who believed that people are driven by "goal-seeking", often towards "superiority" in wealth and power.

Cornfeld's personal goal was already formulated: "To make a very great deal of money." His catchphrase in persuading others to part with their money – "Do you sincerely want to be rich?" – was a crude application of Adlerian analysis.

After graduation Cornfeld returned briefly to sea, and then began his financial career as a salesman for a mutual funds business. Mutual funds were then in vogue as a way of bringing investment opportunities to small savers: selling them was not incompatible with Cornfeld's professed radicalism.

He also had a short stint as a social worker for the Jewish philanthropic institution B'nai B'rith in Philadelphia – an interlude he later capitalised on shamelessly.

In 1955, with a few hundred dollars in his pocket, Cornfeld moved to Paris, where the next year he established the nucleus of IOS, attracting salesmen from among the Bohemians and misfits of the expatriate American community and finding natural customers among the relatively well-paid US military personnel.

Two years later IOS moved its headquarters to Geneva, expanded its sales force and began to tap into offshore capital attracted by the discretion of Swiss banks. IOS was initially an agent for the Dreyfus Fund, a New York investment house noted for having bought Polaroid shares at $32, which eventually rose to $6,372.

From 1960, however, Cornfeld and his colleagues began to develop their own funds, beginning with the International Investment Trust, a loosely assembled vehicle, registered in Luxembourg, which eventually attracted investments of $700 million.

Two years later they launched the Fund of Funds. This was ostensibly a mutual fund which invested only in other high-performing mutual funds, thereby offering, according to the salesmen's logic, diversity of risk combined with the possibility of the highest performance. But the greatest beneficiary was in fact IOS which, by creating its own "proprietory" funds for the Fund of Funds to invest in, could charge double slices of management commission and brokerage and conceal a multitude of imprudent speculations.

The activities of IOS expanded to include banks and insurance companies (100,000 British investors signed up for Dover Plan life insurance policies) as well as such madcap ventures as oil and gas exploration rights in the Canadian Arctic – the blatant overvaluation of which was a major factor in the collapse of the company.

Many of IOS's investments proved unmarketable, having been made chiefly for the benefit of the firm's directors and their friends. In an era when offshore investment and currency trading were strictly controlled, rules were constantly infringed.

The growth of IOS funds was driven by a pyramid-selling system, in which salesmen (of whom at the zenith there were 16,000) were lavishly rewarded with commissions and stock options, and were often themselves heavy investors in IOS schemes. Cornfeld's personal wealth was estimated to have reached $150 million.

The collapse and disgrace of his empire began with a public offering of $110 million of IOS shares in September 1969. The prospectus indicated that the cash was to go towards further development of the business. In fact a large portion of the shares sold were those which had already been issued to IOS employees under the stock option scheme. Some $30 million of the issue proceeds went straight to Cornfeld and 489 of his salesmen, many of whom became millionaires. Cornfeld's own slice of the takings was $7.8 million.

Early in 1970 rumours of mismanagement and over-valuation abounded. Profits for 1969 turned out to be substantially less than the issue prospectus had forecast. Heavy selling of stocks in which IOS was known to be an investor hastened the decline, and caused panic on the London Stock Exchange. It was revealed that most of IOS's remaining cash had been lent to directors for their personal ventures – including, in Cornfeld's case, the purchase of a BAC 1-11 airliner fitted out to rival the Playboy chief Hugh Hefner's "Black Bunny" jet.

Cornfeld was forced off the IOS board at an acrimonious meeting of shareholders. Expressing concern for investors and denying wrongdoing, he struggled unsuccessfully to regain control.

After a three-year investigation by the Geneva State Prosecutor he was arrested and spent 11 months in preventive custody before being granted bail of SFr 5 million, the highest in Swiss legal history. At the trial in 1979, however, he was acquitted of fraud in relation to the share issue, other charges of dishonest management and incitement to speculation having been dropped.

IOS had passed into the hands of the financier Robert Vesco, who was initially welcomed as a white knight. He later absconded to Puerto Rico with $225 million. Those IOS investors who could be traced eventually received a few cents in the dollar by way of refund.

Although describing himself as a "professional defendant", Cornfeld continued to dabble in film production, real estate development and other ventures, including the marketing of a range of vitamin pills claimed to be capable of doubling the average person's sex drive. His riches still ran to several million dollars, which supported him and his nubile friends in luxury on both sides of the Atlantic.

His philandering was curtailed in the early 1980s by marriage to a model, Lorraine Armbruster, by whom he had a daughter, Jessica. But after their separation he returned to his sybaritic ways.

In 1987 he was reported to be sharing his Californian house with eight women, and to have two more companions in London. Shortly before the heart attack which finally incapacitated him in 1994, he was sighted in his Rolls-Royce accompanied by his two leather-clad lesbian chauffeuses.

March 2 1995

VIVIAN STANSHALL

VIVIAN STANSHALL, who has died aged 52, was a picaresque musician, satirist and all-round eccentric.

Like Peter Cook, Stanshall was a godfather of the irreverent and surrealist comedy later popularised by Monty Python's Flying Circus. He could declaim like John Betjeman and play the ukulele like George Formby, but listed his chief influences as "Ivor Novello, Noël Coward and Little Richard".

Stanshall's heyday was the mid-1960s, when as the singer of the Bonzo Dog Doo-Dah Band he brought his anarchic humour to a wide audience, hitting the charts in 1968 with "I'm the Urban Spaceman" – perhaps the only top-ten single ever to feature a hosepipe solo.

Roger Ruskin Spear (who performed on saxophone

and with exploding sculptures) recalled the early days of the band: "The Bonzos started from the throw-outs of various jazz bands. We were all thrown out for playing too loudly and too badly, and we ended up playing together."

To begin with the Bonzos concentrated exclusively on novelty foxtrots, covering old 78s, but after going electric in 1966 they branched out into rococo parodies of more mainstream pop. The Bonzos owed much in spirit to the work of Spike Jones, but the group's unique appeal was largely the result of Stanshall's eclectic tastes and his considerable talent as a mimic. He was capable of unsettlingly accurate impersonations of Coward, Elvis Presley and Jack Buchanan, among others.

With songs such as "Cool Britannia", "Can Blue Men Sing the Whites (or Are They Hypo-crites)" and "My Pink Half of the Drainpipe" – and a truly wild stage act – the Bonzos came to the attention of Paul McCartney, who cast Stanshall in the Beatles' television film *Magical Mystery Tour* (1967).

After the Bonzos split up in 1970 Stanshall enjoyed a brief renaissance introducing the instruments on Mike Oldfield's hugely successful *Tubular Bells* ("Grand pi*a*no," he intoned, "mandol*i*n, two slightly dis*tort*ed guitars").

In the 1970s and 1980s he found himself increasingly unable to cope with the pressures of popular success. As with Spike Milligan, his zany talent masked deep depression.

The highpoint of Stanshall's later career was the cult film *Sir Henry at Rawlinson's End* (1980), which starred Trevor Howard as Stanshall's bizarre alter ego Sir Henry ("If I had all the money I've spent on drink," ran a typical line of Sir Henry's, "I'd spend it all on drink").

But Stanshall never lost the respect of his many

devoted admirers, who included James Cameron, John Cleese, Jack de Manio and Stephen Fry.

Stanshall always devoted much of his energy to practical jokes. In the 1970s he was frequently joined in these by his best friend Keith Moon, the drummer of The Who, whose wealth and recklessness allowed Stanshall to indulge his quirky sense of humour on a wider stage. Stanshall had particularly fond recollections of his "trouser testings".

Though the routine was not so formalised as to preclude improvisation, in its purest form the prank consisted of Stanshall's entering a West End tailor's and asking to see "the strongest pair of trousers in the shop". Despite the apparent implausibility of such a request, most shopkeepers were, as he remembered, "only too eager" to provide him with a garment in what they considered their most durable fabric. Stanshall would then enlist the assistance of a bystander (Moon), and together they would "test" the garment so thoroughly that it would disintegrate, leaving each of them holding a leg.

The tailor's cries of anger and surprise were, Stanshall recalled, the cue for the second accomplice – a one-legged man, hired from a theatrical agency – to come into the shop and exclaim: "Just the job! Wrap them separately!"

Vivian Stanshall was born on March 21 1942 and grew up in north London. On leaving school he spent a year in the Merchant Navy earning the money to send himself to art school. In later years he would recall heroic drinking sessions with Melanesians in the New Hebrides.

In 1962 he enrolled at the Central London School of Art, where he met Rodney Slater, "Legs" Larry Smith and Neil Innes (who would become the core group of the Bonzos). They began to perform in the evenings in such south London pubs as the Tiger's Head, Catford. Stanshall spent his free time studying for an A level in Ancient Greek at the Camden Working Men's Institute.

The band's growing popularity – particularly in the United States – led to overwork and high living. Consequently Stanshall resorted for many years to alcohol and tranquillisers.

In the 1970s he made a number of increasingly crazed solo records and developed his skills as a broadcaster, conducting exercise classes for old jokes and sometimes deploying freshly minted ones. At a chemist's shop near Broadcasting House, for instance, where he was seeking one of his innumerable prescriptions, he once heard a man in front of him say: "I'm going on holiday and I need an insect repellant." The chemist gave him a tube of something called *Wasp-ese*.

Fascinated, Stanshall approached the counter and said "As a matter of fact, I'm just off to Africa, and I'm a bit worried about being pestered by big game." He then demanded an aerosol spray called *Repel-ephant*, and a tube of *Rhin-no*!

All this was incorporated into his wireless routine the next day, which began with a mock advertisement: "Hi! Having pachyderm problems?"

Barred from the set of *Sir Henry at Rawlinson's End*, for which he had written the script, Stanshall retreated to a converted First World War Irish Navy patrol boat at Chertsey, where he remained for nearly two years, unable to work and so stricken by anxiety attacks that he could barely pluck up the courage to go out and collect his post.

After drying out at Weston-super-Mare in 1986, Stanshall recovered sufficiently to complete two new episodes of *Sir Henry* for BBC Radio. He also had an unsuccessful comic opera, *Stinkfoot*, produced at the Bloomsbury in 1988 (a project financed by Stephen Fry and Pete Townshend).

Stanshall's main source of income was from voice-overs for advertisements. In 1992 he did a total of three hours' paid work. But after he appeared on Jools Holland's New Year's television show in 1993, Bella Freud, the fashion designer, declared that 1994 would be "the year of Vivian Stanshall as spiritual leader".

It proved to be the year of Vivian Stanshall as promoter of Ruddles Ale – in a series of television commericals which he wrote and performed, and which, uniquely for an advertisement for alcohol, featured scenes of spectacular drunkenness.

Recently he divided his time between a bedsitting-room in Muswell Hill and his mother's bungalow at Leigh-on-Sea in Essex, which was not entirely to his taste: "I have to endure the floral carpet, the floral upholstery and the floral wallpaper."

Last year in a Wimpy bar in Leigh-on-Sea he was set upon by a gang of youths whom he had lectured on the inadvisability of ethnic cleansing. "A fight took place. I acquitted myself. My eyes blazed. My fists were clenched ... then out came the Stanley knives. They cut me all over, ruined a perfectly good shirt. The encounter ended when one party ran away. I will leave it to you to decide which one it was. Little did they know with whom they were tangling: Vivian Stanshall, star of a beer ad."

March 7 1995

RONNIE KRAY

RONNIE KRAY, who has died aged 61, formed with his twin brother Reggie one of the most notorious criminal partnerships of modern times.

Distinguished from their youth by a willingness to "go the limit" in a fight, the "well-known sporting twins from London's East End" – as the press euphemistically termed them – brought to the hitherto parochial British criminal scene a taste of American organised crime.

Ronnie was sentenced to life imprisonment after being convicted at the Old Bailey in March 1969 of the murders of George Cornell and Jack "The Hat" McVitie; Reggie was given the same sentence for the murder of McVitie and for being an accessary after the murder of Cornell.

The twins were criminal entrepreneurs, controlling clubs and public houses, dealing in stolen American bonds, and running swindles and blackmail rackets. Their commercial success was based on their reputation as exponents of violence. Amateur boxing champions, they eschewed the traditional razor as ineffective and, besides employing the knife, cutlass and broken bottle, developed an early affection for guns.

Obsessed with publicity, the Krays contrived an image inspired by transatlantic gangster fiction – at the height of their fame they swanned around in the company of George Raft, the star of the film *Scarface*.

Ronnie Kray was a compulsive fantasist, who loved his nickname "The Colonel" and behaved as if directing a film of his own life. At the Regal billiard hall (an early venture), he would sit on a throne, urging people to smoke until the hall resembled the haunts of the Chicago gangsters he admired.

Publicly polite, patriotic, devoted to their mother and dressed in sober suits, the Krays developed an uncanny double act replete with controlled menace; it spawned a whole genre of fiction, and gained them a cult following. They were an integral part of the "Swinging Sixties", an era in which the jaded palates of high society sought stimulation in the morally decadent company of criminals.

They mingled with such politicians as Tom Driberg and were at the heart of the sex scandal involving Lord Boothby. Ronnie, who talked grandly about "a politics of crime", particularly relished these connections.

Ronnie was sensitive about his sexual peccadilloes – "I'm not a poof; I'm an homosexual," he asserted. He seduced the East End boys he recruited as spies, and his parties were "highly sophisticated".

Reggie had orthodox business acumen; but he was in thrall to his twin, who was drawn to violence and saw killing as the ultimate proof of manhood. "We never hurt innocent people," explained this paranoid schizophrenic. "The men we killed were other villains. Jack McVitie liked to hurt people."

This romantic view of themselves was frequently echoed by others. But a more reasonable attitude was that of the judge at their trial, Sir Melford Stevenson, who said the Krays had told the truth only twice: when one twin referred to a barrister as a "fat slob", and when the other twin muttered that the judge was biased.

Ronald and Reginald Kray were born on October 17 1933, at Hoxton, in the East End; their elder brother, Charlie, was a long-standing business associate. Their father, Charlie, earned a living as a door-to-door "pesterer"; their adoring mother, Violet, came from Bethnal Green, to which the family moved.

The twins were educated until 14, at Daneford Street School, where they impressed the headmaster as the "salt of the earth". The local vicar remembered them as "extremely kind boys who would do anything for me except come to church".

During the Second World War their father evaded service and the twins became adept at lying to the police. Violet's only concerns were that they be well mannered, clean and polite.

As boxers, the twins never lost a fight until they turned professional at 16. In 1950 they were charged with a brutal assault; witnesses later retracted their statements, a common phenomenon in cases involving the Krays.

In 1952 they were called up for National Service. On entering their barracks they determined to go home to Violet, and flattened the corporal who tried to stop them.

They spent their Army years AWOL or in detention. Ronnie filled the long hours by pretending to be mad.

In 1954 the Krays set up business at The Regal. Within a few years many East End businesses were paying them protection money, and the twins were courted by the "Boss of Britain's Underworld", Jack Spot, then expecting a confrontation with his henchman Billy Hill. But he refused to start the bloody war Ronnie sought.

Ronnie had taken to drawing up lists of people he intended to kill when time permitted. In December 1956 he was sentenced to three years after nearly murdering a teenager. He was caught driving around clutching a gun. "Careful," he said to the police, "it's loaded."

He showed signs of paranoia and depression, and was

certified insane. At Winchester prison he made the first of several suicide attempts.

In 1958, Reggie organised his twin's escape. When Ronnie was recaptured he convinced doctors he was not mad, and was allowed to complete his sentence.

Reggie launched the twins' first club, the Double R, in the East End, which was popular with such home-grown talent as the actress Barbara Windsor. But Ronnie still preferred extortion or grandiose schemes, and once attempted to found a city in the Nigerian desert.

In 1960, the twins took over Esmeralda's Barn, a Mayfair gambling club. Lord Effingham joined the board and the Krays established close relations with Tom Driberg, Labour MP for Barking, and several peers.

In 1964 the *Sunday Mirror* alleged that Lord Boothby had conducted a homosexual affair with Ronnie Kray. Represented by Arnold Goodman and the future Labour Lord Chancellor, Gerald Gardiner QC, Boothby (who would appear to have committed perjury during the case) won £40,000 in libel damages.

In 1965, to Ronnie's disappointment, Reggie married Frances Shea; she committed suicide soon after.

The following March Ronnie walked into the bar of the Blind Beggar in Mile End and shot dead George Cornell, an associate of the Richardson gang, who had dismissed him as a "fat poof".

Ronnie later offered Jack "the Hat" McVitie £500 to shoot the Krays' business manager, Leslie Payne, whom he suspected of betrayal. McVitie failed to carry out the commission and was seen brandishing a shotgun and emitting vague threats against the Krays.

In October 1967 the twins lured McVitie to a flat in

Stoke Newington. Urged on by Ronnie, Reggie stabbed him, pinning him to the floor through the throat. Such was the violence of the attack that McVitie's liver fell out.

Superintendent "Nipper" Read thought that it would only be when both twins were remanded that witnesses would come forward. It was May 1968 before he had a strong enough case. When the police came Ronnie was asleep with his latest fair-haired catamite.

The twins were imprisoned together at Parkhurst; Ronnie was certified insane and sent to Broadmoor.

The Krays published the ghosted *Our Story* (1988), notable for its pathetic arrogance. The proceeds from this and the film *The Krays* (starring the Kemp twins from the pop group Spandau Ballet) was reputed to have earned them £1 million.

Ronnie produced lurid paintings, and published a selection of his poetic meditations. In 1993 he published *My Story*, in which he pondered the ethics of murder, concluding that "we just did what we had to do".

While in Broadmoor, Ronnie Kray married twice. Neither marriage was consummated.

March 18 1995

DAVID HERBERT

DAVID HERBERT, who has died aged 86, was an interior decorator, an actor manqué, an international playboy and the "Uncrowned Queen" of Tangier, where he spent the latter part of his life as doyen of the Western expatriates.

Herbert pitched camp at Djamaa el Mokra, within

striking distance of the casbah in what was then Morocco's International Zone. He lived in an exquisite villa, decorated in vivid shades of pistachio pink and mangrove green. The interior was hung with pictures by his old friends Cecil Beaton and Patrick Procktor, as well as the occasional Van Dyck, delicate porcelain and other ravishing imports from his ancestral seat of Wilton.

Paul Bowles, another Tangerine figure, praised Herbert for his stamina and his "devouring social curiosity".

Flighty, charming and mercurial, David Herbert was a classic case of the "younger son" syndrome. He readily acknowledged his lack of ambition, and richly fulfilled Edith Olivier's prediction that he would be a failure in life.

Between the wars he had been a social figure in England, memorably caricatured by Lord Berners in his public school spoof *The Girls of Radcliff Hall* (1937), in which he appeared as Daisy Montgomery: "Daisy, when about to perform some action that was particularly mischievous, invariably pretended that she was acting with the highest ends in view."

David Alexander Reginald Herbert was born on October 3 1908, the second son of Lord Herbert, who was in turn the elder son of the 15th Earl of Pembroke and 12th Earl of Montgomery. He spent his childhood in Ireland before his father inherited the earldoms and the family seat of Wilton – perhaps the most beautiful house in England.

The precocious young David's first memories were of the great house, with its magnificent Double Cube Room by Inigo Jones. It was then used as a hospital for casualties of the First World War, and he recalled flirting with the wounded officers.

At nine he was sent away to a private school at Wixenford, where he acquired an abiding mistrust of learning. He then spent four years at Eton, where his most vivid memories were of being birched by the head-master.

Herbert was as unsuccessful in the classics as he was as a "wet-bob" – he scuppered one race by being "incurably sociable" and waving to friends ashore. As a stage-struck schoolboy he often absconded to the theatres of London.

Having sabotaged his parents' attempts to have him crammed for Sandhurst, he ended up at an Army college in Farnborough. In 1926, when he was spending all his spare time in London night clubs, he was shocked by his father's bankruptcy.

Herbert decided that he had a vocation for acting. On the strength of "the glint in his eye", the romantic novelist Elinor Glyn (a family friend) contracted him for two films, *Knowing Men* and *The Prices of Things*, in which he played second lead without distinction – despite Glyn's coaching and attempts to set his receding chin into prominence.

Eventually, in 1930; he found employment as social secretary to the German banker Otto Kahn in Berlin, a short-lived job followed by stints as an English coach on various German films. It was the era of "Herr Issyvoo" and Sally Bowles. Herbert shared a flat in Berlin with Christopher Sykes, an honorary attaché at the British Embassy, and befriended Cyril Connolly, who wrote plays for the three of them to perform in Harold Nicolson's apartment.

Herbert found the "divine decadence" much to his liking. After a brief engagement to Ruth Landshoff, leader of Berlin's young smart set, he had a stint as a *kabaret* performer.

Back in London Herbert met Peter Spencer, an actor and opium addict some 20 years his senior. They set off for New York, where disaster struck when money and job offers failed to materialise.

Herbert had recourse to a remote relation for assistance, Mrs Cornelius Vanderbilt. He took up interior decorating for rich New York ladies, and threw himself into the Bohemian life of Manhattan, renewing a friendship with Tallulah Bankhead.

Friends from England arrived: Beaton (whom Herbert had met at a ball at Wilton, where the young photographer had been thrown into the river by a group of hearties); and Stephen Tennant, the fey aesthete whose insouciant ways with cosmetics shocked even New York.

Herbert's hedonistic life attracted equivocal comments from family and friends. Edith Olivier noted that he was "the happiest of creatures . . . But I see no future for him. His gift is to be young."

Having more or less disgraced himself in New York, he moved into the Park School, an 18th-century "Pavilion of Pleasure" at Wilton, which he renovated to his own taste, painting one room black. "Don't tell my mother," Herbert told Tennant, who commented: "Rather silly, really – all she had to do was to walk round the corner and look in the windows."

On a voyage with his cousin, Sir Michael Duff, Bt, Herbert discovered Tangier and immediately fell in love with the place, which Truman Capote described as giving a refuge to "all manner of humankind – *outré* or decadent, elegant or abandoned to *hashish* or sex, or both of these at once. A little on the scary side too . . ."

Herbert revelled in the El Minzah Hotel and its barman, Dean; in the mysterious Tangerine hostesses, Feridah and Jessie Green; and in the native pashas and dignitaries, with all of whom he struck up friendships.

In the spring of 1939 Herbert and Beaton rented a house in Tangier and worked together on Beaton's spoof *My Royal Past*. Later that year Herbert enlisted in the Merchant Navy – to do, as he put it, "a good job without necessarily killing anybody, and with luck, seeing no bloodshed".

He served as a wireless operator in the Indian Ocean and elsewhere. In 1942 his ship, the *Strathallan*, was sunk by enemy action and he was one of the few survivors. He romanticised his exploits considerably – talking, a friend observed, as if he were Rupert Brooke.

Herbert told Edith Olivier how the chief engineer had smuggled his two pet canaries on to a life-raft under his cap. Olivier thought that Herbert's experiences had matured him: "David has found the traditional Herbert power of leadership – without losing their equally traditional gaiety of spirit."

In 1947, blaming his "dictatorial mother" for his inability to remain in Wiltshire, Herbert decided to settle in Morocco, where he became the toast of Tangerine society. In that "oriental Cheltenham" (as Beaton called it) he was often to be found arranging flowers for one of Barbara Hutton's rooftop parties in the casbah.

A goatishly youthful figure, communicating in an excessively anglicised and affected French, he lived his later life as though the second half of the 20th century had not happened. He took as close an interest in the natives as in the more celebrated expatriates.

To the annoyance of his brother, the 16th Earl of

Pembroke, Herbert allowed himself to be described as "Lord Herbert"; from his brother's death in 1969 until the birth of his nephew's son and heir in 1978, he was heir presumptive to the Earldom of Pembroke.

Immensely hospitable, he would regale his guests with anecdotes in a style which combined cultivated heartiness and bitchiness. The guest room had a portrait by Cecil Beaton of Mick Jagger's posterior, executed in shades of green and blue.

He enjoyed his evening visits to the cafés of the souk, as well as games of patience and the novels of E. F. Benson.

Twice a year he would return to England to stay with his sister, Patricia Viscountess Hambleden – a long-serving lady-in-waiting to Queen Elizabeth the Queen Mother – but was always eager to return to his adopted home.

In 1972 Herbert published *Second Son*, an anecdotal autobiography as carelessly social as its author; a further volume, *Relations and Revelations* (written in the form of advice to a great-niece), was published in 1992.

In recent years time made inroads into his hairline, and to protect himself from the sun he wore a sadly ill-fitting wig; his withered hands grew ever more encrusted with rings.

Herbert once said of his life: "I realise that I may not have achieved much, but I have certainly had a great deal of fun . . ."

April 5 1995

BAPSY MARCHIONESS
OF WINCHESTER

BAPSY MARCHIONESS OF WINCHESTER, who has died in India aged 93, became the third wife of the 16th Marquess of Winchester in 1952, when he was in his 90th year, and spent much of the next decade engaged in public squabbles with her husband's friend Eve Fleming.

An enthusiastic self-publicist, Lady Winchester was prone to circulating documents extolling her own virtues. One described her as "a great and gracious lady . . . an unofficial ambassador for India . . . recognised for her beauty and grace . . . for her wealth and fabulous jewels". Another listed the many heads of state who had received her, including Calvin Coolidge, the King of Afghanistan, King Farouk of Egypt and Emperor Haile Selassie.

Lady Winchester ensured that even her marital disputes were widely broadcast. While she was wintering in India in 1953 her husband went to Nassau to visit Eve Fleming, the mother of Ian Fleming. Lady Winchester followed him, and stalked the pair, rather in the manner of the native lady, forever staring, in Somerset Maugham's short story *The Force of Circumstance*.

According to Ivar Bryce, a neighbour, "There was almost always an overweight Indian lady clad in a dingy sari, pacing the main road . . . occasionally pausing to raise and shake her fist towards the main house."

She wrote vitriolic letters to her husband: "May a viper's fangs be forever around your throat," she raged, "and may you stew in the pit of your own juice."

Lady Winchester claimed that Eve Fleming had made Lord Winchester a prisoner, and forced him to stay in courier rooms at hotels while she took comfortable suites. When Bapsy Winchester saw her rival press the Marquess's left thigh in 1954 she sued her for enticement. The litigation continued in various forms over the next four years, and in 1957 the case came before Mr Justice Devlin at the High Court in London.

Lady Winchester proved a temperamental witness, sometimes talking ceaselessly, at other times stubbornly mute. When in communicative mood she claimed that her husband had at first worshipped the ground she walked on, and then "murdered" her. At one point the judge became so exasperated that he threatened her with a night in prison.

Lady Winchester's counsel told the court that his client had been portrayed as "a sort of mixture of Jezebel, Sapphira and Mrs Malaprop". In fact, he said, she was "a wronged woman distraught . . . like Dido – with a willow in her hand upon the wild sea banks and wafting her love to come again to Carthage".

The court found against Mrs Fleming, but to Lady Winchester's fury the verdict was later reversed in the Appeal Court. Lord Winchester and Mrs Fleming retired to Monte Carlo, with Lady Winchester still in pursuit. He died in 1962, just short of his 100th birthday.

Bapsybanoo Pavry was born at Bahrat, India, in 1902, the daughter of Khurshedji Erachji Pavry, whom she claimed was High Priest of the Parsees in Bombay; Lord Winchester maintained that his father-in-law was merely the priest of a fire temple.

Young Bapsy was educated at Columbia University, New York, and in 1928 was presented at court to King

George V. In 1930 she published a book, *Heroines of Ancient Iran*, for which she was awarded the Iranian Order of Merit 25 years later. In 1947 she was a delegate at the Unesco Paris Peace Conference.

When she married in 1952 she circulated a document claiming that she was the first non-European ever to become a marchioness.

Her husband was by no means the most distinguished in his line. William Paulet, created Marquess of Winchester in 1551, had been Lord President of the Council under Henry VIII, and served as Lord Treasurer under Edward VI, Mary and Elizabeth. "By truth," Elizabeth said of him, "if my Lord Treasurer was a young man, I could find it in my heart to have him as a husband before any man in England." He was still in office when he died, in his late eighties, in 1572. He had built Basing House, near Basingstoke, which the 5th Marquess held for Charles I during a prolonged siege.

The younger son of the 14th Marquess, who was born in 1801, Montagu Paulet succeeded as 16th Marquess in 1899, when his elder brother was killed in the South African War. "Monty" Winchester's first two wives died in 1924 and 1949 respectively, without children.

When he died in 1962 the marquessate passed to a kinsman. From then on Lady Winchester divided her time between London and Bombay, escorted by her brother Dasturzada, Dr Jal Pavry. In London the pair lived at the Mayfair Hotel, and doggedly solicited invitations to public functions. When her brother died in 1985 Lady Winchester put out a statement that she had "received messages of sympathy from all over the world".

She was a member of the Council of World Alliance for International Peace through Religion, and in 1989 made an endowment to Oxford University, in memory of herself and her brother, for the study of international relations and human rights.

Lady Winchester wrote hundreds of letters to celebrated figures, and usually received replies from their secretaries. But her extensive archives, presented to the City of Winchester between 1974 and 1995, did include such triumphs as Christmas cards from King Olav of Norway, a reproduction portrait of herself by Augustus John, and photocopies of thank-you letters from George Bernard Shaw.

September 9 1995

BRIAN LENIHAN

BRIAN LENIHAN, who has died aged 64, held more cabinet posts in the Irish Republic than any other individual since the foundation of the state in 1922.

As Deputy Prime Minister and Minister for Defence in 1990, Lenihan was sacked after he lied about the telephone calls he had made eight years previously to the President, Dr Patrick Hillery, asking him to delay dissolving the Dail. The "Dublingate" affair was seen as symptomatic of the corruption of the ruling Fianna Fail party. It cost that party – and Lenihan – the presidential election.

At first the Prime Minister, Charles Haughey, said that it was "up to my old friend Brian" to decide whether he should resign or not. When Lenihan showed no inclination to go, Haughey sacked him. Haughey won the ensuing vote of confidence by 83 votes to 80, with

Lenihan and his sister providing the margin of victory. The machinery of Fianna Fail's politics continued to function smoothly regardless of personal differences, as it had always done.

In 1970 Lenihan (who from time to time usurped Haughey's nickname of "Houdini") offered comfort and support to the Taoiseach, Jack Lynch, during the gun-running crisis. Haughey, then Minister for Finance, and Neil Blaney, Minister for Agriculture, were dismissed and later arrested and charged with conspiracy to import arms and ammunition. In 1977 Lynch rewarded Lenihan, who had lost his rural consituency, with the safe seat of Dublin West, which he held until his death.

Haughey's rise to leadership in 1979 proved no obstacle to Lenihan, who continued to enjoy senior positions. He was made Haughey's deputy in 1983, after staunchly backing him in a sulphurous leadership struggle.

Once described by the Irish historian Joseph Lee as "an amiable virtuoso of shadow language", Lenihan had the gift of seeming both forceful and affable, without actually committing himself to any position. His rhetorical skills made him the regular front for the Fianna Fail Government in sensitive television debates, particularly those concerning Northern Ireland.

Abroad, he was less circumspect. Soon after his appointment as Minister for Foreign Affairs in 1979 he issued a communiqué in Bahrain announcing that his Government recognised the PLO as representatives of the Palestinians. His use of the phrase "Palestine state" provoked protests from Israel.

The Prime Minister, Menachem Begin, sent a forceful message via his ambassador in London. An hour-long meeting between Lenihan and the envoy, Shlomo Argov, was later described as unprecedented in diplomatic exchanges between friendly countries.

Brian Joseph Lenihan was born on November 17, 1930 at Dundalk, Co. Louth. He grew up at Athlone, Co. Westmeath, where his father ran the Hodson Bay Hotel and a local garage.

After studying law at King's Inns in Dublin, Lenihan practised as a barrister, and was elected a county councillor in Roscommon in 1955. He won a senate seat in 1957, and was elected a member of the Dail for Roscommon in 1961, losing his seat in the redrawn constituency of Roscommon–Leitrim in 1973.

The same year he was elected to the European Parliament, and was leader of the Fianna Fail delegation to Strasbourg until 1977. He was elected to the Dail in Dublin West in the landslide victory Fianna Fail enjoyed that year, after the party had pledged to abolish rates on private houses.

Lenihan, whose wavy hair resisted the slicked-back, seal-like style favoured by most Fianna Fail politicians of the 1960s, was one of the "mohair and Mercedes" generation which emerged from the shadow of Sean Lemass, Haughey's father-in-law. He was also part of a formidable political family. In 1963, he welcomed his own father into the House as the member for the two neighbouring counties of Longford and Westmeath. His sister, Mary O'Rourke, later inherited her father's seat.

Lenihan was parliamentary secretary to the Minister for Lands from 1961 to 1964. In his next appointment, as Minister for Justice, he was panicked into a policy of arrests and fines, almost at random, during the Irish Farmers' Association campaign for higher prices for their produce.

This was the first time Lenihan had raised his head above the barricades of political protocol. He was to do it again and again.

In 1968, as Minister for Education, Lenihan angered Dublin University's Trinity College, an institution dating from Elizabethan times, when he suggested that a "merger" between the college and its much younger Roman Catholic rival, University College Dublin, would be "completed within six months".

The announcement, made at the sensitive venue of the National University Graduates' Club in New York, was seen as a calculated insult to Trinity, and a gratuitous one, since the merger never took place. When Lenihan later made a speech at Trinity, he was forced to escape from an angry crowd of students by climbing through a lavatory window.

In opposition in 1983, Lenihan again drew opprobrium with his handling of a telephone bugging affair. He suggested that the Garda had been involved in tapping the phone of Seamus Mallon, an SDLP Member of the Commons. This infuriated both the Government and the police.

He attacked the extradition of terrorists and described the Supreme Court judgment which sent Dominic McGlinchey to Northern Ireland as "a debacle". His criticism of the participation of the Republic's armed forces in the Remembrance Day ceremony in 1983 was seen as an appeal to the rabidly nationalist elements of the electorate.

The loss of his rural seat was attributed largely to his treatment of farmers. But a contributing cause was the Government's miscalculation in sacking the Irish state television authority: one of its members was a local newspaper editor in Lenihan's area.

Lenihan's catch-phrase – "no problem" – caused considerable irritation both within and without his own party.

But his value to Fianna Fail far outweighed his liabilities. In 1980, when the second meeting between Mrs Thatcher and Charles Haughey produced a notably opaque joint statement agreeing that new Anglo-Irish "institutional" structures would be studied, Lenihan suggested that the words "constitutional" and "institutional" were interchangeable. This gloss engendered among Fianna Fail supporters an agreeably fuzzy image of possible British compromise on the status of Northern Ireland within the United Kingdom.

The same year, Haughey tried to have Sean Donlon, the Irish Ambassador to Washington, removed. Donlon had fought a successful campaign in the United States to end support for the IRA. His powerful friends, including Tip O'Neill, the Speaker of the House of Representatives, forced Haughey to back down. Lenihan then denied that any change had been mooted.

Lenihan's local knowledge and political resource occasionally failed him. In 1982 Charles Haughey made a daring bid for an extra seat to secure his narrow majority. He offered the EEC Commissionership to an opposition deputy in Lenihan's constituency. Richard Burke eagerly accepted. This, Haughey believed, opened the way to a by-election victory.

Lenihan weighed into the campaign. He went over the heads of the local education authority to promise a new school. Trees were planted in a new housing estate on the eve of the election. Fianna Fail lost the by-election, and the next day the trees were dug up by the company from which Lenihan had borrowed them.

In 1983 Lenihan showed considerable physical courage on a trip to Londonderry as a member of the New Ireland Forum, when he was attacked and beaten with flagpoles by members of Ian Paisley's Democratic Unionist party. His grit was also evident in his election victory in June 1989. Two days after receiving a liver transplant at the Mayo Clinic in Minnesota, and too ill to be interviewed, he arranged to be dressed and photographed to establish credibility with the electorate. He topped the poll with a sympathy vote, became the first deputy to be elected to the 26th Dail, and flew home just two days before the vote for a new Government.

Charles Haughey failed to gain an overall majority in that election, but Lenihan's instincts helped in the formation of the coalition Government with the Progressive Democrats, a party which had been formed by dissident members of Fianna Fail.

By suggesting that he would run in any contest for an alternative to Haughey, Lenihan played on the fears of colleagues who knew that the monolithic and essentially tribal nature of Irish politics was the secret of Fianna Fail's success. Many felt that a political bloodbath would ensure the party's defeat.

It could be argued that his failure as presidential candidate in 1990 was as much due to the proportional representation system as to any public antipathy to Fianna Fail in the wake of the telephone call scandal. The main opposition party's choice of a particularly weak contender – Austin Currie – ensured the victory of the outsider, Mary Robinson, who benefited from protest votes.

Lenihan's fall from grace came in 1990, when he told a university research student that, after the fall of Dr Garret FitzGerald's Government in 1982, he had telephoned Hillery and attempted to persuade him to postpone the dissolution of the Dail. Lenihan subsequently denied that he had admitted making the call. He was shown to be lying when the student produced a tape recording of the interview.

The affair compromised Lenihan's credibility as a candidate for the highest office. In particular, his phrase "mature recollection", which he used to describe his revision of events, became a national joke.

Lenihan married, in 1958, Ann Devine. They had four sons and a daughter.

November 2 1995

BARBARA SKELTON

BARBARA SKELTON, who has died aged 79, published three works of fiction and two striking volumes of autobiography, remarkable chiefly for the light they shed on her career as a *femme fatale*.

Her memoirs, *Tears Before Bedtime* (1987) and *Weep No More* (1989), rarely erred on the side of discretion. In particular she penned an hilariously funny portrait of Cyril Connolly, her first husband who divorced her on grounds of her adultery with the publisher George Weidenfeld.

She then married Weidenfeld, who in turn divorced her on grounds of adultery with Cyril Connolly. Finally she was briefly the fifth of the millionaire physicist Derek Jackson's six wives.

Skelton enjoyed love affairs with King Farouk of Egypt; the painters Felix Topolski and Michael Wishart; Alan Ross, founder of the *London Magazine*; and Bob Silvers, founder of the *New York Review of Books*. The cast also included a metropolitan policeman – "sex is a great leveller," she reflected.

Anthony Powell admired the "peculiarly incisive malignity" of Skelton's memoirs. It has even been suggested that she might have afforded certain characteristics for the lethal Pamela Flitton, who drives men to their death in Powell's *A Dance To the Music of Time*.

However irresistible others found her feline sex appeal, Skelton herself was dismissive of her beauty – "bun-faced, with slanting sludge-coloured eyes". She was also distinctly unappreciative of conventional male good looks.

Rather, she liked to dwell in detail on her lovers' physical shortcomings – on Connolly's elephantine torso and Chinese coolie legs, or on Weidenfeld's hands and pallor intruding "like flaws or speckles in an otherwise perfect photograph".

Skelton's conversation was as sharp and funny as her writing. She enjoyed sharing the fruits of her wide reading; and however sullen and sulky she might appear, good humour would instantly return in the company of anyone who could make her laugh.

The daughter of an Army officer and a Gaiety Girl of Scandinavian origin, Barbara Skelton was born in 1916.

She was a passionate and uncontrollable child, on one occasion running at her mother with a carving knife in a jealous rage. Fascinated from an early age by the havoc-wreaking possibilities of passion, she was expelled from her convent school when a bundle of love letters was found in her desk.

The letters, written by herself and addressed to herself, showed a degree of moral corruption which the nuns were unable to countenance. Her education thus ended, Miss Skelton was given a job as a model at a Knightsbridge dress-shop.

Her patron, a rich friend of her father's, quickly established his protégée as his mistress, and Barbara Skelton was launched on her career of petulant promiscuity.

Cocktails and tangos at the Savoy soon palled and were followed by a brief sojourn with a paternal military uncle in India, where she broke the heart of a poetic and peace-loving soldier. An attempted elopement resulted indirectly in the death of her admirer.

She returned to London and an erratic modelling career, which included a spell working for Schiaparelli.

During the first years of the Second World War she set up house with an unsurprisingly unattractive Free Frenchman – "a balding stocky man with a pale reptilian face". Recruited to the Foreign Office by Donald Maclean, she was posted to Egypt as a cypher clerk at the embassy.

Friendship with King Farouk flourished after a chance encounter at a restaurant, much to the disquiet of her Foreign Office superiors, who transferred her to Athens. She was to renew her acquaintance with Farouk some years later, when she joined him at Monte Carlo. He whipped her with a dressing-gown cord, providing material for her first novel, *A Young Girl's Touch* (1956), in which the heroine is beaten in similar fashion by King Yo-yo.

After the war Skelton lived a hectic and bohemian social life in London, consorting with, among others, Peter Quennell (whom she nicknamed "The Bastard") and the film maker John Sutro. In 1969 Skelton's novel *A*

Love Match was withdrawn when Sutro and his wife threatened to sue her for libel.

Skelton's acquisition of a red Sunbeam Talbot convertible resulted — according to Nancy Mitford — in the captivation of Cyril Connolly. They were married in 1950, and for the next four years lived together in her cottage in Kent.

In her memoirs Skelton describes Connolly lying abed morning after morning sucking the sheet and crying out in an ectoplasmic voice, "I wish I was dead", or more simply, "Poor Cyril".

Rage seems to have presided over the ill-starred marriage from the very beginning. When Skelton one day asked her husband what he had all over his face (it was in fact red wine), he furiously replied: *"Hate!"*

Visits to other people's houses were invariably disastrous. "Do come back when you're less cross," suggested one hostess. Nevertheless Skelton retained a residual affection for Connolly: "he had such enormous charm and intelligence," she wrote, "and he never bored me".

Her affair with George Weidenfeld began with the tortured permission of Connolly. "I am simply obsessed with him sexually," she noted of her new admirer. "I no longer remark on his hands or his toenails. And I have told him that he must grow some new black hair on his back. I have even threatened to smear him with bone lotion to further the process."

A Young Girl's Touch was dedicated to Connolly and published by Weidenfeld; and in 1956 Skelton divorced the first and married the second. "A feeling of utter despair followed the ceremony," she recorded. During the honeymoon she chanted "Until Death Us Do Part" at her husband through clenched teeth.

Weidenfeld's attempts to make her behave like a smooth social hostess – "Gush, *gush*," he would whisper to her at dinner-parties – were to no avail. She continued to play with Connolly, and in time the publisher sued for divorce.

Skelton's marriage to Weidenfeld and her affair with Connolly both ended in 1961. She then embarked on a series of liaisons with younger men, and took up with Kenneth Tynan, who maintained that "sex means smack and beautiful means bottom and always will".

Subsequently, Skelton lived for some years in New York, where she worked variously as a dental nurse, secretary and elderly lady's companion. She also wrote a book of short stories, *Born Losers* (1965), about the sex war in New York.

Of her third foray into matrimony in 1966 Barbara Skelton observed: "A marriage can be founded on many things ... It was not for love that I married Professor Jackson." The union, dominated by Skelton's menagerie of small violent mammals, was of brief duration.

Skelton then went to live in a farmhouse in Provence, where for more than a decade she shared the favours of the French journalist Bernard Frank with Françoise Sagan. Cyril Connolly visited her there shortly before his death, and spent an afternoon rummaging through her papers. "You certainly were a sexpot in your day," he concluded.

In 1993 Skelton returned to Britain, where she divided her time between a flat in the King's Road and a cottage in Worcestershire. Her affection was chiefly bestowed on two cats – her "pussers", as she called them.

January 29 1996

DR KALIM SIDDIQUI

DR KALIM SIDDIQUI, the self-styled radical Islamic leader who has died aged 65, became notorious by calling for the enforcement of the death sentence against Salman Rushdie.

Widely seen as Iran's man in Britain, Siddiqui was very nearly prosecuted in 1989 after asking Muslims at a meeting in Manchester to raise their hands if they endorsed the *fatwa* against the author of *The Satanic Verses*. What was not widely appreciated at that time was that Siddiqui had been partly instrumental in encouraging the Ayatollah Khomeini to issue his death sentence.

On February 13 1989 Khomeini had seen a television report of the anti-Rushdie riots in Islamabad in which five demonstrators had been shot dead by police. The Iranian leader telephoned his senior advisers, including Dr Seyyed Mohammad Khatemi, a long-serving cabinet minister responsible for Islamic guidance, to ask for information about the author. Dr Khatemi told Khomeini: "Kalim Siddiqui is in town. I will go and ask him."

In fact Siddiqui was preparing to fly back to London from Teheran after attending a two-week conference on Islamic thought. Much of Teheran was covered in snow when he arrived at the capital's Mehrabad airport at 5 a.m. on February 14.

According to his version of the events (supported by Iranian sources), Siddiqui was astonished to find Dr Khatemi waiting for him in the VIP lounge. "What do you know about Salman Rushdie and his book?"Khatemi demanded.

Siddiqui replied that he had read only photocopies of the most offending pages, but that, on the strength of these extracts, he certainly disapproved of the author. After their 10-minute talk, Dr Khatemi left the airport. Later in the morning Siddiqui's flight was cancelled and he was taken back to his hotel. While he was having lunch, someone rushed in to announce that Khomeini had issued a *fatwa*.

"Absolutely the right thing to do," Siddiqui commented, tucking into his *chello kebab*. "It had to have been something important for a cabinet minister to come at 5 a.m.," he said later. "I can only surmise that Khatemi went straight back to the Imam."

Siddiqui's great strength was that he learned to manipulate the media, especially television, by making extreme statements which he knew producers would find irresistible.

Yet at home in Slough, he lived the life of the suburban man, maintaining two semi-detached houses, living in one and working in the other. On a table he kept delicious pistachio nuts from Iran. Though hate mail poured in, he claimed that his English friends continued to invite him to dinner.

Siddiqui liked to appear a cuddly figure, donning wellington boots and weeding his vegetable garden. Those interviewing him discovered an avuncular academic, with a white beard and a reedy chuckle.

He cherished what he regarded as Britain's finer values, professing particular admiration for British liberalism. This did not prevent him from espousing the cause of the mullahs and daring the British Government to prosecute him. He calculated that, if they did, he would emerge either as a hero or as a martyr.

Kalim Siddiqui was born in 1931, near Hyderabad, south India, and grew up in Sultanpur, Uttar Pradesh, in northern India, where his father was a junior police inspector.

In 1942 Siddiqui had his first brush with British authorities when, he claimed, he was shot at during a nationalist agitation. He was one of the millions of Indian Muslims who fled to Pakistan during the murderous Hindu–Muslim conflicts at the time of partition in 1947.

In Karachi he spent three years selling vegetables and sleeping rough on the streets. This experience drove him into student politics, and he edited a broadsheet called the *Leader*. In 1954 the group he worked for sent him to Britain to learn the rudiments of journalism.

His first job was on the *Kensington News*. He also worked for the *Wokingham Times*, the *Northern Echo* in Darlington, and the *Slough Express*.

In 1964 he sent Bill Webb, the *Guardian*'s literary editor, a review of a book by Fenner Brockway, then Labour MP for Slough. Colin Putz, the night editor, called him in, pointed to an empty desk and said: "If you are interested, sit down and start working." He did, and stayed eight years.

In the 1960s Siddiqui studied at the LSE and obtained a PhD from University College, London, by developing Max Weber's view that "society has a better chance of performing well when it is in a state of conflict". His thesis was later developed into a book *Conflict, Crisis and War in Pakistan*.

"Conflict is like sex," he wrote, "it is everywhere. Also like sex it should be enjoyed and not suppressed." Curiously, in the light of later developments, he showed himself at this stage to be against the mullahs, whose narrow legalism he blamed for the lack of dynamism in Pakistan's economy.

In 1972, convinced that there was "a deep-seated anti-Muslim animus in Western culture going back to the Crusades," Siddiqui quit both the *Guardian* and journalism.

In 1973 he set up a Muslim Institute in Bloomsbury, for which he initially gained Saudi finance. But it was alleged that, instead of beginning a series of studies of the prophet Muhammad, as had been promised, Siddiqui had used the first instalment to buy property for the Institute.

Certainly the Institute made property investments. Despite the Koran's ban on gambling as "an abomination devised by Satan", the Institute acquired the freehold of a betting shop in the Fulham Palace Road.

Later the Institute became a pro-Iranian vehicle, though in recent months Teheran began to distance itself from the firebrand leader.

Since he lacked any spiritual authority Siddiqui presented himself as the intellectual leader of Britain's Muslims. In *The Muslim Manifesto: A strategy for survival* (1990), he set out his views on everything from the need for a Muslim parliament to separate schools, dress and inheritance rights.

In 1992, in the heat of the conflict generated by the publication of Salman Rushdie's *Satanic Verses*, Siddiqui established the Muslim parliament to "define, defend and promote the interests" of Britain's Muslims. But fellow Muslim leaders condemned it as an attempt to create a state within a state.

Moderate Muslims dismissed Siddiqui as a fanatic or

an "Iranian stooge", and even the Council of Mosques in Bradford, where *The Satanic Verses* was burnt in 1989, considered him a liability.

Siddiqui argued that Khomeini's utterances crystallised everything he felt about the relationship between the Christian and Muslim cultures. Critics accused him of jumping on the fundamentalist bandwagon and held that he did more than anyone else to harm relations between British Muslims and the rest of the population.

Kalim Siddiqui married in 1960, and is survived by a son and a daughter. His younger son suffered a brain haemorrhage when he was four and died in 1990, aged 10. "Our faith", Siddiqui reflected, "helps us to live through these very hard personal experiences."

April 20 1996

TIMOTHY LEARY

TIMOTHY LEARY, who has died aged 75, was one of the most vocal and charismatic spokesmen of America's counter-culture during the 1960s and 1970s – and immortalised by a song in the "tribal love rock musical" *Hair*.

His championing of the hallucinogenic drug lysergic acid diethylamide (LSD) made him a *bête noire* of the Establishment on both sides of the Atlantic, and brought him the close attention of law-enforcement agencies around the world.

Tall, handsome and soft-spoken, Leary in his prime was a tenacious and irrepressible figurehead for the movement that advocated the drug lifestyle, and was himself a consumer of LSD on a grand scale.

His most famous slogan was "turn on, tune in, drop out", which he thought up one day over lunch with Marshall McLuhan, the media commentator. The phrase became the rallying cry of a generation.

With an astute understanding of the power of celebrity and media manipulation, Leary reinvented himself several times. From a Harvard professorship in the late 1950s, conducting experiments on psilocybin with the likes of Aldous Huxley and Allen Ginsberg, he moved swiftly to a more "hippy"-like stance, announcing in 1966 that he had founded a new religion, called the League of Spiritual Discovery.

Devotees of the league, he said, would smoke marijuana for an hour every day and would devote Sundays to taking LSD.

Later Leary took a more overtly political line, and in 1972 declared that he would run as California's first psychedelic governor. He never did, but he well understood the shock value of such an announcement; and to the end he relished his ability to upset the Establishment.

"Envy me, man," he said in 1994, after managing to get himself arrested in Austin, Texas, for smoking a cigarette in an airport as a protest against political correctness and the demonisation of smokers. "I bet you wish that at 73 years old you'll be banned for being a threat to public morals." On that occasion, however, he admitted that the situation was not without irony. "It was kind of odd. The cops were sort of like my grandchildren."

In 1995 Leary was diagnosed as having terminal cancer. In pain and undergoing chemotherapy, he kept his fans informed of his deteriorating condition via the Internet, on which he also posted his daily diet. It included: 44 cigarettes; three cups of coffee; one beer; two glasses of wine; one cookie; one marijuana joint; one Tylenol PM; two prescription pain killers; 12 balloons of nitrous oxide (laughing gas); and three "Leary biscuits" – Ritz crackers topped with cheese and marijuana.

Leary entertained the idea of having his head preserved cryonically, but changed his mind after deciding that cryogenicists "have no sense of humour. I was worried I would wake up in 50 years surrounded by people with clipboards."

Timothy Francis Leary was born at Springfield, Massachusetts, on October 22 1920, the son of a US Army captain. He was educated at the Jesuit-run Holy Cross college, before entering West Point Military Academy.

He left West Point after 18 months and in 1942 took a bachelor's degree in psychology at the University of Alabama. After serving as a psychologist at a US Army hospital during the Second World War, he gained his MA at Washington State University in 1946, and his doctorate at Berkeley four years later. He was then appointed an assistant professor at the University of California.

From 1955 to 1958 Leary was director of psychological research at the Kaiser Foundation Hospital in Oakland, California, where he wrote monographs on personality testing. One of the tests he devised was adopted by private and governmental agencies, including the CIA, and was administered to Leary himself during a later brush with authority.

A decisive point in his career came with the suicide of his first wife, Marianne, in 1959. Leary spent a year in Spain, returned to the United States as a psychology lecturer at Harvard, and began to experiment with psychedelic drugs in the form of psilocybin mushrooms, which he had first encountered in Mexico.

He set up research projects to experiment with mescaline and psilocybin, inviting students – as well as such figures as Ginsberg, Aldous Huxley, William Burroughs (*qv*) and Arthur Koestler – to participate, and soon set up similar experiments with LSD.

But the Harvard authorities, unnerved by the increasing notoriety of the psychology department, terminated Leary's contract, and in 1963 he moved into a large mansion in New York State – placed at his disposal by a young millionaire sympathiser – and established a fluctuating community of LSD enthusiasts.

Frequently raided by the local police, the house became the headquarters of the Brotherhood of Eternal Love (successor to the League of Spiritual Discovery) and the International Federation for Internal Freedom – "If-If", for short.

In 1970 Leary was sentenced to 15 years' jail for drug smuggling. But after a few months he walked out of prison, in an escape organised by an underground group called the Weathermen, who charged the Brotherhood of Love £20,000 for the service.

Shortly afterwards, he turned up in Algiers, as a guest of Eldridge Cleaver, the fugitive leader of the Black Panther movement, and only after seeking asylum in Switzerland and Afghanistan was he finally arrested and returned to the United States. Under pressure from the FBI, he co-operated in helping to entrap other drug users, and after a year was released on parole.

During the 1980s Leary was rehabilitated in the eys of fashionable society. In 1983 he published his autobiography, *Flash Backs*, and appeared in *Return Engagement*, a film documenting a lecture tour he had made with his old enemy G. Gordon Liddy, one of the FBI agents who had arrested him (and who masterminded the Watergate break-in).

Latterly, Leary transferred his attention to digital technology. From his mansion in Beverley Hills he predicted the rise of the personal computer, then moved on to virtual reality, and recently championed the Internet. "It's about taking the power of global communication away from the mass media," he said, "which has always been the technique of controlling, manipulating and programming minds."

In his seventies he admitted to the onset of senility, but refused to see this as a negative feature in his life: "Senility is wasted on the old. For me it's a thrilling adventure."

Leary was married, by his own account, "five and three-quarter times" and had at least three children.

June 1 1996

JESSICA MITFORD

JESSICA MITFORD, who has died in California aged 78, was the most rebellious of the celebrated Mitford sisterhood, to the extent of embracing Communism and marrying an American.

As a writer and journalist "Decca" Mitford gloried in the sobriquet "Queen of the Muckrakers". But she showed in her autobiography, *Hons and Rebels* (1960) that she had inherited her full measure of the family's ruthless wit.

In addition she sparked lively controversy with her

investigations of American consumerism. In *The American Way of Death* (1963), she laid bare the gruesome and exploitative antics of the self-designated "grief-therapists", who bled the bereaved of their last cent.

Jessica Mitford's exposé of this monstrous cuckoo-land, where "the trappings of Gracious Living are transformed, as in a nightmare, into the trappings of Gracious Dying", provoked apoplectic attacks from the funeral trade. Magazines with titles such as *Mid-Continent Mortician*, *Casket and Sunnyside*, and *Concept: The Journal of Creative Ideas for Cemeteries* condemned the "Mitford blast" as a Red Plot.

The morticians found an ally in Congressman James B. Utt of California, who read a two-page statement about Jessica Mitford's subversive background into the Congressional Record. "I would rather be buried by one of our fine upstanding American morticians," he concluded, "than set foot on the soil of a Communist country".

Mitford was overjoyed. "Enemies are as important as friends in my life," she said, "and when they die I mourn their passing."

The book became a best-seller. The author basked in her macabre celebrity, and was especially proud when a company produced a simple, cheap coffin which was called the "Jessica Mitford Casket".

She recalled being approached by a stranger in a dress shop. "Are you shopping for a shroud?" the man demanded.

Jessica Lucy Freeman-Mitford was born on September 11 1917, the fifth daughter of the 2nd Lord Redesdale and his wife, Sydney, the models for Uncle Matthew and Aunt Sadie in Nancy Mitford's novels.

In the 14th century the family was established in

Northumberland. It first came to prominence in the 18th century, when John Mitford was Speaker of the House of Commons and (as Lord Redesdale) Lord Chancellor of Ireland. His son was raised to an earldom in 1877, but nine years later both titles became extinct. The property passed to a cousin, Bertie Mitford, whose great-grandfather was William Mitford, celebrated as the author of *The History of Greece*.

Bertie Mitford had a distinguished career in the diplomatic service, married a daughter of the 5th Earl of Airlie, fathered nine children and was created Baron Redesdale (of the second creation) in 1902. His second son David, Jessica's father, married Sydney, daughter of "Tap" Bowles, the founder of *Vanity Fair* and *The Lady*.

Of their children, Nancy, the eldest, won renown as a novelist; Pamela was devoted to riding and the country; Tom, the only boy, was killed in Burma in 1944; Diana married Sir Oswald Mosley; Unity fell in love with Hitler, shot herself on the declaration of the Second World War and died in 1948; and Deborah ("Debo"), the youngest, is the present Duchess of Devonshire.

By her own account Jessica had "a perfectly horrid childhood". She was brought up in the barrack-like house built by her father at Swinbrook, near Burford, Oxfordshire, almost entirely cut off from everyone save her own family. Her father would foam at the mere mention of outsiders.

This category, as Jessica explained, "included not only Huns, Frogs, Americans, blacks and all other people's children, the majority of my older sisters' acquaintances, almost all young men — in fact the whole teeming population of the earth's surface, except for some, though not all, of our relations and a very few tweeded, red-faced country neighbours". Anything, or anybody, that smacked of the literary or artistic was dismissed as "Damn sewer! Stinks to merry hell."

Apart from a few months at Oakdale, an establishment near High Wycombe, Jessica never went to school – a source of great grievance. Her parents were no less adamantly opposed to the notion that she should wear spectacles to alleviate her short sight.

Marooned at Swinbrook, she was entirely dependent for company on her brother and sisters. Nancy was invariably waspish; Pamela wanted to be a horse; Diana was the favourite sister; Unity joined her in inventing a private language called Boudledidge; Debo, nearly three years younger, was a playmate rather than a friend.

The main excitement was afforded by occasional visits to the family house in London, at 26 Rutland Gate.

At Swinbrook life was rugged. Before she was 10 Jessica had broken both arms in her attempts to learn to ride. "Poor little Decca," reflected her mother, "she doesn't seem to have much bounce."

At 12, Decca opened a "Running Away Account" at Drummonds Bank, and saved with single-minded determination. She even profited when her appendix was removed and presented to her in a jar of alcohol.

"You are *so* lucky to have a *dear* little appendix in a bottle," the envious Debo complained. In no time Decca had sold it to her for £1, which had been safely deposited at Drummonds by the time Nanny flushed the organ down the lavatory.

Mitford turned to Communism in her teens, partly in reaction to the burgeoning Fascist sympathies of her sister

Unity. The two sisters took turns with a diamond ring to carve the appropriate political insignia on the windowpane of their shared sitting-room.

Marxism appeared to help Decca make sense of her mad beginnings. "Farve," she would announce at the breakfast table, "d'you realise that as well as being a Sub-Human you're a Feudal Remnant?" In the circumstances it was not surprising that she did not enjoy being a debutante.

A spell at the Sorbonne in Paris also failed to provide the necessary drama. *"Ma petite, il vous jetera sur un divan et il vous violera,"* her landlady promisingly warned of one middle-aged admirer, but for once the French failed to deliver.

The longed-for release came in 1937 when Decca, at 19, met her second cousin Esmond Romilly, a nephew of Winston Churchill and a born anarchist. He too was 19, and had already founded a subversive magazine, run away from school (Wellington), and spent six weeks in a remand home. He had just been invalided home after fighting for the Republicans in the Spanish Civil War. Of course Jessica found him irresistible.

They fell in love and ran away to Bilbao, Jessica having announced to her parents that she was spending a couple of weeks with friends in Dieppe. When her sister Unity relayed the terrible news to Hitler, the Führer sank his head in his hands and sighed *"Armes Kind"* ("Poor child").

"Find Jessica Mitford and persuade her to return," telegraphed the Foreign Secretary, Anthony Eden. "Have found Jessica Mitford, impossible to persuade her to return," replied the British Consul. Even the arrival of a destroyer, the captain of which attempted to lure her aboard with promises of chicken and chocolate cake, left her unmoved.

Eventually the refugees escaped to St Jean de Luz, where they were met by Nancy, whom the family had despatched with her husband, Peter Rodd, to reclaim them. This she failed to do. Soon afterwards Jessica and Romilly were married at Bayonne, at a ceremony graciously attended by both mothers.

Jessica Mitford never saw her father again. Shortly before his death in 1958 Lady Redesdale asked her daughter if she would like to see him, and Decca replied that she would "as long as Farve promises not to roar". "Since you have such impossible conditions," her mother wrote back, "I shall not arrange for you to see your father."

In 1939 the Romillys emigrated to the United States. They worked as bartenders and sold silk stockings door to door. Romilly, "belligerent, bullying and brave" (in the words of Nancy Mitford's biographer Selina Hastings), proved a remarkably successful salesman, Jessica less so.

In 1940 Romilly left America to join the Royal Canadian Air Force, glumly observing to his wife: "I'll probably find myself being commanded by one of your ghastly relations". He was killed in action in November 1941.

Jessica Mitford remained in Washington where, the previous February, she had given birth to a second daughter (the first died in infancy). During her time in the maternity ward of Columbia Hospital she organised a "bedpan strike". Angered by the callous behaviour of overworked nurses, she persuaded the entire ward to wet their beds when a nurse failed to respond to the bell. The nurses came to heel.

Between 1941 and 1943 Jessica Mitford worked as an

investigator in the Office of Price Administration, first in Washington and then in San Francisco. In 1943 she married an American Jewish lawyer, Robert Treuhaft, and together they joined the Communist Party.

The Treuhafts moved to Oakland, California, and became deeply involved in the Civil Rights movement. During the late 1940s and early 1950s Jessica Mitford served as executive secretary in Oakland of the Civil Rights Congress, and in 1949 she was instrumental in bringing about the first state investigation into charges of police brutality.

In her second volume of autobiography, *A Fine Old Conflict* (1977), she described how she ducked subpoenas in the McCarthy witch-hunts. The Treuhafts left the Communist Party in 1958, not in a fanfare of disillusion, but to concentrate their energies on the Civil Rights movement.

In 1955 Jessica Mitford brought her husband and children to England, her first visit for 18 years.

Her writing career took off in 1960 with the publication of *Hons and Rebels* – at once a very funny book about English upper-class idiosyncrasy and a poignant account of her first marriage.

But it did not please everyone. "What surprised me," Evelyn Waugh wrote to Nancy Mitford, "was that she not only gives a nasty impression of the people against whom she has conceived grievances, but about those she presumably loves."

In 1969 she published *The Trial of Dr Spock*, and four years later produced *The American Prison Business*, a grim study of what happens to men and women behind bars.

She also wrote for magazines such as *Atlantic*, *Life*, *Esquire* and *McCall's*. Militantly eclectic in her choice of targets, she exposed fraud in a second-rate restaurant one month and in the Supreme Court the next.

An article exposing corruption in the Famous Writers School, which promised propserous writing careers to the illiterate in return for large sums of money, resulted in the school's filing for bankruptcy.

Her later books were *The Making of a Muckraker*, a collection of journalism; *Faces of Philip, A Memoir of Philip Toynbee*; *The Story of Grace Darling, Heroine and Victorian Superstar*; and *The American Way of Birth*.

Jessica Mitford kept a more than transatlantic distance between herself and her sisters, although her childhood favourite, Diana, married to the Fascist leader Sir Oswald Mosley, was the only one from whom she remained estranged.

When the Mosleys were released from prison in 1943 Jessica Mitford wrote to Winston Churchill: "They should be kept in jail, where they belong." Nancy reprimanded her for this "not very sisterly" approach, despite having herself been in part responsible for Diana's arrest in 1940.

Jessica Mitford was once telephoned in California by an English journalist who was writing an article about sisters. The journalist had already spoken to Nancy who had said, "Sisters stand between one and life's cruel circumstances." Decca was startled into saying that surely sisters *were* life's cruel circumstances.

Jessica Mitford is survived by her second husband and their son, and by a daughter from her first marriage.

July 25 1996

SIR PETER GREEN

SIR PETER GREEN, who has died aged 71, was chairman of Lloyd's at a time of crisis and reform.

But, although he was once called "the father of the new Lloyd's", revelations about his own business arrangements later associated him with the kind of practices which had tarnished the reputation of the old Lloyd's.

A powerful figure in the marine section of the market, brusque in his manner, Peter Green was treated with some reverence by brokers seeking to place business with his syndicates. If Green's stamp was on the underwriting slip, the rest of Lloyd's would generally follow.

He had a reputation for straight dealing and liked to impress on prospective underwriting members the significance of the market's unlimited liability by asking them to write a blank cheque. Pocketing it, he would tell them: "That's the risk you are now undertaking as a Name at Lloyd's."

Green became chairman of Lloyd's in 1979, declaring his intention of restoring the damaged trust between market participants. He helped to secure the passage of the 1982 Lloyd's Act and chaired the committee which planned the new Lloyd's building.

He was, however, notably forgiving towards those in the market who were alleged to have erred. In the case of Oakley Vaughan, an agency whose syndicates had been underwriting more business than their capital could support, the inquiry findings and subsequent reprimands were all handled in private.

In the case of PCW syndicate, the subject of a multimillion pound fraud investigation, Green declared after his own short inquiry that he had found "no dishonesty". DTI inspectors later disagreed, but rejected suggestions that Green had been guilty of a cover-up.

In 1983, the Bank of England persuaded Lloyd's to appoint a chief executive from outside the market, Ian Hay Davison. Green was obliged to disclose for the first time to the 1,000 Names for whom he acted that he had placed reinsurance on their behalf with a Cayman-registered company, Imperial Insurance, in which he had a 7.6 per cent interest. Cover for oil rigs in the Gulf of Mexico had benefited Green by $182,000.

Inquiries by the Inland Revenue followed. Later that year Green announced his resignation from the chairman-ship; he was awarded the Gold Medal of Lloyd's, an honour (involving the double ringing of the Lutine Bell) bestowed only eight times in 50 years.

But a disciplinary tribunal later found that Green had failed over a period of five years to ensure that the reinsurance arrangements were fair to his Names. The tribunal declared this to be "discreditable conduct" and fined him a total of £50,000.

Green vigorously contested this verdict, but later remarked: "I may have been sailing a bit too close to the wind . . . I thought I was trying to do my Names a lot of good but, you know, you learn by your mistakes."

It was generally acknowledged that what he had done was far from unusual in Lloyd's. It was pointed out that almost all the candidates to succeed him as chairman were also the subject of Inland Revenue investigations.

Peter James Frederick Green was born on July 28 1924. His forebears had been involved in shipping and shipbuilding since the 18th century; his great-grandfather, Sir Frederick Green, was the owner of the Orient Line. Peter's father, Toby, was the underwriter of the Janson Green syndicate which traced its origins to 1892.

Young Peter was educated at Harrow and Christ Church before joining the Royal Navy in 1943. He served as a sub-lieutenant on Russian convoys and in the Mediterranean.

On leaving the Navy he joined his father in Lloyd's, becoming an underwriting member in 1947. On his father's death in 1966 he succeeded as chairman of Janson Green. He became a member of the Committee of Lloyd's in 1974.

Green was knighted in 1982. He retired from active underwriting in 1984 but remained chairman of Janson Green until 1988.

Green was a founder member of the Admirals Cup challenge, in which he competed several times.

Peter Green married first, in 1950, Pamela Ryan, who died in 1985. He married secondly, in 1986, Jennifer Whitehead.

July 30 1996

SPIRO T. AGNEW

SPIRO T. AGNEW, the former Vice-President of the United States who has died aged 77, was Richard Nixon's choice as running mate, and proved worthy of his master.

Nixon had never met Agnew before 1968, the year he was elected President. He was impressed, though, by the way in which Agnew, then Governor of Maryland, handled riots in Baltimore after the murder of Martin Luther King.

Agnew had called a meeting of the state's black leaders and berated them as "circuit-riding, Hanoi-visiting, caterwauling, riot-inciting, burn-America-down type of leaders"; they had "broken and run" when they should have been preventing the riots.

Nixon was enraptured. "That guy Agnew's a really impressive fellow," he commented. "He's got guts. He's got a good attitude." In no time Agnew was being considered as Vice-Presidential candidate, though completely unknown to the nation at large.

A self-made man, he could be presented as the fulfilment of the American dream; a representative of a border state, he might appeal to both north and south. More importantly, his tough stance on law and order promised to neutralise the threat posed to the Republicans by Governor George Wallace of Alabama.

But Nixon knew, even in 1968, that Agnew had received commissions from contractors in return for state works awarded to them. Nixon regarded this practice as an unavoidable in Maryland politics. "I did not dream", he claimed, "that Agnew would go on accepting the contributions after he became Vice-President."

When Nixon announced that Agnew would be his running mate, the Republican convention expressed some dissent. "The name of Spiro Agnew is not a household name," the candidate himself admitted. "I certainly hope it will become one within the next couple of months."

In the ensuing presidential campaign Agnew acted as Rottweiler, while Nixon assumed the part of statesman, remote from the dirty business of politics. The two of them hardly met between the convention and the election.

Agnew accused Hubert Humphrey, the Democratic candidate, of being "squishy soft, soft on inflation, soft on communism and soft on law and order." He described student dissenters as "basically parasitic ... they take their tactics from Fidel Castro and their money from daddy." A Nixon presidency, Agnew promised, "would bring an end to civil disobedience of any kind".

He referred to Poles as Polacks, and addressed a reporter as "the fat Jap". As for social concern, "when you've seen one slum, you've seen them all". Liberal America was noisily outraged; the silent majority, shaken by the mayhem on the streets in 1968, remained encouragingly silent.

After Nixon won the election by a whisker, Agnew resumed his barrage of abuse. Opponents of the Vietnam War were "an effete corps of impudent snobs". Television commentators were "the most superficial thinkers I've ever seen", while newspaper reporters were anathematised as the "nattering nabobs of negativism".

Nixon never showed any disposition to involve Agnew in government. "I'm off to the White House now," the Vice-President observed on leaving a party. "It's autumn, and they need someone to sweep up the leaves."

But in attacking pornography, pot and permissiveness Agnew struck a chord with many voters. Sixty-seven per cent of voters over 50 gave him credit "for having the courage to speak out and against radical blacks and students where others don't dare".

So Nixon, having toyed with the alternative possibility of John Connally of Texas, again chose Agnew as his running mate in 1972. But by April 1973 the Department of Justice was investigating allegations of bribery, extortion and tax fraud against the Vice-President.

Nixon's instinct was to defend Agnew. This was not so much because he was grateful for the Vice-President's unswerving loyalty during the Watergate crisis, as because Agnew's reputation acted as a kind of insurance policy. Liberals could hardly rejoice in the prospect of destroying the President if Agnew was to succeed.

In July 1973 Agnew advised Nixon to destroy the White House tapes: "You've got to have a bonfire right now," he said. It was the best counsel he ever gave, but Nixon took no heed.

By this time the Vice-President's own career was doomed: the Justice Department was ready to indict him on 40 different counts. For a time Agnew blustered, denouncing the charges as "damned lies" and promising to fight them.

For a moment it seemed that both the President and the Vice-President might be impeached, and there was talk of the Presidency passing to the Speaker of the House of Representatives. This was Carl Albert, who was under treatment for alcoholism.

In the event, though, Agnew showed no stomach for the fight, and made a deal under which he resigned the Vice-Presidency (on October 9 1973) in return for the Department of Justice accepting a *nolo contendere* plea to one count of having knowingly failed to declare income.

Agnew was put on probation for three years, fined

$10,000, and disbarred from practising as a lawyer and from voting. He also forfeited membership of the Royal and Ancient Golf Club.

Nixon never saw him again, though he did express sympathy. "I do not believe," he later remarked, "that Agnew deserved the almost hysteria that went on in the US Attorney's Office and everywhere else that he had commited the crime of the century. But with the problems I had there was nothing I could do for him. I only wish I'd been stronger. If I had been I would have stopped him from going."

One of the lawyers involved in the investigation of Agnew's affairs was more direct. "The man is a crook. There is no question about that at all, and the country is well rid of him."

Spiro Theodore Agnew was born on November 18 1918 in Baltimore, the son of an immigrant Greek restaurateur whose name was originally Anagnostopoulos. His mother was from Virginia.

The Agnews ran a café which failed in the Depression, but they made a comeback and were able to finance Spiro at Johns Hopkins University, where he studied chemistry.

Afterwards Agnew attended evening classes at the Baltimore Law School, working as a clerk by day. Later he was a supermarket manager and a claims assessor with a timber company.

In the Second World War he fought in France and Germany, becoming a company commander with the 10th Armoured Division and being awarded the Bronze Star.

He graduated in law in 1947 and was soon prospering in his office in the Baltimore suburb of Towson. After flirting with the Democrats he joined the Republicans, and in 1961 was elected chief executive mayor of Baltimore County. He proved an energetic administrator.

In 1967 Agnew contested the governorship of Maryland against a segregationist; as a champion of civil rights he managed to take 50 per cent of the vote against his opponent's 40 per cent – in a state where Democrats outnumbered Republicans three to one.

Agnew began as a governor with a social conscience, pouring money into housing and anti-poverty schemes. He also repealed state laws banning racial intermarriage, liberalised the abortion laws and overruled death sentences.

But during his second year of office, as America was torn by racial and civil strife, Agnew emerged as an unbending conservative. In April 1968, when black students marched on the statehouse in Anapolis, he had 227 of them arrested.

At the same time he strengthened police powers, cut down on health and welfare expenditure, and attacked President Johnson for allowing "the so-called poor people with Cadillacs" to camp in Washington. Commentators decided his new political stance was linked with the presidential elections of that year.

Agnew supported Governor Nelson Rockefeller for the Republican candidacy until Rockefeller withdrew. He was then delighted to discover that he had impressed Nixon.

After his disgrace, he worked for a firm called Pathlite in Maryland, and acted as an international trade consultant. He managed to repay his debts.

In 1976 he published *The Canfield Decision*, a novel about a Vice-President who is accused of criminal actions:

"I thought it best to write of those things I knew about," he said. Another book, *Go Quietly, Or Else* appeared in 1980.

Spiro Agnew married, in 1942, Elinor Judefind; they had a son and three daughters.

September 19 1996

ALGER HISS

ALGER HISS, who has died aged 92, was a US State Department official suspected of spying for the Soviet Union; his case sharply divided American opinon – not least because Ricahrd Nixon established his reputation in pursuing the charge.

During the 1930s Hiss was the quintessential New Dealer, and went on to play an important role at the Yalta conference and in the setting up of the United Nations. So when he was accused of being a Communist spy the American establishment was outraged.

The storm broke in August 1948, during the testimony of a senior editor of *Time* magazine, Whittaker Chambers, before the House Committee on Un-American Activities. Chambers, a self-confessed former Communist agent who had abandoned his creed to become an anti-Soviet polemicist, was a pudgy, unprepossessing man regarded even by his allies as obsessive and unreliable.

Chambers appeared before the committee to elaborate allegations which he had first made privately after his defection from the Communists in 1939 – that seven Government employees had been involved in "Communist infiltration of the American Government". The most distinguished of these was Alger Hiss.

Chambers declared that his work as a Communist had brought him into close contact with Hiss and his wife, Priscilla, whom he also accused of being a Communist. "I was very fond of Mr Hiss," he insisted.

Radiating confidence, Hiss protested on oath that he had never met Chambers. When he finished speaking, the courtroom burst into applause. Most observers, including President Truman, felt the committee had overreached itself.

But Hiss had aroused the hostility of one of the committee's junior members, Congressman Richard Nixon. The young Californian from the wrong side of the tracks resented Hiss's suave East Coast manner and persuaded the committee to let him set up a sub-committee to question Chambers in private.

Chambers then revealed a detailed knowledge of the Hisses' life druring the 1930s. He recalled, for example, that they were amateur ornithologists and "to their great excitement," had once spotted a prothonotary warbler.

Under pressure, Hiss changed his story. He might have known Chambers, he admitted, under the name of George Crosley, a writer. And he had, indeed, once seen a prothonotary warbler, "a gorgeous bird".

Finally, Chambers and Hiss confronted each other. After an extraordinary charade in which Hiss made Chambers read aloud and examined his teeth, he identified him as Crosley. Then, shaking with emotion, he dared Chambers to repeat his charges in public. Chambers duly did so on the radio programme *Meet the Press*.

At the end of September 1948, Hiss filed a libel suit

against Chambers. Three months later one of Hiss's lawyers finally thought to ask Chambers if he had documentary proof of his accusations. To the lawyer's consternation, Chambers replied that he had: 65 pages of retyped State Department cables, and four handwritten notes.

Before anyone had time to examine these documents in detail, Chambers told the committee that he possessed "another bombshell". He melodramatically led the committee's investigators to the pumpkin patch of his farm in Westminster, Maryland, and reached into a hollowed-out pumpkin.

Out came microfilm of copies of State Department documents from the mid-1930s, some in Hiss's handwriting. Taken as a whole, they covered a vast area of international affairs: the Sino-Japanese war, Germany's takeover of Austria, the Spanish Civil War and, crucially, America's intentions towards the Soviet Union.

Chambers's story was straightforward: Hiss had stolen the documents from the State Department, where he worked for the Assitant Secretary of State, before leaving work in the evening, and had returned them the next morning.

Overnight, they were photographed or copied by Mrs Hiss on her typewriter before being handed to Chambers, who was supposed to pass them to the Russians. In fact, Chambers explained, he kept the documents as a "life preserver", so that he could blackmail the party if threatened.

Hiss could not be charged with espionage because the three-year statute of limitations had expired. But after experts had testified that samples of Priscilla Hiss's correspondence and the documents were typed on the same Woodstock typewriter, a grand jury voted unanimously to indict Hiss for having lied twice – when he said he had not stolen the documents, and when he denied having seen Chambers after 1935.

For his trial, which lasted from May to July 1949, Hiss assembled an impressive collection of character witnesses, including two Supreme Court judges. But there was nothing he could do about Woodstock N230099, which was discovered after a frantic search and which, experts decided, was undoubtedly the instrument in question.

The jury voted eight to four to convict Hiss, which meant that there would have to be a second trial. Nixon was furious, claiming that the jury foreman was a former Left-wing activist determined to acquit Hiss irrespective of the evidence.

The second trial opened in November 1949, by which time the discovery of Russia's atomic bomb and Mao's victory in China had intensified the anti-Communist mood. There was a new judge, a new witness – Hede Massing, a former Soviet agent who testified to meeting Hiss at a Communist meeting in 1935 – and, effectively, a new defence.

The new Hiss line was that Chambers was mad, an argument developed at great length by Dr Carl Binger, who produced a diagnosis of "psychopathic personality" based partly on his own observations of Chambers's behaviour in the courtroom and partly on readings of Chambers's translations of German novels.

This argument was easily demolished by the prosecution. On Jaunary 21 1950, Hiss was found guilty and sentenced to five years in jail. In fact he served 44 months in Lewisburg Penitentiary – a good corrective, as he remarked, to three years at Harvard.

Alger Hiss was born at Baltimore, Maryland, on November 11 1904 and was only two years old when his once-prosperous father Charles, by then unemployed, killed himself by cutting his throat. But the boy worked hard, and won prizes at Johns Hopkins University and Harvard Law School.

In 1929 he went to work for Justice Oliver Wendell Holmes, and later that year married Priscilla Fansler Hobson, a divorced Yale graduate with strong Left-wing sympathies.

By the early 1930s Hiss was combining a career at a New York law firm with work for a radical laywers' group at night. In 1933 he travelled to Washington for a post in the New Deal bureaucracy.

Three years later Hiss became assistant to Francis B. Sayre, Assistant Secretary of State, where he had access to a wide variety of telegrams from diplomats and military attachés.

From 1939 until 1944, Hiss served as aide to Stanley K. Hornbeck, political adviser to the Far Eastern division of the State Department. In 1944, he was appointed deputy director of the office of Special Political Affairs.

At Yalta, Hiss was chiefly concerned with advising on the setting up of the United Nations, and later that year was a natural choice as temporary secretary-general of the UN, organising conferences at San Francisco. On his return, he took over as director of the office of Special Political Affairs.

But it was in 1945 that the FBI received allegations

of Hiss's Communist activities from two informants, neither of whom knew Whittaker Chambers: Igor Gouzenko, a Russian code clerk who had worked at the Soviet Embassy in Ottowa; and Elizabeth Bentley, a former Russian agent.

By late 1946 the rumours circulating in the State Department made it impossible for Hiss to continue working there, and in February 1947 he succeeded John Foster Dulles as President of the Carnegie Endowment for International Peace. He had been there little more than a year when Chambers's allegations were made public.

After his release from prison Hiss found it impossible to rebuild his career, and by 1960 he was selling office stationery. He continued to protest his innocence, but it was not until Nixon's election as president in 1968 that interest in the case revived. To radical Democrats, Hiss – who was now identified with the anti-Vietnam lobby – appeared as Nixon's first victim.

Several pro-Hiss books appeared, many concentrating on Chambers' unreliability as a witness. Hiss enjoyed a new career as a campus celebrity and in 1975 became the first lawyer ever readmitted to the Massachusetts Bar after a serious criminal conviction.

In 1978, however, his cause sustained a damaging blow with the publication of Allen Weinstein's *Perjury*. A liberal historian, Weinstein had originally been convinced of Hiss's innocence, but soon changed his mind.

Much of his investigation focused on the Woodstock typewriter produced at the trial, which conspiracy theorists had long argued was an FBI forgery. Weinstein concluded that such a forgery was a scientific impossibility, and suggested that if anyone was guilty of conspiracy it was Hiss's brother, Donald, who had been the first to track down the Woodstock but had then concealed the discovery.

Weinstein unearthed many suggestive details. In 1945, for example, during a conversation between Andrei Gromyko, Soviet ambassador to the UN and Edward Stettimus, the American Secretary of State, the former said he had "a very high regard for Alger Hiss, particularly for his fairness and impartiality".

Moreover, during the latter stages of the war, Hiss had consistently sought access to highly sensitive intelligence files on atomic energy and the internal security of America's allies – documents which had little or nothing to do with his own responsibilities.

If Hiss was a spy, he could have done enormous damage to American interests. In particular, he would have given the Russians the priceless advantage of knowing the details of American negotiating positions long before Yalta.

At best, Hiss was a liar. As Weinstein wrote: "The evidence proves that he did in fact perjure himself when describing his secret dealings with Chambers, so that the jurors in the second trial made no mistake in finding Alger Hiss guilty as charged."

The Hisses separated in 1959; they had a son. After Priscilla's death in 1992, Hiss married Isabelle Johnson.

November 18 1996

TINY TIM

TINY TIM, the American pop singer who has died aged 66, specialised in horrendous falsetto vocalisations of sentimental songs, and cultivated an appearance of utter ghastliness to match.

His greatest success, in 1968, was a version of "Tiptoe through the Tulips" which had first been recorded 39 years before. Critics wrote of the surreal awfulness of the performance. But for a year or two Tiny Tim was a weird enough phenomenon to compel attention, even in the heyday of hippiedom.

Although he washed obsessively, no one would have guessed it by looking at him. Tiny Tim's frizzy hair tumbled down over his shoulders, framing the gigantic nose which dominated his face. One critic who saw him on stage was reminded of a 16-stone floor mop; another remarked that he teetered about like a pregnant gazelle.

Off-stage, Tiny Tim clutched a shopping bag which contained his ukulele and his cosmetics. Long before the heavy metal bands of the 1970s, he was affecting white make-up – which he was still wearing when the 1970s bands were being resurrected for nostalgic fans.

In a way he was always consistent. "As a singer only one thing stands between him and success," it was observed, "complete and utter failure."

Tiny Tim was born Herbert Buckingham Khaury in New York on April 12 1930, the son of a Roman Catholic Lebanese father and a Polish Jewish mother. He was never a handsome boy, and his looks were not improved when, on a school outing, he slipped and broke his nose on a cannon that had once belonged to George Washington.

As a young man he gained some notoriety in the homosexual clubs of Greenwich Village with his cracked falsetto renderings of classic songs. "Why'd you gotta sing like a fairy?" his mother demanded.

Khaury adopted a number of pseudonyms in those early days: Larry Love, Darry Dover, Emmett Swink, Rollie Dell, Julian Foxglove and Winifred Lee. His idiosyncratic interpretations of "Be My Baby" and "Sonny Boy" attracted notice, and in 1968 he appeared as Tiny Tim in the film *You Are What You Eat*, which celebrated the more radical manifestations of black power and flower power.

Taken up by Reprise Records, he made an album called *God Bless Tiny Tim*, which included his unforgettable reworking of "Tiptoe Through the Tulips". As a single this number made the Top Twenty for six weeks, though it never went higher than No 17. That year, 1968, he made an appearance at the Royal Albert Hall.

A reviewer of that concert, while noting Tiny Tim's gift for summoning up the half-forgotten songs and gestures of such crooners as Rudy Vallee and Al Jolson, found that he seemed to love his audience rather more than they loved him. In America a critic likened him to "a haunted house, inhabited by ghostly song-and-dance men".

No one was ever quite sure how serious Tiny Tim was trying to be. "I am really a vampire of songs," he reflected, "and vampires suck blood. When I sing 'Great Balls of Fire' I enter the body of Elvis Presley for a moment."

Aside from music, Tiny Tim presented himself as a Biblical fundamentalist: "I found Christ in 1953," he would say. He also supported America's involvement in Vietnam. "Even in the days of King David," he explained, "there were religious wars and people had to fight."

At the end of 1969, Tiny Tim was married before a television audience of millions on the Johnny Carson Show. His bride, Vicki Budinger, had stood in line to meet him in a Philadelphia store. The couple promised to be "sweet, gentle, kind, patient, not puffed up, charitable, slow to anger and swift to forgive".

But Tiny Tim refused to kiss his betrothed until the knot had been tied. "I am a weak person and if I kiss a girl it might lead to the ultimate. I can't allow that to happen until I marry." After the wedding, he announced that he and Miss Vicki would sleep in separate rooms for three days, "as dictated by the Scriptures".

It later transpired that he had interpreted the Scriptures with even more rigour than he professed. "Nothing happened to us sexually for six months," Miss Vicki vouchsafed. They had a daughter, Tulip, in 1971, but separated in 1972 and, against Tiny Tim's wishes ("I'm a 'Till Death Do Us Part' man"), divorced. "I blame Women's Lib," he said. "They're getting women further and further into men's domain."

Meanwhile Tiny Tim had appeared at the Isle of Wight Pop Festival in 1970 leading a crowd of 250,000 in a rendering of "Land of Hope and Glory". Two months later, though, at Batley Variety Club in Yorkshire, a former Coldstream guardsman decided to "shut him up" for "running England down" and knocked the microphone out of his hand. Deeply affronted, Tiny Tim cancelled the rest of his tour and returned to America.

By that time his career was entering steep decline – though only the year before he had been earning $50,000 a week at Caesar's Palace, Las Vegas. In 1975 he was back in Greenwich Village, living in the spare room of his mother's apartment. "Why'd you gotta look like a nut?" she remonstrated.

In the next two decades Tiny Tim's only notable achievement was to set a world record for non-stop singing: in 1988, at Brighton, he clocked in at three hours 11 minutes.

He married a second time, and this time divorced without resistance. But for nearly 30 years, unknown to Tiny Tim, a fan had been waiting for her chance. "When I was a girl," Sue Gardner explained, "all my friends liked the Rolling Stones and Jimi Hendrix. I thought they were out of their minds. When Tiny came on he sang songs that were happy and wholesome, and nice for children. I loved him even then. I always wanted to meet him but I never knew how to find him."

In 1995 she finally obtained his number through a newspaper, and telephoned on impulse. They were married shortly afterwards. Tiny Tim wore a purple suit and serenaded the guests with "Sweet Sue".

Subsequently, a new record, "Girl", was sufficiently well received to inspire hopes of a tour. "I've made 27 come-backs already," Tiny Tim said in 1996, "maybe this will be my year." But his heart was playing up, and when his doctor ordered him to cut down to one glass a day, he acquired a bigger glass.

In September he collapsed on stage after suffering a heart attack at a ukulele festival in western Massachusetts.

December 2 1996

JOHN VASSALL

JOHN VASSALL, who has died aged 72, spied for the KGB as an Admiralty clerk for seven years after being blackmailed about his homosexuality.

Vassall was 29 when he was sent to work in the British Embassy in Moscow in 1954. His homosexual habits were quickly discovered through the help of Sigmund Mikhailski, an interpreter at the Embassy who was a KGB agent. Vassall was then photographed drunk at a homosexual party.

Homosexual activity was not only a criminal offence in Britain and Russia at that time, but the security services' positive vetting was meant to establish that no Embassy staff were homosexual. In retrospect, it seemed ludicrous that the British failed to detect Vassall's signs of homosexual behaviour when they were only too obvious to the Soviet enemy.

Vassall was decisively set up by the KGB on March 19 1955, the night of the St Patrick's Ball at the American Club in Moscow. He was introduced to a soldier, a stranger, and taken to a flat. As Vassall said later: "There was nothing faked about his love-making. Suddenly the light went out. Somehow I knew it was not a power failure. I was suddenly cold and terrified. I started to shiver."

Two secret policemen had entered the flat, and they told the naked clerk that he was guilty of an offence which was taken very seriously in Russia. At that moment Vassall thought suicide might be a way out and made a dash for the window, but he was hauled back. So began a long process of threats and promises that led him more firmly into the clutches of the KGB.

In his diaries, Sir William Hayter, then British ambassador in Moscow, later wrote about Vassall: "There was no excuse for him. If he had come to me or the Naval Attaché and told us he was being blackmailed by the Russians, he could have been sent home at once without any opposition from the Soviet authorities. One or two similar cases occurred during my time."

Vassall's account of it was that he felt unable to approach the ambassador or the Naval Attaché because he felt their attitude was too distant to make a confidence possible. A few months after his treachery began, the Foreign Office departmental report on his activities was favourable. "A pleasant young man of first-class appearance and manners. Never ruffled. Always helpful. His moral standards are of the highest."

Vassall's state of mind during the succeeding years was a strange one. He kept doing his work. The KGB offered alternately threats of arrest or torture and small favours. They arranged holidays for him. They gave him small amounts of money (£50 at Christmas 1955), more to compromise him further than as an enticement.

"Who on earth would do it for money?" Vassall asked in his (naturally self-serving) autobiography. "The whole thing is an illusion, a stay of execution, nothing more."

Vassall tried to distract himself by visits to the ballet. He visited Rome, and was delighted to see the Pope, believing that, whatever he had done, he was still a Roman Catholic. (He had been received into the Church in 1953.) But he felt unable to go to confession for seven years, until after his arrest.

John Vassall

After the completion of his two-year tour of duty in Moscow, Vassall was posted to London. There he continued to be fascinated by homosexuality. Mikhailski had sometimes supplied him with willing partners in Moscow.

Back in London he drank in Soho clubs frequented by homosexuals, such as the Rockingham Club, the Music Box and the Alibi Club. His nickname among those who knew him well was "Vera". Vassall later claimed he was friendly with two unnamed MPs, to whom he was introduced by a homosexual friend, during the years of his spying.

In London Vassall was given a job in Naval Intelligence, in which he spent almost a year. He was then appointed assistant private secretary to Thomas Galbraith, the Civil Lord for the Admiralty, who had some responsibility for intelligence material. They got on well; Galbraith felt obliged to resign in 1962 when Vassall was exposed, even though there had been nothing improper in his behaviour.

After two years with Galbraith, Vassall was given a job in 1960 at the Military branch of the Admiralty. All this time he was making regular contacts with his Russian minders "Gregory" and "Nicolai". He photographed secret papers for them, and sometimes he took them away to be copied. "I never had any trouble taking the secrets out," he wrote. "I put them in my documents case, or rolled them inside an evening paper, and walked out unchallenged."

The KGB payments continued. Vassall had always liked foreign travel, but holidays in Capri, New York, Florence, Brussels, Rome, Vienna, Geneva, Cairo, the Riviera and Spain on his pay of £700 a year attracted attention. He was also said to own 36 Savile Row suits. Unknown to Vassall, MI5 agents burgled his flat in Dolphin Square and found incriminating documents.

On September 12 1962, while on his way back to the Admiralty from the Post Office in Trafalgar Square, where he had gone to draw money for another holiday, he was approached by two men in macintoshes. They showed him a warrant and asked him to get into a car with them, next to the statue of Captain Cook.

They took him to Scotland Yard where, with the help of tea and sandwiches, his long interrogation began. Even then he wondered if he might be able to persuade the security services to let him off and help him to start a new life abroad.

With the hope of hiring a good barrister, Vassall accepted an offer of £5,000 from the *Sunday Pictorial* for his story. During his trial he was asked if money and lust kept him tied to the Russians. "No, it was a trap that I could see no way of getting out of," he replied.

He was found guilty of four charges under the Official Secrets Act and sentenced to 18 years, of which he served 10.

William John Christopher Vassall was born on September 20 1924 at St Bartholomew's Hospital, where his father was Anglican chaplain. He felt that his mother and father did not get on, and this made his childhood unhappy.

He was educated at Monmouth School and failed to gain a place at Keble College, Oxford. He spent a year in banking and served as a photographer in the RAF during the Second World War. He then joined the Civil Service and applied for a posting with the Admiralty at Moscow.

As an economy measure, an applicant was sought who, like Vassall, was single.

Prison life for Vassall was to some extent ameliorated by a little flower garden he tended, and by his religion.

In Maidstone jail, Vassall was somewhat taken by Frank "the Axeman" Mitchell. "He was a colossal figure and arrived in white T-shirt and smart slacks, with a chest expander under one arm and a record player under the other," he remembered. "I could see he was somebody exciting and I was terribly curious to see how he ticked."

Vassall was also befriended by the Earl of Longford (then chairman of the publishing house which later published Vassall's autobiography). On his fourth application for parole he was released in October 1972.

After his conviction a tribunal under Lord Radcliffe had been appointed to examine Vassall's case. The spy agreed with some journalists that the Radcliffe Tribunal exposed few facts that might upset the Establishment or hamper the security services.

Naturally no details of what Vassall had passed to the Russians were made public. The political correspondent of *The Sunday Telegraph*, Ian Waller, went so far as calling the tribunal "a massive cover-up".

On his release from jail, Vassall spent some time in a monastery writing his book, *Vassall*, published in 1975. Meanwhile he changed his name to John Phillips and found a job as a clerk at the British Records Association, an organisation representing archivists, in Charterhouse Square, near Smithfield, to which he travelled each day, unrecognised, by Underground from his flat in St John's Wood. A picture of Churchill hung over his mantelpiece and he often went to Lord's to watch cricket.

He denied rumours that he received an Admiralty pension. He continued to spend periods staying in a guest room at the Charterhouse monastery in Sussex.

In 1980 the BBC screened a drama documentary in which Vassall was played by John Normington as weak, vain and keen to be thought a gentleman.

The prosecution at Vassall's trial summed up his downfall by saying: "He was entrapped by his lust, and thereafter cash kept him crooked." Vassall's own verdict on his life was: "Well, I've done the best with the body and mind that I was given."

December 6 1996

PAMELA HARRIMAN

PAMELA HARRIMAN, the American ambassador in Paris who has died aged 76, was proudly described by her second husband as "the greatest courtesan of the century".

From obscure, if aristocratic, beginnings in Dorset, she became in turn Winston Churchill's daughter-in-law, the lover of some of the world's richest men, a powerful Washington hostess, a multi-millionairess and finally a successful diplomat.

All this, and much more, Pamela Harriman achieved through the clear-sightedness with which she marked down her quarries, the ruthlessness with which she pursued them, the seeming indifference with which she shrugged off criticism, and the courage and energy with which she accepted reverses and marched on to new conquests. She was never guilty of self-pity.

Red-haired, but with a tendency to dumpiness,

Pamela Harriman was far from being an overwhelming beauty – though "the best facelift in the world" (as friends described an event which she herself refused to acknowledge), together with her undimmed vitality, made her an exceptionally striking 70-year-old.

Her secret lay in her ability to make any man at whom she set her cap feel that he was the sole object of her attention. Women tended to be less impressed. Yet part of her skill was to subsume her own ambitions in those of her conquests.

"She's interesting because she has fantastic taste," Truman Capote considered, "but she has no intellectual capacities at all. She's some sort of marvellous primitive. I don't think she's ever read a book or even a newspaper except for the gossip column. Pamela's a geisha girl who's made every man happy."

The talent ran in her family. She was born Pamela Beryl Digby at Farnborough, Kent, on March 20 1920, the first of four children born to Edward Kenelm Digby, who succeeded as the 11th Lord Digby two months after her birth. Pamela's mother was a daughter of the 2nd Lord Aberdare.

"Something in all the Digbys caused them to win renown by being at odds with society," wrote the biographer of Sir Kenelm Digby (1603–65). The rogue gene was still active in the 19th century when a Jane Digby became one of the great adventuresses of her time, leaving a trail of husbands and lovers from Bavaria to Syria.

Pamela Digby was much struck by Jane Digby's career; at first, though, she did not seem destined to emulate it. She spent her infancy in Australia, where her father was military secretary to the Governor-General. She learnt to talk by mimicking a loquacious white parrot, the first fruits of a talent which would later be practised on Sir Winston Churchill.

At Cape Town on the voyage home from Australia, the three-year-old Pamela sank her teeth into the calf of a black man on the quay, on the theory that he was made of chocolate. Thereafter she was brought up at Minterne Magna, the family home in Dorset. By chance, in the early 17th century it had been bought by John Churchill, grandfather of the 1st Duke of Marlborough.

Pamela Digby's father's interests were hunting and horticulture (especially carnations). Though Pamela became an excellent horsewoman, her boredom was relieved only by the visits of fox-hunting Americans, who appeared to her as the epitome of glamour.

She was sent away to Downham School in Hertfordshire, before being "finished" in Paris – an episode later inflated into "post-graduate work at the Sorbonne". She also went to Germany where, she claimed, Unity Mitford introduced her to the Führer.

In 1938 Pamela Digby returned to do "the Season". "She was very plump and so bosomy that we all called her 'the dairy maid'," one of her contemporaries remembered. "She wore high heels and tossed her bottom around. We thought she was quite outrageous. She was known as hot stuff, a very sexy young thing."

On coming out she was taken up by Lady Baillie, whose Leeds Castle set was a rival to that at Cliveden. Pamela Digby was delighted to be drawn into the ambit of men of power and influence.

In 1939 she met Randolph Churchill, and notwithstanding dire warnings on every side married him three weeks later. Nine years older than she, he already had a reputation as an alcoholic roustabout, and it did not help that he insisted on reading Gibbon aloud to her during their honeymoon. Fidelity he never even attempted.

Worse, his capacity for accumulating debts left her constantly short of money, breeding in her two enduring characteristics: insatiable avarice and a dislike of English men which eventually came to embrace the entire country.

Nevertheless, she established excellent relations with her parents-in-law, Winston and Clementine Churchill, and while Randolph was away lived at 10 Downing Street and Chequers. Her alliance with the Prime Minister was sealed by the birth of young Winston in October 1940.

As Pamela Churchill's marriage deteriorated, she amused herself with American servicemen; Sir Charles Portal, the British Chief of Air Staff, was also much struck. But she did not confine herself to the military; her American admirers included William Paley, the president of CBS, Jock Whitney, who would later be American ambassador to London, and the broadcaster Ed Murrow.

Her most notable conquest was Averell Harriman, President Roosevelt's Lend-Lease envoy, and 28 years her senior. Their liaison was encouraged by Lord Beaverbrook, who gave her money for clothes, and condoned by Winston Churchill, who saw Pamela's potential as a conduit of information between the Allies. The affair ended when Harriman was sent as ambassador to Moscow in 1943.

By this time her attitude to Randolph had become vitriolic. "Panto [Pamela] hates him so much that she can't sit in a room with him," recorded Evelyn Waugh in May 1942. And Harold Nicolson noticed Randolph's "little wife squirming" in embarrassment as she listened to him in the House of Commons.

They were divorced in 1946, though Pamela always

remained loth to relinquish the name of Churchill. For a while she worked for Beaverbrook on the *Evening Standard*'s Londoner's Diary, but her journalistic career did not survive her conquest of Prince Aly Khan.

In 1948 she moved to Paris and pursued an affair with Gianni Agnelli, heir to the Fiat empire. But though she nursed him back to health after a serious car crash, and even joined the Roman Catholic Church (which duly produced an annulment for her), he would not contemplate marriage. When she became pregnant she had an abortion.

She became a friend of the Greek shipping magnate Stavros Niarchos, and the lover of the French banker Elie de Rothschild. But de Rothschild, like Agnelli, preferred to finance her as a mistress rather than indulge her as a wife. "They just don't want to marry her," Truman Capote gleefully observed.

By the late 1950s the British establishment regarded her as a scandalous figure. In 1956, when Queen Elizabeth the Queen Mother was on a visit to Paris, Lady Jebb, the ambassador's wife, found it impossible to invite Pamela Churchill to lunch at the Embassy.

Pamela Churchill did not repine: she turned to America, where she settled on Leland Hayward, a theatrical impresario and the producer of *The Sound of Music*. He had been married five times (though only to four women); and in 1962 the number increased to six.

Though he turned out to be less than colossally rich – and such fortune as he possessed was speedily diminished by her taste for interior decoration – the marriage was a success. Pamela Hayward looked after her husband devotedly as his health failed.

When he died in 1971, she moved speedily into

action. Spurned by Frank Sinatra, that August she found herself – whether by chance or design – sitting next to her old flame Averell Harriman (now 79, recently widowed and one of the richest men in America) at a Washington dinner party given by Katherine Graham of the *Washington Post*. The opportunity was not wasted; they were married at the end of September 1971. In December Pamela Harriman became an American citizen.

Averell Harriman was a pillar of the Democratic party, to which Pamela, though instinctively conservative, now conformed. Their house in Georgetown, Washington, became the unofficial heart of the party in exile during the years of Reagan and Bush.

Pamela Harriman proved herself an imcomparable hostess and fundraiser, and invitations to her parties became as prized as those to the White House. Though still no intellectual, she began to acquaint herself with foreign policy issues, and accompanied Harriman on trips to the Soviet Union. In consequence, when Raisa Gorbachev visited America in 1987 she had tea with Pamela Harriman rather than Nancy Reagan.

Averell Harriman had died in 1986, leaving her a fortune and a leading position in the Democratic party. Her choice for the 1988 nomination was Al Gore; in the event she had to make do with Michael Dukakis, who caused her considerable alarm on his visit to her house by threatening to slip off a narrow podium into her proudest possession, Van Gogh's *White Roses*.

In 1992 Pamela Harriman gravitated to Bill Clinton, who delighted her by picking Gore as Vice-President. After his election President Clinton appointed her the American ambassador in Paris, the post once held by Benjamin Franklin and Thomas Jefferson.

Her energy and social adroitness ensured her success in Paris. Although she was embarrassed by two failed spying operations, she helped America and France to reconcile their differences over trade in audio-visual and farm products, thus making possible the successful conclusion of a Gatt deal. Impressed by her accomplishments, the French Government cited her "passion, ardour and intelligence" in appointing her a Commander of the order of Arts and Letters in the *Légion d'honneur*.

But Pamela Harriman had become embroiled in controversy over the management of trusts which Harriman had left her, and from which his two daughters drew income. At first all went well, but between 1989 and 1993 $21 million of the trust money was poured into a hotel and conference centre in New Jersey that failed.

In 1994 the Harriman heirs, whom Pamela Harriman had treated with disdain, instituted a lawsuit alleging that she had squandered the family funds. A settlement was reached at the end of 1995, but the cost was evidently considerable: Pamela Harriman sold three of her paintings (a Picasso, a Renoir and a Matisse) for $11 million, as well as one of her two houses in Georgetown.

In April 1996, after three years in Paris, she told the *Washington Post* that she was "ready to go back to Washington. It's been nice, but there's a limit to how long you can live a public life. You're 'on' most of the time." In May, though, the American Embassy in Paris "categorically denied" that her resignation was impending.

February 6 1997

GUY WAYTE

GUY WAYTE, who has died aged 89, fulfilled his ambition when in 1968 he bought the *Tatler*; but a few years later he was called an "unscrupulous humbug" by the judge who sentenced him for falsifying circulation figures.

Humbug or not, Wayte delighted the fashionably genteel when he began to publish the *Tatler* again after a three-year gap, with advertisements on the front cover under the familiar knee-breeched figure with his quizzing glass, and a price of 5s. At Wayte's insistence most of those photographed in its glossy pages had to be titled.

Tatler was the icing on the cake of Wayte's Illustrated County Magazine Group. He realised profits depended on advertising, and that advertisers were interested in circulation. The circulation figures of the *Tatler* and the *Nottingham Observer* were falsified over eight years. Sometimes this was done by the simple expedient of putting the figure 1 to the left of the real sum; thus the *Nottingham Observer*'s true monthly circulation of 2,000 copies was inflated to 12,000. The *Tatler*, instead of selling the 295,570 claimed for a six-month period, in reality sold 100,069.

An accountant who was one of those charged at the same time as Wayte, but acquitted, blamed him for putting pressure on him to sign false returns sent to the Audit Bureau of Circulation: "Wayte would be jumping up and down. He was a bloody swine."

Wayte blamed the bringing of the case on a disgruntled printer. But in February 1980 Wayte was given a

nine-month suspended sentence on two counts of conspiracy to defraud advertisers.

William Guy Alexander Wayte was born on April 4
1907, the elder son of an Anglican parson who went over
to Rome. His grandmother was a daughter of Sir Joseph
Paxton, the architect of the Crystal Palace.

Young Guy was educated by tutors and by the age of
19 was running *The Oxford and Cambridge Magazine*,
selling space during the day, and in the evenings knocking
on the doors of famous writers asking for contributions.

Wayte then started up a magazine called *Society*. This
was followed by another, *Hunting*.

After serving in the Second World War, Wayte began
to publish from his home in Ruddington, Nottinghamshire, his only trade publication, the *Paint Journal*. The
next step was to start, with his brother Humphrey, the
first of his monthly county magazines, the *Leicester
Graphic*. This covered hunting fixtures, parties and local
business events. Eventually there were 17 county magazines.

The style of some of the regional titles may be judged
from the column called Edgbaston Commentary in the
Birmingham Sketch: "Radiant day ... wrote diary in full
sunshine with *mirabile dictu* a tortoiseshell butterfly alight-
ing on the page and honey bees sipping the flowering
daphne."

After the 1st Lord Thomson of Fleet had bought and
closed down the old *Tatler* after trying to modernise it,
Wayte managed to acquire the name for a song, and in
1968 it appeared again with a policy of turning the clock
back to unashamed snobbery.

After the circulation debacle, the *Tatler* was sold, and

was soon turned into something completely different, much to Wayte's sadness.

Wayte and his wife, Marjorie, were generous hosts at Colston Bassett Hall, the Palladian house in Nottinghamshire which he had bought and restored in the 1960s.

Under the piratical image he liked to project, Wayte had a soft heart which he tried to hide, sometimes successfully. In manner he was a sort of Regency figure, immaculately dressed and priding himself on being one of the last of the "heavy swells". He lived life to the full, hunting and playing tennis well into his eighties.

Guy Wayte married, in 1944, Marjorie Sunderland. There were no children.

March 6 1997

JOLIE GABOR

JOLIE GABOR, the mother of Magda, Zsa Zsa and Eva who has died aged 97, was always determined that her daughters should achieve celebrity.

"You will be rich, famous and married to kings," she told them – and to that end insisted that they should master every possible accomplishment. "I wanted them not just to skate," she said, "but to skate like Sonja Henie; and I wanted them to play the piano so magnificently that a Rubinstein would be green with envy."

No talent was too arcane to be overlooked. "When will you be able to do that?" she demanded after taking her daughters to watch a fire-eater at a circus. This maternal solicitude bore fruit; if none of the girls married kings, they all became show-business personalities, with the keenest instinct for publicity.

No doubt there was an element of frustrated ambition in Jolie Gabor's hopes for her daughters. Born Jolie Tillemans into a prosperous merchant family in Budapest, she wanted to be an actress, only to have her dreams dashed when, at 17, she was married off to Vilmos Gabor, a former cavalry officer who owned a jewellery business.

"In the back of my mind I had the idea to get a divorce six months later," she remembered. "But like a fool I fell pregnant and had a daughter. Then I had another daughter and another. And all the time I wanted sons." Six months stretched out to 22 years.

Jolie Gabor finally divorced her husband in 1939, and escaped to America with no possessions beyond $100 in cash, a sable coat and a 30-carat diamond. Fortunately her daughter Zsa Zsa had preceded her to New York and married the hotel tycoon Conrad Hilton within three weeks of stepping off the boat. "Her heart is so big," Jolie observed, "I believe she would have married Connie Hilton just for my sake."

Subsidised by Zsa Zsa, Jolie Gabor started a small jewellery shop on Madison Avenue. Soon it was a big jewellery shop. "When you look as beautiful as my daughters, you don't struggle," Jolie Gabor reflected. "The best combination in the world is brains and looks. And also to know how to enjoy yourself."

She cast a benevolent eye over her daughters' copious matrimonial adventures, reserving a special affection for the actor George Sanders, who married both Magda and Zsa Zsa. "You know, Jolie," Sanders wrote to her, "I think marriage is for very simple people, not for great artists like us."

Zsa Zsa, however, cast a colder eye on her third husband. "Ven I vas married to George Sanders, ve vere both in love with him. I fell out of love vith him, but he didn't."

In 1957 Jolie Gabor married Count Edmond de Siegethy, who had escaped from Hungary in 1956. He arrived in New York with only $27 and proceeded to spend $20 on flowers for Jolie.

"Any man who could be so generous had to be special," she concluded, "so I married him."

The match, she noted proudly, took the matrimonial score of herself and her daughters to 13; eventually the daughters would notch up 19 marriages on their own account.

It hardly boded well for Jolie's marriage to de Siegethy that, at a family reunion in Vienna in 1958, she told Vilmos Gabor that he had always been her *real* husband. Nevertheless her second marriage endured. "You see, my darling," she explained to a journalist in 1973, "he insists every day that I take 14 vitamin pills, and that I use only the best lotions on my face. The Hungarians worship beauty."

Jolie Gabor expressed outrage at suggestions that her daughters married for money. Zsa Zsa, for example, never took any alimony. And Eva (who died in 1995) concluded that men were a necessary evil: "Sex," she said "is very good for pimples."

Jolie Gabor loved parties and was always ready to pawn a diamond to pay for champagne.

"Life's a gamble," she held, "you must know how to

play it." She spoke of her daughters with pride, yet she knew what was due to herself: "I too am a success."

April 3 1997

HUGHIE GREEN

HUGHIE GREEN, who has died aged 77, was the creator and smiling compere of the television talent show *Opportunity Knocks* which gave a range of stars their first big break and was watched at its height by 25 million people.

The tone of the programme was set by his customary reassurance to viewers, delivered in his trademark mid-Atlantic accent, "I mean that most *sincerely*, folks."

The show ran on ITV from 1956 to 1978 and was appreciated for its innovative style – the "clapometer" which measured audience enthusiasm, the voting by viewers, and Green's flirtatious on-screen relationships with such fellow presenters as the diminutive Monica Rose.

The stars it launched included such luminaries as Little and Large, Peters and Lee, Freddie Starr, Tom O'Connor, Pam Ayres, Lena Zavaroni, Frank Carson, Mary Hopkin and its biggest find, Les Dawson, whose wife had told him that the show represented his last chance at a career in comedy.

Each week Green introduced six new acts of varied quality and content. Among those featured were a chef who "cooked a complete veal dinner in under three minutes", a margarine sculptor and a dancer "who kept tropical fish and danced the sailor's hornpipe". The actress

Su Pollard tried her luck but finished second to a singing dog.

On the screen, Green's unctuous treatment of performers ("Isn't that wonderful folks? Let's have a hand for Bob!") did seem to put amateurs at their ease but was thought by the fastidious both servile and patronising.

Green never baulked at sentiment and was increasingly tempted to use his programmes as a platform for his fervently patriotic opinions. He used to end the show with the words, "Bye, bye, buy British," later asking, "What is offensive about that? I've never heard of anyone being *too* patriotic."

ITV advised him to eliminate the jingoistic finales of *Opportunity Knocks* after Green (accompanied by a brass band) had given a rendition of one of his own songs. "It went like this," Green recalled. "'We are still the nation, / That bred a generation, / Who in 1940 dark, / Made a torch of one last spark, / Fanned it into life to mark, / Freedom! Freedom! Freedom in victory!' Now who could possibly complain about that?"

Off screen, Green had little in common with his oleaginous television persona. Describing himself as "a hard-nosed businessman", he lived well, piloting his own aircraft, keeping a yacht anchored on the south coast and driving a Rolls-Royce.

Hugh Hughes Green was born in London on February 2 1920. His father was a Glaswegian, his mother a stage-struck Irish colleen. Young Hughie spent his early years in Canada, where the family was staunchly Conservative; his godfather was the First World War militia minister Sir Sam Hughes and his grandfather was later the first constituency campaign manager for the future prime minister John Diefenbaker.

The boy was educated back in London but at the age of 12 turned down a scholarship to Westminster School in order to make his stage debut. The following year he approached the BBC, demanding an audition for himself and his troupe of child actors, and by the age of 14 was top of the bill at the Alhambra Theatre.

He made his screen debut in 1936, as *Midshipman Easy* in Carol Reed's film, saving Margaret Lockwood from Spanish bandits. He went on to appear in *Melody and Romance* (1938), *Down Our Alley* (1939) and *Tom Brown's Schooldays* (1940). He also formed three touring theatrical companies (The Hughie Green Gangs) and at one point employed 200 people.

In 1940 he joined the Royal Canadian Air Force and spent the Second World War ferrying aircraft across the Atlantic, sometimes with undertrained Russian crews who "had a disconcerting way of making up for their lack of skill with an abundance of zany courage". The aircraft in which he trained, Stranraer Flying Boat 921, now rests in the RAF Museum at Hendon.

After the war, Green returned to films with *If Winter Comes* (1948) and made his radio debut in 1949 with his own talent-spotting show, *Opportunity Knocks*.

Green spent the next year unsuccessfully trying to persuade the BBC to show the programme on television. In 1950 he brought a court action against the BBC, claiming that they were "conspiring to prevent the show being screened". Green invested a fortune in legal fees but lost the case and was declared bankrupt.

In order to pay off his debts he returned to Hollywood and began working as a stunt pilot. He appeared on Broadway and in several American television shows, but his film career never revived after he played a small part in *The Master of Lassie* (1950).

By the mid-1950s Green had become esatblished in America as a quiz-master. He returned to Britain in 1956 when ITV agreed to screen *Opportunity Knocks*. Over 10,000 acts were auditioned each year, of which 175 were chosen by Green for the show.

Each act was introduced by a sponsor whom Green would question before the act began — "Tell me Betty, what was the proudest moment of your life? . . . Isn't that wonderful, folks?" This embarrassing formula proved an immediate success with the public.

Green also hosted *Double Your Money* in the mid-1950s and, from 1968, *The Sky's The Limit*. By the early 1970s it was clear that Green and the producer of *The Sky's The Limit*, Jess Yates, had differing ideas about the production of the show.

Yates urged Green to modernise the presentation. Green claimed that Yates (known to his colleagues as "The Bishop") was trying to "introduce elements of sex" into the programme. "To my shock and horror Yates said the show had to be jazzed up", Green recalled, "and he sacked our singer Audrey. I know she was corny but the people loved her."

By 1974 relations between the two had become so strained (it was later alleged that Green was actually the father of Jess Yates's daughter, Paula), that they were arguing regularly about everything, even the colour of Green's shirts. On one occasion Green almost refused to appear after Yates introduced what Green described as "dolly-birds in purple wigs and a giant rocket on castors". Yates left the show in 1974 and *The Sky's The Limit* was taken off the air.

In 1978 *Opportunity Knocks* was also removed from schedules because, according to Green, "TV's been taken over by anti-patriots. The Reds aren't under the beds, they're right in there running programming. Why else did they stop me praising our heritage, and giving viewers good old rousing patriotic stuff to get this country back on its feet?"

Although Green complained that television had become "overwhelmed with filthy and salacious shows", his scruples did not prevent him accepting the part of Bob Scratchitt, the host of a television chat show, in *What's Up Superdoc?* (1978): "I knew it was what's called 'soft porn' when I accepted the part. But it's a funny film and after all I am an actor."

By the end of the 1970s Green's performing career had stalled. But he still maintained a variety of business interests. He kept up a keen interest in broadcasting and continued to lobby against what he described as "Communist subversion on television" and to scrutinise the small screen for "evil people putting over anti-British propaganda".

Green returned to television in 1987 when he was employed by the BBC as a consultant on the new *Opportunity Knocks* presented by Bob Monkhouse. But his appointment was short-lived. "They knew I didn't approve of Monkhouse," he recalled, "but they went ahead and offered it to him anyway. They didn't listen to a word I said."

In 1989 Green leapt to the defence of his interest in *Opportunity Knocks* when he discovered that the New Zealand Broadcasting Company were screening a show which copied it in every detail, including the catchphrase "It's make your mind up time" and the clapometer. Green

declared himself "horrified" that his ideas were not protected by copyright laws. He appeared at the Edinburgh
Festival to talk about the pirating of television formats and
brought a case against NZBC for "stealing his ideas".

By 1990 Green had spent £250,000 on legal fees but
he lost his case when it reached the Judicial Committee of
the Privy Council. The court ruled that it was impossible
to copyright a gameshow because it was unscripted and
did not constitute a dramatic performance. Green
described the court's ruling as "a thieves' charter".

The next year he began a battle to change Britain's
copyright laws. Backed by an all-party group of MPs, he
petitioned for the restructuring of laws to protect British
game shows from foreign television companies.

In 1996 Green received an apology from the BBC after
a character in the comedy series *The Vicar of Dibley* was
heard to observe, "There hasn't been a bus through the
village since Hughie Green died."

His wife Claire, his childhood sweetheart whom he
married in 1942 (dissolved 1975), died in 1995; they had
a son and a daughter.

May 5 1997

SIR JOHN JUNOR

SIR JOHN JUNOR, who has died aged 78, was editor of
the *Sunday Express* for 32 years, from 1954 to 1986, and
one of the last survivors of the Fleet Street generation that
came to prominence under Lord Beaverbrook.

There is room for debate about Junor's success as an
editor, for the circulation of the *Sunday Express* actually

halved (from four million to two million) under his leadership. But as a columnist on that paper from 1973 to 1989 he won a keen following for the blunt manner in which he wrote what so many readers thought, but would never have dared to say quite so forcefully themselves. His pieces, and especially the abusive passages, profited from being read out aloud in Junor's rich Scottish tones.

He dismissed homosexuals as "poofs", "powderpuffs" and "pansies", and expressed the view that Aids was the punishment ordained by God for sodomy. In particular he anathematised those "who flaunt their homosexualism and try to subvert and convert other people to it. These are the people I have an utter hatred for, because I think they are spreading filth."

Other categories which aroused his wrath included Anglican bishops — "trendy old women"; the Irish — "wouldn't you rather," he demanded after the Brighton bombing, "admit to being a pig than to being Irish?"; the Press Council — "po-faced, pompous, pin-striped, humourless twits"; and the Greenham Common women — "sluts".

Taxed with racism, Junor would point out that the President of Gambia was a friend. But he did not disdain general principles: "Never trust a bearded man," he would tell subordinates, or "Only poofs drink white wine". Concerned by the rising crime statistics, he wanted to hear more of "the whack of birch on bare backsides".

Particular *bêtes noires* were Lord Denning — an "unctuous old humbug"; Lord Attenborough — "ancient, affected, side-whiskered trendy"; the Archbishop of Canterbury, Dr Runcie — "a pathetic old man" who deserved "a kick up the backside"; and the Bishop of Durham — "a vain old fool", "a really nasty piece of work, an evil man", whose ordination had provoked the Almighty into hurling a thunderbolt at York Minster.

Viscount Whitelaw "would not be two-faced if there were a third one available"; Neil Kinnock was "a weak, wet Welsh windbag"; and President Bush appeared as "a neutered old tabby". Further down the hierarchy, Jonathan Dimbleby featured as "a bumptious little twerp", while Sara Keays was excoriated as a "vicious, vindictive, scheming bitch".

"Pass the sick bag, Alice" was the stock conclusion to these reflections on the passing scene. Alternatively, "Aren't there times when you truly feel like pulling the duvet over your head and turning your face towards the wall?"

By contrast, erring heterosexual men, such as Cecil Parkinson, conspicuously failed to provoke his disapproval. Junor appeared to find comfort in the reflection that, according to the Church of Scotland, "marriage is a contract, not a sacrament". He himself had a keen eye for the other sex – although, in the words of a friend, he was not so much a lover as a plunderer of women.

On the positive side, Junor believed that Britain was "the greatest nation in the world", though he also nursed a surprising weakness for the French. Mrs Thatcher, the Princess of Wales and Selina Scott all aroused his passionate enthusiasm. Mrs Thatcher reciprocated by knighting him in 1981, writing a foreword to *The Best of JJ* (1981), and turning up at a dinner party to celebrate his 25 years as editor.

"The moralist of the suburbs", as Junor was called, also found room in his column for inside political gossip, dollops of romantic slush and occasional maudlin reflections on the wonder of bird life ("the miracle of the swallows"), the sufferings of animals ("those poor, dumb reckless creatures") and the cuteness of children ("little mites"). But it was rage that drove him. Aware of this, he always carred a tape recorder so that he could catch his fury on the wing. The style that resulted was once described as that of a Rotarian on Ecstasy.

Junor's greatest strength as a columnist was that his contempt for the chattering classes was even more intense than theirs for him, so that he never cared a scrap about provoking their disdain. Nor did he make cowardly calculations of self-interest. No good journalist, he used to say, should ever go anywhere without his resignation in his pocket.

He was the last journalist to be summoned before the Bar of the House of Commons, as a result of an article he wrote in the *Sunday Express* in 1956, which charged MPs with doing very well out of their supplementary petrol allowances at a time when the rest of the country was severely rationed. He acquitted himself before the House with dignity, offering a statement that was half apology, half defiance.

Junor liked to dwell on Auchtermuchty, a small town in Fife, as the repository of the Calvinist virtues which he upheld against the depradations of modern life. But it was observed that the closest he usually permitted himself to come to this paradise was to drive through it on his way to the Royal and Ancient at St Andrews.

For all the theoretical glories of his native Scotland, Junor lived in England – in Surrey – and remained there even after leaving the editorship of the *Sunday Express*. The Scots, he decided towards the end of his life, had become "a bunch of whingeing third-raters".

Yet though Junor enjoyed the good life and the best

restaurants, he never fogot his humble origins, or the fact that the majority of his readers did not enjoy the salaries and expenses of Fleet Street. He himself never ceased to count the pennies. "Now tell me something," he asked a journalist who had told him the cost of lunch at a restaurant, "does that figure include vegetables?"

John Donald Brown Junor was born in a Glasgow tenement on January 15 1919. His father was foreman in a steel roofing works, but it was his mother, a fanatical whist player, who was the dynamo of the family. She pushed her three sons to work hard, so that John and his brothers (one became a schoolmaster, the other a doctor) all went from state school to university.

Junor read English Literature at Glasgow University, where he became President of the Liberal Club and discovered a talent for public speaking. In the summer vacation of 1938 Lady Glen-Coats, prospective Liberal candidate for Orkney and Shetland, invited Junor to tour her constituency and to speak on her behalf. For this he received a cheque for £30, and an insight into a way of life beyond the tenements of Glasgow.

In 1939, after graduation, Junor acted as private secretary to Lady Glen-Coats (receiving £4 a week and his car). They visited Berlin together just before the Führer marched into Poland.

Junor joined the Navy as a midshipman (RNR), serving in the armed merchant cruiser *Canton*, a converted P&O liner. Later he transferred to the Fleet Air Arm.

His training revealed that he was by no means a natural pilot. Yet he survived a critical moment when his aircraft's directional instruments failed in pitch darkness. There was nothing to do but to pray, "my mouth quite dry". Salvation duly arrived in the shape of another plane, which guided him in to land. "I came to the conclusion," Junor said, "that someone up there had decided I had some purpose still to serve in life."

"I was a devout coward," he admitted. Relief from the hazardous business of taking off and landing on aircraft carriers came when he was appointed editor of *Flight Deck*, the Fleet Air Arm magazine.

In 1945 Junor was demobbed as a lieutenant, but not before he had fought Kincardine and West Aberdeenshire for the Liberals at the general election of that year, losing to the Tories by only 642 votes. He went on to unsuccessful contests at East Edinburgh in 1948 and Dundee West in 1951.

Meanwhile he had been working in London for an Australian newspaper and news agency, and in 1947 had joined the *Daily Express* as a reporter under Arthur Christiansen. In 1951 he was still undecided over a political or a journalistic career. "If it is politics," Beaverbrook told him, "you will reach the highest echelon. But if it is journalism, I will put on your head a golden crown."

Junor chose the golden crown. He was Crossbencher on the *Sunday Express*, and then assistant editor of the *Daily Express*. In 1953 he moved to the *Evening Standard* as deputy editor, and the next year became editor of the *Sunday Express*. But though he served his master well he was never guilty of the sycophancy which distinguished so many Beaverbrook acolytes, including many on the Left.

Junor claimed in his memoirs, *Listening for a Midnight Tram* (1990), that he ran the *Sunday Express* very much according to his own lights. "I had always been totally unreasonable," he wrote. "I had never once taken on the staff anyone I didn't personally like. I always took the simplistic view that if I didn't like him then other members of the *Sunday Express* staff might not like him either."

He would take the trouble to call his writers to tell them that their work was "piss poor". But as Michael "Inspector" Watts recalled, "the one thing we used to dread from him above all was praise – oh *God* it was awful. Because you knew that after praise, within a week or fortnight, would come the lash." Nevertheless, Junor was always good company, and could be kind as well as irascible.

In 1963, unable to stomach the thought of supporting Harold Macmillan at the forthcoming election, Junor resigned. Before he had worked out his six-months' notice, however, Macmillan was struck down with prostate trouble and left office. Junor returned to a post that had been eagerly coveted by Arthur Brittenden and Derek Marks.

But under his leadership the *Sunday Express* notably failed to move with the times. Well into the 1980s the paper was still fighting the Second World War, with tales of military derring-do illustrated by line drawings. There were also contemptuous references to artists and "long-haired" pop stars, and advertisements that seemed to concentrate heavily on garden sheds.

Junor's own column, though, retained its punch and popularity, and he continued with it after he gave up the editorship in 1986.

In 1990, outraged that Lord Stevens of Ludgate should have appointed a new editor without consulting him, Junor took his column to the *Mail on Sunday*. He always stressed the importance of insisting on one's own worth.

"If you can walk over a man once," he believed, "you can walk over him as often as you like." His column lost none of its force in its new habitat.

Junor married, in 1942, Pamela Welsh; they had a son and a daughter, both of whom became journalists.

May 5 1997

OSCAR BEUSELINCK

OSCAR BEUSELINCK, who has died aged 77, was a celebrated show business solicitor, known for his fierce negotiating skill and his boisterous and often unprintable bravado.

He acted for clients as diverse as John Osborne, Sean Connery, *Private Eye* and Robert Maxwell, and dealt with matters ranging from divorce and contract to tax and libel.

Beuselinck handled all four of Osborne's divorces. In his autobiography, the playwright recalled their first meeting at Beuselinck's office in Ludgate Hill: "His secretary and the switchboard girl were both sullen and looked like neglected evacuees, ignorant and ill-fed. The second thing he said to me was: 'You think I'm Jewish don't you?' And then grinning all over his face, 'Well I'm not. You should look at my chopper.'" (Beuselinck was always keen to dispel the impression created by his name and neat olive face.)

Beuselinck's advice to his clients was nothing if not straightforward. "If you must see her," he would tell male divorce clients, "keep your thing in your trousers." Or, as he asked Kathleen Tynan when she went to see him for a divorce: "Now, who have you been having it off with?" When tackled on the propriety of such an opening gambit, he would say that these were necessary legal questions, asked in a way designed to cause minimal embarrassment.

Osborne used aspects of Beuselinck for characters in several of his plays. Much of Beuselinck's background and some of his lewd catch-phrases found their way into his portrait of the embittered womanising solicitor Bill Maitland in *Inadmissible Evidence*.

Beuselinck was cheeky and instinctive, rather than boorish. Over-emotional and unorthodox, he would often become involved in stand-up rows in court. For women clients, he appeared a cross between a teddy bear and a knight in shining armour, who took both them and their complaints seriously.

One of five children, Oscar Albert Beuselinck was born in London on October 10 1919, the son of a Flemish Catholic father – a chef with the Union Castle shipping line – and a determined Cockney mother known as "Fighting Win". He grew up in a cramped flat in Holborn. "I never had a proper bath until I was 14," he recalled. "One room and mice by the thousand. I was the original Jimmy Porter."

From Rosebery Avenue primary, he won a scholarship to grammar school, but was unable to take it up because his father was not British by birth. Instead, at 14, after a stint as a tailor's trotter, he became an office runner at Wright & Webb solicitors, whose clients included MGM and Columbia Pictures.

Five years later, he was a junior litigation clerk, while

studying law at night school. "I wore a trilby," he recalled, "and changed my shirt twice a week. I thought that very posh."

During the Second World War, Beuselinck served in the Royal Artillery and later the Intelligence Corps, working on the preparations for D-Day and later on the de-Nazification of Germany.

Returning to his firm in 1946, he was admitted a solicitor in 1951. Almost immediately he set up on his own in the offices of the impresario Jack Hylton, who introduced him to clients such as the Crazy Gang, Arthur Askey and Oscar Lewenstein – the last of whom recommended him to John Osborne.

It was at Beuselinck's suggestion that Osborne and Tony Richardson set up Woodfall Film Productions to make the film of *Look Back in Anger*. The company, of which Beuselinck was a director, went on to film *The Entertainer*, *Saturday Night and Sunday Morning*, *A Taste of Honey*, *The Loneliness of the Long-Distance Runner* and *Tom Jones*.

Such was Beuselinck's success meanwhile that by 1963 he was able to buy his old firm, which by then was called Wright Webb Syret. By the late 1960s his clients included two out of the five major American studios and a host of stars.

In 1970 he flew to Hollywood to negotiate Sean Connery's return as James Bond. He also lent Harry Saltzman money to buy the film rights to the James Bond stories, though without asking for a percentage of the profits. Before long he was fighting Saltzman on behalf of his co-producer Cubby Broccoli. Later, however, he represented Saltzman and his wife in a battle against Adnan

Kashoggi, and eventually brought him on to the board of Woodfall Films.

Around this time Beuselinck sued *Private Eye* for libel on behalf of Wolf Mankowitz. During the 1970s, he brought libel actions on behalf of Richard Harris, Sean Connery, Willis Hall and Telly Savalas.

After suing *Private Eye* on behalf of Penelope Keith, Beuselinck was invited to an *Eye* lunch (he had acted for Peter Cook on theatrical matters). Beuselinck would become *Private Eye*'s principal solicitor, and was deemed to be so effective that the Express Group and others were soon beating a path to his door.

When Robert Maxwell sued the magazine for libel in 1986, Beuselinck was determined that they should fight it while launching a scathing attack on Maxwell. His vehemence eventually persuaded Peter Cook and Richard Ingrams, who by that time were fighting shy of libel actions. But *Private Eye* had very little evidence to support its offending story, and Maxwell won.

Beuselinck thought it scandalous that mention of Maxwell's dishonesty, as detailed in a Department of Trade and Industry inspector's report, was inadmissible for the purposes of mitigating damages.

Maxwell later unsuccessfully sued Beuselinck for professional malpractice, alleging that Beuselinck had exploited a friendship with a Mirror Group executive to press Maxwell on the discovery of hitherto undisclosed payments to the Labour party.

But these battles were soon forgotten. With seemingly indecent haste, Maxwell, who was worried by the growing number of libel suits against his papers, retained Beuselinck as the Mirror Group's in-house lawyer. This, to say the least, lowered Beuselinck in the esteem of those at *Private Eye*.

At the Mirror Group, Beuselinck was responsible for giving George Carman one of his first libel briefs. Beuselinck resigned from the *Mirror* in 1991 following a BBC *Panorama* programme about Maxwell, although Maxwell persuaded him to stay on as a consultant. In 1993, two years after Maxwell's death, he returned to private practice at Davenport Lyons, where he built a leading defamation practice.

In 1989 Beuselinck represented Carmen Proetta, the eyewitness who gave an account of the shooting of IRA terrorists in Gibraltar, in her successful libel action against the *Sun*, which had suggested she was involved in vice and drugs.

Beuselinck was a stout defender of his own reputation. When he was sued in 1971 by Margaret Duchess of Argyll, over tax advice which, she alleged, he had given her about her memoirs, he obtained full vindication in a trial lasting two and a half weeks. He then sent copies of the judgment to his friends.

Beuselinck was a nimble dancer, and at showbusiness parties seemed to know everyone. At the theatre, he would often fall asleep. Even on holiday he was not comfortable in informal clothes, reverting in the hottest climates to sober blue suits. He hardly ever drank. "I don't drink or smoke," he said. "I just pay alimony."

His instinct for settling other people's lives did not carry over into his own, which was colourful and at times chaotic. He listed his recreations in *Who's Who* as "getting married and Mozart", and he was notoriously boastful about his sexual exploits.

While Beuselinck was explaining Osborne's poor

chances for a divorce, the telephone rang. Cupping his hands over the receiver, Beuselinck whispered: "This is my bank manager. I'm screwing his cashier only he doesn't know that." Then after he put the 'phone down: "No Johnco, if I don't get it three times a day I feel physically ill, I really do." His closing remark, as he saw Osborne out, was: "Have you ever had it on the kitchen table?"

"You couldn't help liking him," Osborne wrote. "Like Max Miller. No inner life to hinder."

Beuselinck was three times married and three times divorced. He remained on friendly terms with all three wives. He had a son from his first marriage, the actor Paul Nicholas, and another son from his second.

July 30 1997

WILLIAM BURROUGHS

WILLIAM BURROUGHS, who has died aged 83, was an eccentrically daring satirist and one of the innovators of the 20th-century novel; alternatively (to quote Victor Gollancz) he was simply a purveyor of "bogus-highbrow filth".

In Britain it was the simultaneous issuing in 1963 of *Naked Lunch, The Soft Machine, The Ticket That Exploded* and *Dead Fingers Talk* that established his scandalous reputation.

Although *Lady Chatterley's Lover* had been published in 1962, no one seemed ready for *Naked Lunch*, a semi-autobiographical portrayal of the horrors of heroin addiction which Burroughs turned into a metaphor for humanity victimised by addiction to money, power and sex.

The characters included the Shoe Store Kid, a drug pusher who seeks out his prey with hands of "rotten ectoplasm"; Dr Benway, a crazed surgeon devoted to Automatic Obedience Processing; and the Lobotomy Kid, who creates the Complete All-American de-anxietised man, an "all purpose blob" of viscous jelly with a black centipede at its centre. The narrative was a nightmarish carnival of fragmented grotesqueries and obscene homosexual fantasies. A man is consumed by his own anus; a city becomes the inside of a sick intestinal system; "larval entities" gather as "the Planet drifts to insect doom".

When *Naked Lunch* was published in America, Norman Mailer heralded Burroughs as a genius, while Mary McCarthy invoked the shade of Jonathan Swift. "There are many points of comparison," she found, "not only the obsession with excrement and the horror of female genitals, but disgust with politics and the whole body politic."

In Britain, though, the *Times Literary Supplement* published a review headlined "Ugh", which sparked off a lively 13-week correspondence. "I do not wish to spend the rest of my life with my nose nailed to other people's lavatories," wrote Edith Sitwell. "I prefer Chanel No 5."

Anthony Burgess complained that Dame Edith was allowing squeamishness to ruin her judgement. "I do not like what Mr Burroughs writes about," he observed, "for that matter I do not always like what I myself write about."

Burroughs's appearance was no more calculated to please than his books. A tall, gaunt, grey and sinister figure, he was once described as a Giacometti sculpture in a demob suit. Years of drug-taking left his skin a hideous grey.

In 1951 he shot and killed his second wife Joan Vollmer (whom he had married in 1945) while "playing a game of William Tell" (trying to shoot a glass off her head) at a drunken party. Joan Burroughs was an old girlfriend of Jack Kerouac's and a "speed freak". Burroughs attributed his act to possession by "the evil spirit", which he set himself to exorcise through writing.

In the late 1950s he succeeded in breaking his addiction to heroin, and subsequently warned of the dangers of hard drugs. He professed to believe that drug addiction could be easily cured save that governments, particularly the United States government, had no desire to forfeit the policing power that a widely touted "drug epidemic" gave them.

Because Burroughs held that some drugs, notably marijuana, were not addictive and should therefore not be illegal, he became a cult figure among the younger generation of the 1960s, assuming for them almost the status of a rock-'n'-roll star. He was an appropriate hero for drop-outs, having lived his own life in revolt from the shaming respectability of his origins in Missouri.

William Seward Burroughs was born on February 5 1914 in the most fashionable part of St Louis. His grandfather had invented the Burroughs Adding Machine, a revolutionary calculating device.

But he had also committed the grave commercial error of selling the rights to the calculator, so that the young William Burroughs, though well off, was never as rich as people believed him to be. As an awkward Midwesterner at Harvard, though, it suited him to be mistaken for the heir to a great American fortune.

In fact his father ran a successful landscape gardening firm in St Louis. William was embarrassed by this business, not least by the classical-style "Grecian" statues which were sold to suburban garden owners.

Later he would complain of having been raised in "a malignant matriarchal society". Beyond the home, he was educated at the John Burroughs School and the Taylor School in St Louis, and at a private college at Los Alamos, New Mexico.

At Harvard he read English literature, attending the lectures of T. S. Eliot, and then in 1936 went to Vienna to study medicine. Oddly he never left any account of the Fascism which he must have witnessed there; the police states in his novels are always distortions of the United States, or of Latin American Republics.

Burroughs's medical studies did not last long, and he returned to Harvard to read anthropology in the graduate school. Soon, though, he drifted into advertising and then into a series of deadbeat jobs – as bartender, reporter, and even cockroach exterminator.

Druing the Second World War he was for three months a glider pilot trainee with the US Army, until discharged as unfit in September 1942. Thereafter he worked in a New York shipyard, where he first used drugs, becoming quickly addicted to what he called "Opium Jones", or "GOM" – "God's Own Medicine".

After the war, Burroughs, by then an addict, went to live in Mexico. In 1949 he began to write the autobiographical *Junkie*. The book was published in 1953 under the pseudonym William Lee – the name of the inventor of the knitting machine, as opposed to an adding machine.

It was in Mexico that Burroughs accidentally shot his wife. The Mexican police brought no charges against him

– though it was whispered that his family had paid large sums to square them.

After this catastrophe Burroughs left Mexico and travelled in South and Central America, "just looking around". In Peru he discovered the mescalin-like drug *yage*, which became the subject of a correspondence with Allen Ginsberg (published in 1963 as *The Yage Letters*). The years in South America provided material for *The Soft Machine* (1963).

Later in the 1950s Burroughs lived in Tangier, with "my old friend Opium Jones. We were mighty close in Tangier in 1957, shooting every hour 15 grains of methadone per day which equals 30 grains of morphine and that's a lot of GOM. I never changed my clothes. Jones likes his clothes to season in stale rooming-house flesh until you can tell by a hat on the table, a coat hung over a chair that Jones lives there. I never took a bath. Old Jones don't like the feel of water on his skin.

"I spent whole days looking at the end of my shoe just communing with Jones. Then one day I saw that Jones was not a real friend, that our interests were in fact divergent. So I took a plane to London and found doctor Dent . . ."

Through Dr Dent's prescription of apomorphine Burroughs was freed from heroin addiction. He had previously undergone several cures which did not work, noting in particular that attempting to cure someone of heroin by giving him methadone was like trying to break a whisky habit by drinking gin. When Dr Dent's treatment succeeded, Burroughs insisted that his publishers print his testimonial to apomorphine in each of his novels.

After a spell in Paris at the end of the 1950s, Burroughs lived for some years in London. When the row about his novels broke in the *Times Literary Supplement* in 1963, people imagined that he must be living in Paris, where the Olympia Press had published his work. They were surprised to find him in a basement flat in Notting Hill Gate.

But he took no part whatsoever in the London literary scene, saying it all seemed "sordid" to him. English novelists, he noted, eked out a living appearing on each other's radio programmes.

Later, in 1970, Burroughs moved to a grander flat on the top floor of a building off St James's. Visiting journalists would often think they had come to the wrong door, finding this well-tailored gent, looking a bit like a (then) more mature and un-pink-cheeked A. N. Wilson. "I do as well as a moderately successful plumber in the United States," he said.

He had what he called an "orgone accumulator" in the flat. This was a chest-high wooden box with a letter-box window and lined with tin. For a few minutes every day he would get inside it to let his "orgone accumulate". This, he found, had a pleasing "energising effect".

Meanwhile Burroughs had developed a curious technique for writing novels, whereby he would cut several pages into quarters and join them up willy-nilly, in the hope that chance would produce some new and poetic effect. This he called "cut up and fold in".

He had taken the idea from Brion Gysin, the painter, when they were living together in Paris at the end of the 1950s. Gysin felt that the novel was 50 years behind painting, having produced nothing like Picasso or Jackson Pollock. But Burroughs never employed the technique as much as his enemies liked to claim. He left little to mere chance, and submitted the results he gained to rigorous editing.

In collaboration with Gysin – "the only man I have ever respected" – he wrote *The Experimenter* (1960). But none of the later books – *Nova Express, The Wild Boys, Exterminator!, The Last Words of Dutch Schultz* and *The Place of Dead Roads*, a surreal 19th-century Western – achieved the *réclame* of his earlier novels.

Though Christopher Isherwood considered that *Cities of the Red Night* (1981) was Burroughs's "masterpiece", others discovered simply repetitive self-indulgent homo-sexual fantasy. *Queer*, published in 1985, was more lucid, but it had been written 30 years before, just after the death of his wife.

Burroughs left London in 1974 and took up residence in the gymnasium of a former YMCA building in New York's Bowery. He lived in "The Bunker" as he called it, with a "minder" and with his unfortunate son, Willy, an alcoholic and a junkie who died in 1981 when a liver-transplant went wrong.

That year Burroughs moved to Lawrence, Kansas, as writer-in-residence at the University of Kansas. The scourge of the bourgeoisie became devoted to his vegetable garden. And when he appeared in public he was invariably wearing a dark suit and tie.

To supplement his income he gave readings of his work, both in the United States and in Britain. Delivered in a flat, elongated drawl, with the weary irony of W. C. Fields and the unsmiling seriousness of Buster Keaton, they pointed up the humour of his writing and proved highly popular.

Notwithstanding his wife's death, Burroughs

remained obsessed by guns. In the 1980s he took up action painting, using a shotgun. He would set tins of paint before a plywood board and shoot them with buckshot, trusting in chance to produce an artistic effect.

After his move to Kansas, Burroughs began to write more conventional narratives, including *Place of the Dead Roads* (1984) and *The Western Lands* (1987). He wrote screenplays and appeared in films, including *Twister*. He was even seen in an advertisement for Nike.

In 1995 he published *My Education: a book of dreams*. One reviewer dismissed him as "a dirty old man". "I wish I was a *dirtier* old man," Burroughs responded. "I'm ashamed to go 24 hours without thinking about sex. It's alarming. It really is."

William Burroughs left his mark on Jack Kerouac and Allen Ginsberg as well as on the hippies of the 1960s and the punks of the 1970s. He also proved something of a prophet of the present times.

The nightmarish, drug- and violence-dominated urban scenes he described in early works seemed in the early 1960s to be the product of a feverish, perverted imagination. The passage of time would verify his imaginings, with "crack wars" in the streets of New York, and the Aids virus appearing like a plague from one of his novels. Burroughs himself claimed that Aids had been manufactured in US government laboratories to kill off homosexuals.

August 4 1997

FRANK SMYTH

FRANK SMYTH, who has died aged 57, was one of the last of a breed: the indigent writer-about-Soho before it was taken over by advertising agencies and expensive bars.

Largely unknown beyond Soho, Smyth's gifts as a raconteur, combined with a gigantic appetite for food and drink and the purposeful pursuit of women, made his bulky and untidy figure a landmark from the 1960s to the early 1980s

Editors anxious for copy past its deadline on his specialist subjects of crime and the supernatural became resigned to following the Smyth trail from pub to afternoon drinking club. The quality of the writing varied.

Cause of Death (1980), a history of forensic science, received respectful reviews for the quality of its writing and research. But an earlier book, *Modern Witchcraft*, which Smyth claimed to have written in four days, was dismissed by the reviewer of one national paper as a disgrace to its publisher.

Clutching a copy of the paper, Smyth approached Sir John Betjeman in the Star and Garter pub in Poland Street with the words: "Have you seen my latest review? Let me buy you a drink." Sir John glanced at the review and replied: "Oh no, dear boy, I think I should buy *you* a drink."

It was Smyth's (fairly consistent) charm, and his gifts as a raconteur and mimic, and a musician who could play most instruments by ear, which ensured him a wide circle of friends prepared to forgive outrageous behaviour. This ranged from overstaying his welcome by months to propositioning his hostess.

His circle included the regulars and barmen of almost every drinking haunt in Soho, as well as such figures as Ray Davies of The Kinks, Brian Innes, the publisher, author and member of the Temperance Seven and the writers Dan Farson (*qv*), Dominic Behan, Colin Wilson and Brian Inglis.

Francis Brendan Smyth was born on May 6 1940 at Morley, Yorkshire, and educated at St Michael's a Jesuit school in Leeds. After working on local papers, he arrived in London aged 19, bearing a letter from Graham Greene praising one of his short stories.

He soon became co-editor of the *Record Retailer* and a ubiquitous figure on the popular music scene. Later, he joined Pro-Ject Publicity, which at that time represented groups such as the Seekers, the Hollies and the Kinks. Peter Jones, then running the firm, recalls the difficulty of persuading Smyth to cut his lank hair and exchange his smelly leather "boozing coat" for a suit more appropriate for promotions.

One of Smyth's party pieces was to read from the script of the early ciné verité film *Don't Look Back*, which recorded a tour by Bob Dylan. Smyth, identified in the film as "Second Drunk", delighted in the exchanges between Dylan and himself after a glass had been thrown from a window in the Savoy Hotel.

In the 1970s, Smyth joined the staff of the magazine *Man, Myth and Magic*, and its stablemate *Crimes & Punishment* and established himself as an authority in those fields.

Smyth was proud of inventing the phantom vicar of Ratcliffe in east London for the BBC 2 television series *A*

Leap in the Dark, a sober examination of the paranormal. Its presenter Colin Wilson was appalled; but the existence of the ghost later appeared as fact in more than one book.

Smyth had no aspirations to home ownership, and spent much of his life staying with friends. In the 1970s however, he enjoyed four years of domesticity in Fitzroy Square with Judy Froshaug, the journalist, by whom he had a son.

He spent his later years at Bridport, Dorset, and was a regular contributor to *Real Life Crimes* and the *Wessex Journal*. For the latter he proved – to the satisfaction of locals at least – the legend that the undertaker's cat had eaten Thomas Hardy's heart before that organ (together with the strangled cat) was buried in Stinsford, Dorset.

Frank Smyth is survived by two sons.

August 9 1997

JEFFREY BERNARD

JEFFREY BERNARD, the laureate of Soho who has died aged 65, won a devoted following for his "Low Life" column in the *Spectator*, and a wider band of admirers when Keith Waterhouse brilliantly adapted that mournfully funny epic of self-destruction for the stage.

Jeffrey Bernard Is Unwell opened at the Apollo Theatre in 1989, with Peter O'Toole as Bernard, and enjoyed a triumphant year-long run (with Tom Conti and then James Bolam taking over the lead). In 1991 O'Toole returned for a sell-out short season.

It might seem strange that a column which presented a catalogue of alcoholic and sexual disaster should have so delighted the *bourgeoisie*. Bernard himself attributed his success to his readers' *Schadenfreude*. "If you're living where the grass is greener," he explained, "it must be reassuring to glance occasionally at the rubbish dump."

For years he had consecrated his days to the Coach and Horses in Greek Street, where he would drink vodka, lime and soda. (After he developed diabetes he cut out the lime.) The most promising time for conversation was between 11.30 a.m. and 1.00 p.m. – after two double vodkas, but before the sixth.

"I absolutely loathe getting drunk," Bernard would say. "It's an inevitable accident that happens every day." The same *faux naiveté* appeared in his relations with women. Somehow – he couldn't really explain why – he seemed to make the silly creatures unhappy.

His wives and mistresses were more forthright: "You make me sick," was their refrain in *Jeffrey Bernard Is Unwell*. Bernard could only wonder at their failure to heed the warning signs – "I mean," he said, "you can see a train when it's coming."

But the danger was part of the attraction. "I think it was because he was such a shit," one besotted victim reminisced. "He was a sod unless you did exactly what he wanted." Bernard steadfastly denied being a shit – "I've never deliberately caused misery."

He was saved by the unblinking honesty with which he regarded the wreck of his life, and by his talent for transmuting dishonour into laughter. His readers, in following the litany of disenchantment, found themselves marvellously released from the burden of ideals.

Marriage, Bernard implied, was incompatible with basic principles of self-preservation; work was an interruption of the serious business of drinking and fornication; aspiration, moral or material, was the province of prigs.

"What on earth makes people think that they have the right to be happy?" Bernard demanded. "Why can't people get it into their heads that life, by and large, is pretty bloody boring?"

This schoolboy nihilism exerted an extraordinary appeal. Bernard was compared to Sterne, Leacock and Wilde, while John Osborne found his eye for physical detail "as astonishing and stimulating as anything in Pepys or Boswell".

Those who met Bernard drunk – aggressive, bitter, and foul-mouthed – might be forgiven for missing the charm. But no one could deny the endurance with which he pursued the downward path. Even the amputation of a leg in 1994 failed to quell his spirit.

The fourth of five children, he was born Jerry Joseph Bernard at Hampstead on May 27 1932. His father, Oliver Percy "Bunny" Bernard, was a stage designer and architect, responsible for the Art Deco interiors of Lyons corner houses, and for an entrance to the Strand Palace Hotel, now in the V&A.

"Bunny" Bernard met his second wife while working at Covent Garden. She was an opera singer bred "by an itinerant pork butcher out of a gypsy"; her maiden name Dora Hodges had been forsworn in favour of Fedora Roselli. There was no shortage of money as long as Bunny Bernard was alive. The marriage, enlivened by vicious rows, was authentically bohemian.

Jerry, as he still was, was only seven when his father died, leaving debts. His mother gamely struggled to keep up a stylish front. "My mother looked like Ava Gardner,"

Bernard would remember. "I actually fancied her when I was 16, so I had an enormous amount of guilt about that."

The young Bernard had relished living in London during the Blitz. "I was a psychopathic little boy," he recalled, "I threw milk bottles off the roof and burned down the summer house."

He attended a number of preparatory schools, the fees paid by charities and friends — Joyce Grenfell among them. His first name provoked mockery at school, being associated with the dreaded Germans; so Jerry became Jeffrey.

In 1946 his mother sent him to Pangbourne Nautical College. It was too late, Bernard had grown accustomed to "the musicians, actors, actresses and similar riff-raff" who came to their house in Notting Hill, "and it didn't take me long to see that they were getting more fun out of life than my Latin master".

Soho, to which his brothers introduced him at the age of 14, "was magic, like walking out of Belsen into Disneyland". He also discovered racing. A boy at school was given 12 strokes for betting; Bernard reflected that anything which merited such punishment *must* be exciting.

In 1948 the reprobate was asked to leave Pangbourne. "Dear Mrs Bernard," wrote the Captain of the college, "While I believe Jeffrey to be psychologically unsuitable for public school life, I believe he has a great future as a seam bowler."

And so Bernard began his career as a full-time truant from life. He revelled in the cast-list of Bohemia: "George Barker, Sidney Graham, Francis Bacon, Lucian Freud,

Colquhoun and McBryde, Sid the Swimmer, Ironfoot Jack, Nina Hamnett, Muriel Belcher, Gaston Berlemont, Frank Norman, and a hundred more."

To survive he offered limited favours to the homosexual artist John Minton. There was never much doubt, however, of his own sexual orientation, or of his powerful appeal to women. "He was stunning, and *surly* – James Dean *before* James Dean," one of his early girlfriends remembered.

National Service intervened in 1950. A trooper with the 14th/20th King's Hussars, he tried to sell his tank's petrol before going AWOL for four months. Through the intercession of one of his brothers his punishment was light and he was discharged.

Bernard celebrated his freedom by marrying, though it lasted only four months. He kept himself in drink through jobs as a dishwasher, a fairground boxer, a navvy, a miner.

He also acquired a criminal record when he stole *A History of Byzantine Art* from a bookshop in Notting Hill and tried to sell it in the Charing Cross Road. From 1956 Bernard had the occasional job as a stagehand; and in the early 1960s he was a clapper-boy in films.

When, in 1964, Frank Norman asked him to a rehearsal of *A Kayf Up West* at Joan Littlewood's Theatre Royal, Stratford East, Bernard created such an impression that by the evening he was in the cast. "It was my first experience of being able to make 500 people laugh . . . I'm ashamed to say I've always *craved* not just success but being well-known."

As the years passed it was increasingly as an alcoholic blur, so that when Bernard was commissioned to write an autobiography, he had to place an advertisement asking if anyone could tell him what he had been doing between 1960 and 1974.

Undoubtedly the most significant event of that period was in 1964, when the poet Elizabeth Smart secured him a racing column in *Queen*. Bernard immediately found his style with a mixture of tips, anecdotes and chit-chat. But he also found that the compulsion to cover paper with words was one illness from which he did not suffer.

Nevertheless, he worked at his journalism with more dedication than he cared to admit. His copy was always typed without revision. He soon found slots – usually short-lived – in the *Daily Mirror* and *Town*.

In 1970 he began a column in *Sporting Life*. Professionally it was a success; as one appreciative reader wrote, he was "the first journalist to understand the average punter – self-destructive, paranoiac, a loser, yet richly human". But to Bernard a racecourse was "simply an *alfresco* piss-up". Eventually the paper sacked him for what the editor described as an "unpardonable exhibition at the point-to-point dinner".

In 1966 Bernard had been lured by his third marriage to desert Soho for Suffolk. The mistake was repeated 12 years later with his fourth wife, with whom he went to live at Lambourn. "We ended up prowling around eyeing each other like hungry watch dogs." On both occasions Soho received him back "with open arms and legs".

There was a further professional breakthrough in 1972, when Bernard began to write for the *New Statesman*, for which he produced some of his best work. After three years he was lured away by the *Spectator*, which set him up as its television critic.

It was soon necessary to find a replacement – Bernard

was far too drunk to watch television regularly – but Alexander Chancellor, the editor, determined to keep him in another role. The "Low Life" column began in August 1978.

Bernard's finances improved – without, however, impairing his facility for cadging on friends. He also attracted the unwelcome attentions of the dreaded "Tax-woman". And in 1986 no fewer than nine policemen and three customs men descended on the Coach and Horses to arrest him for making a book without a licence. He was fined £200 and ordered to pay £75 costs.

Behind Bernard's parsimony lay a determination to avoid absolute disintegration. He might boast that he met a better class of person in the gutter, but for him a first-class single to the gutter cost a minimum of £10,000 a year – "and that's without paying tax, rates, telephone, electricity, gas and unnecessary expenses like clothing and food". He was a stickler for clean clothes.

His own room was hung with many pictures of himself with Graham Greene, Lester Piggott and other notables. As his brother remarked on being asked whether this was Jeffrey's room: "Either that or it's someone's who likes him very, very much."

From time to time Bernard made a stab at suicide. "I've never tried to commit suicide sober," he reflected, "I'd be too frightened, because I don't really want to die."

In 1965 Bernard suffered agonisingly from pancreatitis, which developed into chronic diabetes. By the end of the 1960s he was six-to-four favourite for the next Soho death, but the opposition constantly made it to the finishing post before him.

Yet for long the doctors remained confounded. "This, gentlemen," the specialist at the Middlesex Hospital would say to his colleagues, "is Mr Jeffrey Bernard, who closes his veins each day with 60 cigarettes and then opens them again with a bottle of vodka." However, in his last weeks, when dialysis prevented his drinking, he was prohibited in the Middlesex Hospital from smoking too – a heartless measure.

From 1974 to 1976 he managed to stay on the wagon. He even took a job as a barman in a club. "There was this dark, angry, sober face behind the bar, deeply disapproving," remembered Geraldine Norman.

In 1986 a collection of Bernard's pieces, *Low Life*, was published, to add to the previous selection (with Taki) *High Life, Low Life* (1981). Graham Lord's somewhat unsympathetic biography, *Just The One*, was published in 1992. Bernard was also celebrated in one of Michael Heath's best cartoon strips, "The Regulars", in *Private Eye*, with its refrain "Jeff bin in?"

A message was planned for his memorial service: "I'm sorry I cannot be with you today due to *foreseen* circumstances."

Jeffrey Barnard married first, in 1951, Anna Grice, who died in 1955; secondly in 1958 (dissolved 1964), the actress Jacki Ellis; thirdly, in 1966 (dissolved 1974), Jill Stanley, with whom he had a daughter; and fourthly, in 1978 (dissolved 1981), Sue Ashley.

Jeffrey Bernard writes: May I add a few words to your excellent obituary of Jeffrey Bernard. I knew him intimately for many years and I feel that many of his more remarkable qualities were left unsung in your review of his messy life.

He was born covered from head to foot in eczema.

One of the first things he did was to wet the bed and he continued to do so until he was 15. A weak, thin-skinned and over-sensitive boy, he had few friends at school.

The only subject at which he excelled was history. His liking for historical biography was an early sign of the paranoia he was to develop.

But his early obsession with sex prevented him from obtaining any worthwhile academic honours. By the time he left school he had become a chain smoker and compulsive writer of fan letters to Veronica Lake.

In 1946 he paid his first visit to Soho and from that point he was never to look forward. Well do I remember his first bouts of drunkenness that usually ended in tears or abortive suicide attempts, and I think it must have been about this time that it was realised that Bernard was not cut out for a career as a naval officer as his mother had hoped.

He spent months at a time accepting small sums of money from homosexuals or friends in work. He developed a greed for unearned money and the conviction he was cut out for better things.

After an undistinguished spell in the Army, from which he was given a medical discharge with his paybook marked "Mental stability nil", he returned to Soho, married, and split up with his wife a few weeks later.

It was during this period that he first became involved with gambling, and the feelings of infantile omnipotence that this prompted were to last for the rest of his life. These feelings were particularly noticeable in his dealings with women and some even said that his life was a never-ending cliché of a search for his mother.

His drinking began to escalate to such an extent that he was unable to hold down the most ordinary job and he was consequently advised to take up journalism. He gradually drifted into writing a series of personal and, at times, embarrassing columns abut his own wretched life.

After a spell in the alcohol and drug-addiction unit at St Bernard's Hospital, Hanwell, he developed the fantasy that from tomorrow it would all be different. Thinking that geographical changes would solve his problems he moved to various "dream" cottages in the country. Unfortunately he was always there too.

He leaves two unwritten books and a circle of detached acquaintances.

September 8 1997

ANDREW FOUNTAINE

ANDREW FOUNTAINE, squire of Narford in Norfolk, who has died aged 78, was from 1957 President of the National Labour Party ("National because we love our country, Labour because we love our people"); later, in 1967, he helped to form the National Front.

Fountaine was obsessed by the notion that miscegenation constituted a threat to the British race. "If it is Fascist to try and stop that," he declared, "then Fascism is a bloody good thing." Among those he deemed racially alien were all Americans, and Italians south of Rome.

The National Labour Party soon amaglamated with the White Defence League to form the British National Party. In 1962 Fountaine organised an Aryan camp on his Norfolk estate, where he raised the symbolic sunwheel of "pure Northern Europeans".

But for all his speechifying in Stepney and Notting

Hill, Fountaine's call went unheeded. In 1967 he merged the British National Party with the League of Empire Loyalists to form the National Front. "Hitler had some first-class ideas," he told the press.

In March 1968 Fountaine became the first National Front candidate to contest a parliamentary seat when he stood in a by-election at Acton. His concern over alien immigrants "living one third off prostitution, one third off National Assistance, and one third off Red gold" won him 1,400 votes.

Soon afterwards, though, he was expelled from the Front by A. K. Chesterton (cousin of G. K. and head of the Empire Loyalists), who accused him of having issued a "ludicrous" directive on the action to be taken in the case of civil war. After that, Fountaine kept his distance from politics for some years.

In 1976 another row in the National Front gave him the chance to make a comeback, as deputy chairman to the leader, John Tyndall. He stood for Coventry North-West in a by-election, but recorded only 986 votes.

The advent of Mrs Thatcher brought no joy to Fountaine, who considered that she was presiding over "the greatest bunch of traitors in history". By contrast, he explained, the ethos of the National Front was based on "love of our country".

Love, however, was not in evidence among his colleagues. After another ignominious defeat at Norwich South in the 1979 general election, Fountaine took it upon himself to suspend Martin Webster, one of the Front's leading figures. Tyndall retaliated by expelling Fountaine, who reacted by forming the National Front Constitutional Movement.

That was Fountaine's last political throw. After 1981

he largely abandoned his efforts to save the British race and concentrated instead on planting trees on his estate.

Andrew Douglas Algernon Maclean Fountaine was born on December 7 1918, into a family established in Norfolk since medieval times. The family seat of Narford Hall was begun by Sir Andrew Fountaine of the Royal Mint in the 1690s and is notable for the painted decoration by Giovanni Antonio Pellegrini; the house was substantially enlarged in the 1860s to the designs of William Burn. Young Andrew's father, Vice-Admiral Charles Fountaine, was naval ADC to King George V. The boy was sent to Stowe; his hopes of passing through Dartmouth Naval College, however, were undermined by glandular fever.

At 17 he drove an ambulance for the Abyssinians, who were under attack from Mussolini – "though now I see that I was on the wrong side". The error was corrected when he fought for Franco in the Spanish Civil War.

He was an undergraduate at Magdalene College, Cambridge, and in 1938 became a Fellow of the Chemical Society.

On the outbreak of the Second World War, Fountaine managed to get into the Navy by persuading a friend who resembled him to undergo the medical examination on his behalf. He rose from Ordinary Seaman to Lieutenant-Commander, as a gunnery officer on the aircraft carrier *Indefatigable* in the Pacific. He was wounded in a kamikaze attack off Japan, and later saw the flash of the atomic bomb which was dropped – unnecessarily, as he thought – on Nagasaki.

In 1946, on his father's death, Fountaine became master of the family estate. The next year, he made his mark at the Conservative party conference, where he introduced a resolution "finally to root out the ever-increasing subversive foreign influence within our own country and the Dominions overseas".

The Tory rank and file cheered lustily before being quelled by Quinitin Hogg. In 1948 Fountaine again delighted the party conference when he described the Labour administration as "a group of conscientious objectors, national traitors, semi-alien mongrels and hermaphrodite Communists".

He was adopted as Conservative candidate for Chorley, in Lancashire. When the National Union refused to endorse him, he stood as an Independent Conservative in the general election of 1950, and failed by only 361 votes to capture the seat from Labour. Soon afterwards he announced his plans to launch a nationalist movement.

Fountaine also made determined efforts to contact Harold Macmillan. "Used to ring him up at his home," Fountaine recalled, "and he'd pick up the receiver, and as soon as he heard it was me, pretend he was the butler."

In 1959 Fountaine (who had been elected to serve on Norfolk County Council in 1951) stood for Norwich South as an Independent Nationalist, declaring that "the man who can gain the allegiance of the Teddy Boys can make himself ruler of England". He failed, though, to gain the allegiance of his own mother, a New Zealander, who vociferously opposed his candidature.

Away from politics, Fountaine enjoyed racing around the country in his Mercedes sports car.

Fountaine married first, in 1949, Anne Senior; they had a son and daughter. He is survived by his second wife Rosemary, with whom he had a son.

September 25 1997

THE REVEREND PETER GAMBLE

THE REVEREND PETER GAMBLE, who has died aged 77, was a colourful priest-schoolmaster who admitted in retirement that his homosexuality had been the mainspring of his personal life.

His brief experiment in running an Anglo-American school in Oxfordshire in the 1960s ended disastrously through a combination of drug-taking by pupils and financial insolvency. He was obliged to spend the last years of his teaching career at Harrow School.

Earlier he had been chaplain and housemaster at Milton Abbey, which he left after a row with the headmaster. This was followed by eight years as chaplain and tutor at Millfield, where his brother, Brian, was also a teacher.

His gifts as a teacher were considerable, as was his appreciation of beautiful boys. Though his autobiography *The More We Are Together* (1993), subtitled "Memoirs of a Wayward Life", indicate he often sailed close to the wind in his relationships with boys, the physical element was limited and never created scandal.

The Anglo-American school project, whose blameless patrons included Sir John Gielgud, Dame Rebecca West, Douglas Fairbanks Jnr, Sir George Thomson and T. E. Utley, was never sufficiently thought through and always lacked adequate financial backing. It was unfortunate for Gamble and those associated with him that when it started in 1967 the extent of the developing drugs problem among older schoolchildren was not widely recognised and there was little experience of dealing with it.

Gamble took a very tough line. During the first year of the school's life four of its 42 pupils (all in the 16–18 age range) were expelled and another two suspended. A member of the teaching staff was dismissed for spending a weekend with a girl pupil. Matters were further complicated when Sir John Tilley, in whose home the school was housed, accused Gamble of being too rigid, and gave him notice to leave the house at the end of the academic year.

New premises were soon found at Barcote Manor, on the Berkshire–Oxfordshire border, and a bank loan financed the purchase. A language school for foreigners wishing to learn English was also established at Carfax, Oxford, enabling Gamble to continue to use an Oxford address. For a time all was well. Pupils came from America and other parts of the world, as well as from Britain, and the regime was unfashionably strict. Academic results were encouraging.

But by 1970 the drugs squad was making inquiries about the extra-curricular activities of some pupils, and Gamble once again employed draconian measures – expelling four pupils, easing out another six, and placing four more on strict probation. This was reassuring to the parents of the innocent, but reduced the school roll to a point where the enterprise was barely viable financially.

September 1971 saw another fall in enrolment and the school went into voluntary liquidation. Gamble, with the then Bishop of Portsmouth, John Phillips, making kindly noises at his side, met the angry creditors who accused him of gross irresponsibility. But eventually Barcote Manor was sold at a favourable price and all were paid in full.

Several months passed before the erstwhile headmaster joined the teaching staff at Harrow, where he was given responsibility for A-level English and Latin. "There were", he later recorded, "many good-looking boys amid my pupils, but it was for Alec that I fell."

Peter John Gamble was born at Streatham Hill, in south London, in 1920. He attended two local private schools and left when he was 16 without any academic qualifications. His first job was in Fleet Street as an office boy with a monthly magazine *The Review*.

Before long he was not only making the tea but also writing some of the book reviews. This was not enough to satisfy the proprietor, who soon dispensed with his services. He then joined *Readers' News*, the organ of the Readers' Union, and after a spell of answering readers' letters he became deputy editor.

In 1940, however, the Readers' Union moved out of London to avoid the wartime bombing and it was decided that the deputy editor's services were no longer required. This left him with a number of problems besides that of immediate employment. He had joined the Peace Pledge Union and was totally opposed to the war, and he had also had some dealings with the British Union of Fascists, which made him the subject of a police investigation.

Having cleared himself of Nazi sympathies – "I only wrote a letter to Hitler" – and registered as a conscientious objector, he was taken on as a teacher at a boys' private school in Wimbledon. His teaching skills at this stage were undeveloped but he got on well with the boys and fell in love with Julien from Belgium. Their close relationship ended when Julien was old enough to join the Belgian Navy.

Gamble himself moved on to Belvedere Lodge School

at Esher, Surrey, but his contribution to the educational life of the nation was not deemed essential and, on appearing before a Conscientious Objectors' Board, he was ordered to join the Westminster Civil Defence, then struggling with the Blitz.

The importance of this task failed to inspire him and he contrived during his off-duty hours to return to the Readers' Union as head of editorial. This brought him into contact with a number of leading figures in London, with time to spare for patronage of the capital's private clubs for homosexuals.

All this came to a sudden end when he was posted to East Devon to join a regional civil defence column then engaged in the relief of bomb-torn Plymouth. Dissatisfied with his lot, Gamble went absent without leave and when traced was sentenced to a month in Exeter prison.

On his release he declined to wear Civil Defence uniform and was jailed for another month. An attempt to make him serve with hard labour was thwarted when his lawyer discovered that such a sentence could not be imposed on a conscientious objector.

By this time the Civil Defence authorities believed they could manage without him and he was sent to work in a coalmine at Bolsover in Derbyshire. This occupied him for just over a year, and then a local tribunal, having decided that he had done his best in the circumstances, released him from the colliery in September 1945 in order to teach at Kingsholme School.

After a good start with English and Latin, Gamble found himself in trouble with the headmaster for kissing a boy. Although this was smoothed over, he left soon after for another preparatory school – Waltons at Banstead. While there he discovered that his war service entitled him to a government further education grant and he secured admission to St Catherine's Society to read English.

Accommodation in the university and the city being severely limited, he lodged at Ripon Hall, the Church of England's liberal modernist theological college, and while there was encouraged to seek Holy Orders. His protestation that he knew no theology and believed very little of the Christain faith was swept aside and, after acceptance by a church selection conference and a few months at another theological college, he was ordained by the ultramodernist Bishop of Birmingham, E. W. Barnes, to a curacy at Erdington.

This occupied him from 1952 to 1954 and, finding no vacancies for school chaplains, he went to Paris as assistant chaplain at the Embassy Church. This involved conducting services at Anglican centres in Belgium, Holland and France. After just over a year he returned to England to resume his chequered career in education and renew his contacts with the homosexual clubs of Soho.

That he was not cut out for parochial ministry was demonstrated when, following his retirement from Harrow, he filled in as a curate. A Remembrance Day sermon in which he condemned the Western powers' reliance on nuclear weapons led to a protest meeting of assorted colonels and other members of the congregation in the churchyard after the service. Other sermons on theological matters were no less controversial.

October 3 1997

ANTON LAVEY

ANTON LAVEY, the founder and high priest of the Church of Satan, who has died in San Francisco aged 67, had begun his career in the circus, putting his head into the jaws of a lion; when the beast removed a chunk of his neck, however, he decided to look for alternative employment.

Later he would look back fondly on the sleaze that he had encountered during those years. Anton Szandor LaVey had been born in Chicago in April 1930, of a parentage he preferred to keep anonymous. Without his circus experiences in California, he felt, he might never have developed his taste for theatrical display or formulated a sufficiently debased view of human nature. Moreover his talents as an organist – he had accompanied the circus acts – helped to turn his thoughts in the direction of a church.

First, though, he gained further experience of human depravity as a photographer with the San Francisco Police Department. When they put him in charge of answering calls about supposed supernatural happenings, the pieces of his life fell into place.

In April 1966, on Walpurgisnacht, when evil is supposed to hold sway over the world, he shaved his head, declared himself a prelate in the House of Satan, and established his headquarters in a former brothel in the suburbs of San Francisco. He developed elaborate rituals for black mass, advocating the use of buxom nude girls as servers, thoughtfully allowing, however, that clothed women might be used should nakedness prove impracticable.

Claiming to be exploring "an untapped grey area between psychiatry and religion", he expressed a distaste for the mindless hippy radicalism of the 1960s. His *Satanist's Bible* (1967) proposed a sub-Nietzschean philosophy, wherein might equals right, and immediate self-gratification constitutes the chief duty of man.

"Be simply animal man," *The Satanist's Bible* instructs, "hate your enemies, and if someone smites you, smash him." Against this ideal he set the weak – "those who arrange their lives so that they are full of bitterness and animosity and self-rebuke, very often transferred to others".

"What we advocate", LaVey elaborated in 1970, "is what most Americans practise, whether they call it Satanism or not. We are the new establishment. We are for law and order, for the stability of society. We are the new conservatives."

The west coast of America proved fruitful of disciples, some of them celebrities. Sammy Davis Jr declared his interest, and so, LaVey claimed, did Marilyn Monroe. But the cult's most prominent champion was Jayne Mansfield.

This alarmed Sam Brody, her lover and lawyer, who vigorously resisted LaVey's influence. When Jayne Mansfield and Brody were killed in a car crash in 1967 – the actress reportedly being partially decapitated – LaVey let it be known that at the time of the accident he had been cutting out her photograph and had accidentally snipped off the top of her head.

In 1968 his movement received a fillip from the film *Rosemary's Baby*. "It did for Satansim what *Birth of a Nation* did for the Ku Klux Klan," LaVey exulted. He himself featured in one brief scene as the Devil – though it hardly advanced his claims as Satan's high priest that he had to be heavily made up for the role.

The Church of Satan gained a place in the San Francisco *Yellow Pages*, and – after LaVey had acted as chaplain at a military funeral – was officially recognised by the US Armed Forces.

But the murders perpetrated by Charles Manson and his followers in August 1969 suggested that such a movement might be rather more dangerous than a sick joke. Years later Susie Atkins, one of Manson's knife-wielding groupies, blamed LaVey for her descent into depravity and murder.

LaVey insisted that Manson's gang were drugged freaks, too weakly vile to qualify as Satanists. But his movement never recovered from the horror of Manson's crime, and gradually dwindled into insignificance.

Early in the 1990s LaVey was driven to bankruptcy by a fight over alimony with his wife Diane, whom he had married in 1962 and who had been associated with his work as high priestess.

Undaunted, he kept up the bad work, prophesying in *The Devil's Notebook* that the world was on the brink of a second wave of Satanism, characterised by a growing misanthropy and an increasing desire for isolation. At other times, however, he would refer to his Church as "simply a living".

LaVey left orders that he should be buried under the epitaph "I only regret the times that I was too nice". His daughter Karla, another high priestess, explained that he had died at the end of October, but that the news had been held over for fear of upsetting his supporters during Hallowe'en.

"If there *is* an after-life," LaVey had held, "it will depend on the vitality and lust for life of the individual before he dies, and on nothing more than that."

November 11 1997

DANIEL FARSON

DANIEL FARSON, who has died aged 70, was a talented television journalist, writer and photographer; he was also a nightmare drunk.

Farson was a prime specimen of Soho at its height, the Soho of Francis Bacon, Dylan Thomas, John Minton, John Deakin, Jeffrey Bernard (*qv*), Muriel Belcher and other strange characters. To Farson, Soho meant home, and he, convinced he was a misfit, never felt at home anywhere else.

From middle age onwards Farson was a fat man – the solid kind rather than sagging jelly. He never lost his hair, which was fair; in old age he presumably dyed it. In London he dressed in a smart suit with sleeves cut long to cover the tattoo of a fish on the back of one hand that he had had done in the Merchant Navy.

He was a brave man even when sober and strong enough to make an antagonist think twice. He would go off at night to such places as a pub nicknamed The Elephant's Graveyard. It was some surprise that, with his alarmingly risky sex life, he had not been murdered.

To encounter Farson at nine in the evening in the Colony Room Club, for example, was to witness a transformation that any film actor in *Dr Jekyll and Mr*

Hyde would have thought strained credibility. Within minutes, fuelled by a rapid series of large gins scarcely diluted by tonic, his polite talks about his great-uncle Bram Stoker or his interlocutor's latest book would turn into a rant of increasing volume and decreasing intelligibility: "I loathe you, I can't stand you," he would roar, gargling in his podgy throat. "You're *so* clever, *so* patronising." Sometimes the late Ian Board, the club's proprietor, would chase him down the steep, dark stairs, belabouring him forcefully with an umbrella.

Often, the morning after, Farson would appear with a cut face, from a fall, a fight with a rent boy or some forgotten tussle with a policeman. But he would return immediately to the alcoholic fray and the never-ending job of seeking work from newspapers or publishers.

Farson could take good photographs. He caught the changing moment and his pictures were often of interest for their subjects – a hungover Jeffrey Bernard, head in hands under the statue of King Charles in Soho Square, or the smoky French pub, with Gaston Berlemont opening another half bottle of champagne for a crowd of overcoated and hatted men and women. Others had poignancy, such as the little boy with a dirty face and a dart in one hand at Barnstaple Fair or the handsome beggar with two peglegs in Barcelona.

Farson, in his books, photographs and conversation, idealised Soho, though he was aware from experience of its destructive power. In *Soho in the Fifties*, one of his better books, he described the round of drinking: from the French pub to Wheeler's for lunch – with luck in the company of Francis Bacon – then on to the Colony Room Club during the afternoon (when the pubs were shut from

3 p.m. to 5.30), back to the Coach and Horses perhaps, and on into the night, at the Mandrake or some shabby homosexual dive.

Farson was fortunate enough usually to have money to pay his way, and was closer to the oysters and champagne side of things than the cadged halves of bitter familiar to the likes of John Deakin.

Farson had an annoying way of claiming intimacy with famous people and writing about them on the strength of it. It was not that he did not know them, but that he wrote, often inaccurately, about private conversations from past years. His book about Bacon was called *The Gilded Gutter Life of Francis Bacon* – which sounded silly, though it was a quotation from a joking telegram that Bacon had once sent him. More recently, Farson set great store by his acquaintance with Gilbert and George.

In later years he lived in moderate peace in Devon (though he was barred from all but one pub in Appledore), writing books. Every now and then, on the pretext of an interview, he would make increasingly suicidal raids on London, getting drunk earlier and earlier in the day. He would miss his train back to Devon, and perhaps return to the country two or three days late.

Over and over again Farson's assaults on London meant drinking all day, picking up a rent boy and very often being robbed by him at his hotel. He was barred from several hotels for trivial offences such as being found with his trousers round his ankles in the corridor.

One Sunday afternoon in the Coach and Horses an angry rent boy (aged about 30) came into the pub and tried to shame Farson into paying for his afternoon's services. Farson was shameless: "But you didn't bloody do anything," he shouted back. "And I bought all the drinks."

The two most admirable things about Farson were his energy and his determination to start his life again each time he ran into a cul-de-sac.

Daniel Negley Farson was born on January 8 1927. His father Negley Farson was an American-born journalist who would bring the boy an elephant's tooth or an embryo alligator from his trips abroad. During one trip on which little Dan accompanied him, the boy was patted on the head by Hitler as a "good Aryan boy".

Negley resigned suddenly from the *Chicago Daily News* in 1935, but then made money from his autobiographical books, *The Way of a Transgressor* being the best known. Of Negley, Dan was to write: "He was a stronger man than I am, free from the taint of homosexuality." But he was also an alcoholic.

Daniel Farson described how he set off with his parents in 1935 to drive across Europe: "I crouched underneath a blanket on the floor at the back, pretending to be asleep – impossible with the arguments raging in the front, my father constantly wanting to stop, seizing any excuse for a drink, while my mother implored him not to. Occasionally he lost his temper, sometimes violently, followed by angry silence and the utter desolations of my mother's sobs, when I did not dare to move. Then there were whispers as they remembered I was there." Dan lived up to his parents' tortured example for the rest of his life.

In 1940, Dan's prep school, Abinger Hill, was evacuated to Canada. During the holidays he was sent to stay with variously unsuitable relations and friends of his father's in the United States. One day he was collected in a car by Somerset Maugham and his secretary Gerald Haxton. They took him to visit another homosexual, Tom Seyster, who, for some reason, was also his godfather. Nothing untoward occurred. The two younger men drank a great deal: Maugham sympathised with the boy's loneliness and responded later with a kind letter to some poetry he had shown him.

In 1942, young Daniel sailed back to wartime England, feeling more comfortable amid its dangers and shortages than in untroubled America. He was sent to Wellington, a ridiculous misjudgment. After a year he persuaded his parents to let him leave.

He desultorily set about learning Russian, but soon landed a job at the Central Press Agency. This decrepit organisation was staffed by an aged skeleton staff during the war, but it had the privilege of sending a lobby correspondent to Westminster. The head of the agency, Guy L'Estrange, had not been to the Commons since the end of the 19th century, and Farson, aged 17, was sent to cover Parliament. This blond-haired youth was a strange sight in the corridors of Westminster, down which he was pursued without success by the predatory Labour MP Tom Driberg.

For a while, though, Farson's career almost progressed backwards. He served in the American Army, during which time he was sent on a journalism course. He went with the Army to Germany, where he discovered the possibilities of photography in the ruins of Munich. He then went up to Pembroke College, Cambridge, aged 21.

Though he took a degree, he thought he had wasted his time academically. He did learn about the realities of sexual relations, but never found a satisfactory way of accommodating his own preferences.

Farson spent a short time at an advertising agency and then in 1951 joined *Picture Post* as a staff photographer. At this time he made such friends as the impossible, drunken, annoying photographer John Deakin, who had utterly broken with his Liverpudlian background on coming to London.

Deakin, arrested for indecency during a raid on a night club, was asked in court if he had not thought it odd to see men dancing together. "How could I possibly know how people in London behave?" he replied; he was acquitted. Farson was sacked from *Picture Post* at about the same time Deakin was sacked from *Vogue*.

In the 1950s, Francis Bacon took to Farson, despite occasional differences. One night in the Gargoyle club, a male friend with whom Farson was infatuated butted in on Bacon's conversation. Farson apologised to Bacon, only to be met by: "It's too bad that we should be bored to death by your friend and have to pay for his drinks, but now you have the nerve to come over as well, when you're not invited." But next day, Bacon bought Farson champagne in the Colony Room Club: "If you can't be rude to your friends, who can you be rude to?"

Farson's next bright idea was to join the Merchant Navy. He joined the crew of 634 on the 30,000 ton *Orcades* and sailed 50,000 miles around the world, crossing the equator four times. He thought for a moment that he had got Soho out of his sytem.

He next found work with the *Evening Standard* and the *Daily Mail*; he persuaded Colin Wilson, the author of *The Outsider*, to speak unguardedly, and published the damaging interview in *Books and Art*. Then he was commissioned to interview Cecil Beaton for *This Week* on television, and a new chapter opened.

Farson could have been made for television of that period. He was quick-thinking, still handsome, with enough charm to beguile interviewees. He drew out Dylan Thomas's widow in a live broadcast which had to be faded out when he provoked her to fury.

Farson went from strength to strength. He caused outrage with a programme, *Living for Kicks*, about coffee bar teenagers, dubbed "Sexpresso Kids" by the *Daily Sketch*. He produced a series *Farson's Guide to the British*.

Always fascinated by misfits, he also presented the series *Out of Step* which dealt with oddities from witchcraft to nudism.

Farson was in the middle of filming a programme about lonely old people at Christmas when he was called to the telephone and heard that his mother had died after falling down stairs at the end of a lunch with Lady d'Avigdor-Goldsmid. A man in a pub told him he had just heard the news on television: "Daniel Farson's mother dies in fall."

In 1962, with money left him by his parents, Farson bought the tenancy of a pub on the Isle of Dogs in the East End of London. The pub was given a boost by a television documentary Farson made called *Time Gentlemen Please!*

The idea of the Waterman's Arms was to stage old-fashioned music hall, but the scheme also appealed as a chance to play the host, drink and meet attractive men. But whatever money the pub made never found its way into Farson's pockets.

The venture lasted a year. In all he lost perhaps £30,000 – enough in 1963 to buy a row of houses. His days in television were numbered too. A documentary he made, *Courtship*, proved "dull". Farson thought he had gone stale and threw in the towel, though many thought he had been sacked for drunkenness or emotional instability.

He moved to Devon, living in his parents' house near the sea, and made an income from journalism and books. He also contrived a television quiz show on art called *Gallery*. He was hit badly when his younger friend Peter Bradshaw, who lived with his girlfriend in Farson's house, died in 1992.

There was life in Farson yet. He traced his father's footsteps over the Caucasus and went to Moscow for a show by Gilbert and George. He went frequently to Turkey, always getting drunk and picking up men there.

Farson knew he was dying of cancer when his autobiography *Never a Normal Man* was published just after his 70th birthday. It begins: "Two nights ago I flew into Istanbul to sort out my life. So far I have not done well." In it he confessed all – or rather confessed to a larger audience than he had been confessing to for years late at night in Soho.

At the same time he held an exhibition of photographs in a Mayfair gallery and went on Radio 4's *Midweek* with such a hangover that his voice sounded as if it came from inside a wardrobe. The title of the book, the reader soon discovered, was a remark made about his father, not him.

On the day of the funeral of Diana, Princess of Wales, Farson went to the Coach and Horses in Soho, straight from a trip to Sweden. He stood at the bar, noisily

411

impersonating a friend, Sandy Fawkes, bursting into tears. Behind him young people told him to shut up because they were trying to hear the speech of Earl Spencer on the television.

November 28 1997

INDEX

Agnew, Spiro T., 322
Argyll, Margaret Duchess
  of, 218
Atwater, Lee, 120

Bernard, Jeffrey, 383
Beuselinck, Oscar, 368
Blackburn, Raymond, 158
Briginshaw, Lord, 173
Burroughs, William, 373

Cage, John, 205
Cook, Robin, 242
Cornfeld, Bernie, 270
Cradock, Fanny, 255
Crisp, Bob, 235

Delamere, Diana Lady, 9
Durdin-Robertson,
  Lawrence, 247

Eastwood, Peter, 133

Fairbairn, Sir Nicholas,
  265
Fairlie, Henry, 73
Farson, Daniel, 404
Fountaine, Andrew, 392
Fratianno, Aladena, 216

Freeman, Nicholas, 59
Frere, James, 252
Fuchs, Klaus, 17

Gabor, Jolie, 353
Galsworthy, Sir John, 191
Gamble, the Reverend
  Peter, 396
Girodias, Maurice, 90
Gold, Sid, 82
Green, Hughie, 356
Green, Sir Peter, 320

Haldeman, H. R., 227
Hamm, Jeffrey, 195
Hammer, Dr Armand,
  106
Harriman, Pamela, 344
Havers, Lord, 177
Haxell, Frank, 26
Hayman, Sir Peter, 185
Hays, Wayne L., 40
Healy, Gerry, 67
Heber-Percy, Robert, 11
Herbert, David, 284
Hinds, Alfred, 115
Hinze, Russell "Big Russ",
  136
Hiss, Alger, 328

Hoffman, Abbie, 46
Hughes, Docker, 205

Ibarruri, Dolores, *La Pasionaria*, 62

Junor, Sir John, 361

Kagan, Lord, 261
Kent, Tyler, 42
King, Cecil, 1
Kray, Ronnie, 280

Laing, R. D., 55
LaVey, Anton, 401
Leary, Timothy, 308
LeMay, General Curtis "Old Ironpants", 99
Lenihan, Brian, 293

MacBride, Sean, 13
Manahan, Dr Jack, 87
Marie-la-Jolie, 29
McLachlan, Charles, 84
Mikardo, Ian, 212
Mills, Wilbur, 188
Mitchell, John, 37
Mitford, Jessica, 312
Montrose, 7th Duke of, 165
Morgan, Seth, 104
Moschino, Franco, 249

O'Brien, Jimmy, 239

Palumbo, Rudolph, 6
Poulson, John, 209

Qing, Jiang, 126

Ray, Cyril, 152
Rees-Davies, William, 162
Riding, Laura, 144
Rizzo, Frank "Big Bambino", 140
Roberts, Allan, 80
Rubell, Steve, 49
Rusbridger, James, 232

St George, Charles, 199
Salerno, Anthony "Fat Tony", 202
Shockley, Professor William, 51
Siddiqui, Dr Kalim, 304
Silkin of Dulwich, Lord, 30
Skelton, Barbara, 299
Skilton, Charles, 70
Skinner, B. F., 97
Smith, T. Dan, 223
Smyth, Frank, 381
Stanshall, Vivian, 275
Stonehouse, John, 20

Teresa, Vincent "Big
  Vinnie", 77
Tiny Tim, 335

Vassall, John, 339
von Thurn und Taxis,
  Prince Johannes, 113

Wall, Pat, 94
Wayte, Guy, 351
White, Sam, 33
Winchester, Bapsy
  Marchioness of, 290